101
Places
to Get
F*CKED UP
Before
You Die

Also by Matador Network

No Foreign Lands:
100 of the Most Inspirational Travel Quotes of All Time

101
Places
to Get
F*CKED UP
Before
You Die

The Ultimate
Travel Guide
to Partying
Around the World

A Book from 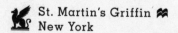 Matador Network
Edited by David S. Miller

St. Martin's Griffin
New York

101 PLACES TO GET F*CKED UP BEFORE YOU DIE. Copyright © 2013 by Matador Network. All rights reserved. Printed in the United States of America. For information, address St. Martin's Press, 175 Fifth Avenue, New York, N.Y. 10010.

www.stmartins.com

Library of Congress Cataloging-in-Publication Data available upon request.

ISBN 978-1-250-03558-5 (trade paperback)
ISBN 978-1-250-03559-2 (e-book)

St. Martin's Griffin books may be purchased for educational, business, or promotional use. For information on bulk puchases, please contact Macmillan Corporate and Premium Sales Department at 1-800-221-7945, extension 5442, or write specialmarkets@macmillan.com.

First Edition: January 2014

10 9 8 7 6 5 4 3 2 1

WARNING LABEL

The depiction of drug and alcohol use, sex, and general debauchery in this book is not meant as a condonement but a truthful accounting of its place in travel culture. Let's get real: many of us have either lost friends or family due to drugs and alcohol, or know of those whose lives have been ruined in moments of bad decision-making while partying—violence, addiction, STDs, unwanted pregnancy, accidents. Consider risks versus rewards carefully while traveling and partying, and make smart decisions. Stay safe out there, people.

Contents

Pre-Party

Let me say outright that there's nothing to defend or romanticize about getting fucked up. Like most everything we do, it's a cliché. Granted there are all different contexts and soundtracks that go along with getting fucked up, a spectrum of motivations and legalities and societal acceptance. But doesn't it all originate from the same elusive wish? To modify the passage of time somehow? To try and seal ourselves a little deeper into it, or perhaps off from it, if only for a while?

But who thinks like this, especially while getting fucked up? The tendency is just the opposite. People roll joints or mix Jack and Cokes or craft homemade IPAs or drop acid and go snowboarding and see themselves and their friends and what they're doing as original. Meanwhile, everyone else is a stereotype.

I was sort of reminded of this on a recent trip to D.C., where my friends and I kept making the same observation: *sloppy drunk dudes in suits everywhere.* Who were these fuckers stumbling around the sidewalks of our nation's capital?

The last night of the trip we sat in a bar called Science Club. The bartender, Meegan, was in her mid-thirties, and despite a thin, stalky body and bleached dreadlocks, she gave off this protective, almost matronly air. The conditions felt potentially epic: I was flying out the next morning, less than eight hours away. Sporleder made a seemingly ceremonial call for Jäger shots. Why not blow it out? Meanwhile, Ross was anchoring the bar like a visiting diplomat, magnanimous, buying drinks for everyone. The music (CL Smooth and People Under the Stairs) seemed just the right volume to allow conversation while almost amplifying the conversation, as if accelerating the night in a certain direction. We talked with a couple of young video producers, both female, about living and working in D.C. (they confirmed our "drunk dudes in suits" assessment). At some point Ross set down his fourth or fifth empty tequila glass and said, almost like a public service announcement, "That's it, I'm officially drunk."

Our tentative plan for late night was some ridiculous sounding club (Opera), but when we conferred with Meegan she said—without a trace of humor or pretense but an almost maternal forewarning—"Opera's great if you want douchebags wearing too much cologne and rhinestone collared shirts all over you."

"Jesus," I said.

"Go to Eighteenth Street Lounge. The guy who owns it is from Thievery Corporation, and they only book good bands."

If there's a goal in this book, it might just be to guide you to the Meegans, to the "good bands" of the world. To accomplish this we gave our travel journalists at Matador a guerilla mission to "assess" how and where people got fucked up all over the globe, and to write about it as transparently as they could. The results were fairly predictable: journalists dialed into certain places "half naked in the back of a stretch limousine with Moët champagne cascading down your tits."

But what surprised me as the book came together was a kind of pathos in many of the stories, a subtext of seeking connections with people.

Several years ago I met this Mexican kid while in the tiny Michoacán town of La Ticla. I assumed he was a local or a surfer, there for the machine-like point and cheap marijuana the kids sold in rolled-up pages of surf mags. But when the inevitable joint came around to him, he smiled and shook his head. It was a gesture layered with meaning, as if he wanted to tell a story, and so when I nodded (approvingly, I hoped, but also questioningly), he began: "This past summer I went on a peregrination for *San Pedro* (peyote). I haven't smoked or drank since." He stared out at the waves for a second and added, "I haven't needed to. It's all *allí nomás.*"

He explained that he didn't just eat peyote but made the entire pilgrimage with the Huicholes for two months from Sierra Madre Occidental to San Luis Potosí, where (and I couldn't help but cringe at this) they were met by gringos trucked in on "spiritual tours."

What's stayed in my memory ever since was the word he used to describe the journey: *solemne.* Solemn. As they walked through the desert, the men and women kept to themselves and stayed quiet, he said. That's the part they leave out of the tour.

When we parted ways I pointed him toward the secret campsite I'd built down the beach. Something was transacted in our brief encounter, an exchange of *buena onda,* a sense of being sealed into that moment. And I think this if anything describes what the authors looked for in these stories, and sometimes found.

DM
Asheville, North Carolina

1: Blowouts

Probably the greatest event I've ever witnessed was the Pan American Surf Championship and bikini contest in Montañita, Ecuador. And it was great not for what you might imagine—the beauty pageant or murderously talented surfers from Brazil, Costa Rica, Panama—but the way the town *transformed,* creating something original without really trying.

Solid head-high swell and sunny days led up to the event (which coincided with *Semana Santa*), and over the course of the week the town's youth waged a continuous, take-no-prisoners water battle across the plazas and over the seawall, launching from rooftops and behind buses and mule-drawn carts. Although members of the opposite sex (of approximately your own age) appeared to be the prize targets, shopkeepers, stoned artisans, basically anyone/anything caught in the crossfire was fair game and only added to the hilarity.

For those few days Montañita behaved less like a town and more like an organism, simply giving in to the anarchy of the water war, the influx of visitors, the long global arc of Carnaval with its roots somewhere in the past but manifesting now as something spontaneous and new, which didn't cost anything to participate in or exclude any participation. If you were there, you were just part of it.

There are all kinds of events. But true blowouts are visceral, participational; they shatter your ideas of how things fit together. As one author described Burning Man, "If you did it right, it's going to take you at least a week to feel normal again. And if you did it right, normality will feel slightly unwelcome." With every blowout event there's a before and after. In between, you have the chance to lose and find yourself all over again.

1. Burning Man

LOCATION: Black Rock City, Nevada
SEASON: First week of September.
IDEAL CONDITIONS: Scorching hot and bone dry with a 75 percent chance of dust storms.
LODGING RECOMMENDATIONS: Recreational Vehicle (for the 1 percent), pup tent, camper van, random flat surface, or better yet—don't sleep.
INGESTIBLES: You're the kid, this is the candy store. . . .

Burning Man is the event. Black Rock City is the place. Burning Man is the art, the music, the people, the party, the intention, the tower of flames that lights the Nevada desert. Black Rock City (BRC)

The wide-open *playa* ready for exploration, with art sculptures throughout the space. Art cars, bikes, and pedestrians all share it with surprisingly few collisions. Photo by James Brian Fidelibus.

101 Places to Get F*cked Up Before You Die

is the flat expanse of barren *playa* that supports this unlikely and otherworldly happening. Got it? Good.

This is the type of scene that you could parachute into stark naked and singing "The Star-Spangled Banner" and upon landing you would be absorbed by the great fifty thousand–person organism—clothed, fed, and imbibed before your 'chute touched the desert ground. It is that kind of party. In fact, fuck that. It's not a party—it's an experiment in living and a radical expression of life-as-art that is so fucking *fun* that it feels like the best memory of your best birthday party, only ninety-nine times better.

Enter the *playa* (no doubt in a creeping procession of thousands of eager burners in dusty vehicles snaking for miles) and see the arch of BRC stretch out toward desert heat nothingness. A semi-circle of a silly pseudo-civilization that only exists for a week or so, BRC is itself a work of art.

Art. You will hear that word a lot at Burning Man. Everything is art, sometimes even when it isn't. But who cares? You don't trek out to the middle of the Black Rock desert to argue the finer foibles of artistic meaning; you come to experience, to interact, to consume, to dabble, and maybe to completely fucking lose yourself.

Find your camp and hug everyone. If you are solo or traveling with a group of friends but have no camp, find a place to park and set up. Set up your tent (or whatever you will pass out in), set up your table with water and a shitty little iPod dock, and set up whatever shade structure you can manage. Start to wander—you should get used to it. BRC is a place for aimless wandering.

Wander past a scraggle of gyrating day drunks and accept a Dixie cup full of pink "jungle juice" that goes down like sugary kerosene. Wander up to a bar and order whatever they are pouring but keep an eye on the bartender if you don't fancy a sneaker dose of ketamine. Wander past a merry gathering of burners wearing tighty-whitey underwear over their clothes who are enjoying a full Thanksgiving spread and would like you to join. Don the underpants and grab some dark meat and gravy. Wander past **BassNectar, Distrikt,** or any of the thumping, big sound camps attracting dancers like thousands of dubstepping human amoebas.

Get dirty, you don't care. Watch the sunrise. Cuddle with strangers. Contrary to popular opinion, it's not all about drugs and buggery, but of course it's there if you want it. It's mostly a matter of going somewhere completely different to allow yourself to shed the robe of predictable, well-behaved banality and reveal yourself as something much more spontaneous. Or just reveal yourself.

Eat some freeze-dried camping food and pineapple chunks from your stash and accept gratefully the hard-boiled eggs, whiskey, psychedelics, pancakes, and coffee people offer gladly. Help cook some communal tamales.

Of course The Man will burn—that's why they call it you-know-what. The Man is a few hundred feet tall, made of wood, and is torched with an orgiastic display of pyrotechnics the penultimate night of the event.

When The Man burns it is the beginning of the end. You will have one more epic descent down the rabbit hole of communal delirium, sober up, and start the process of transition all over again—this time to go home.

NOTES FROM A VETERAN

As you enter Black Rock City you are welcomed Home by a team of grinning greeters. It doesn't matter if you are a veteran or virgin, when you set foot in Black Rock City you're Home—where you belong: where you are accepted, loved, and free to be. Come Home once and you are a local for life.

FUCKED UP FIRSTHAND

I shoot whiskey to mitigate the sobriety gap that eating magic mushrooms sometimes creates—you never know when the funky fungus is going to kick you in the brain and so you nervously wait, drinking whiskey. Suddenly I am dancing in a crowd of Santa Clauses and a mostly naked mad scientist is spraying champagne down my throat from a five-gallon tank he wears on his back. The shrooms kick in as a golf cart converted into a mobile bar and decorated with dildos swings by and I am on a stool introducing myself as The Last Human while accepting a concoction of not-strictly-alcohol from a yellow-and-red McDonald's cooler. "What's in it?" I ask. "I don't know!" he squeals.

VERDICT

If you really want to know, just go.

Josh Johnson

2. Coachella

LOCATION: Indio, California
SEASON: April.
IDEAL CONDITIONS: Hot as hell in the day, warm at night.
LODGING RECOMMENDATIONS: Camping out at the festival keeps the FOMO away.
INGESTIBLES: Acid, shrooms, ecstasy, and weed are the drugs of choice. Festival food that will have you making spicy pies of your own later.

Ordinarily, getting messed up and listening to emotionally stirring music in your grandparents' retirement community is reserved for going to their funeral receptions. But for two weekends in April every year, Indio turns itself from a Palm Springs satellite where retired CEOs go to avoid their wives into one of the world's greatest gatherings for drugged-out hippies running away from the responsibilities thrust upon them by "having a job" and "being an adult." Few places in the world allow for dropping acid and following a seven-foot man in a yellow tutu anywhere, but at Coachella that man may just lead you to a stage where Florence and the Machine perform right before Snoop Lion and a resurrected Tupac.

There are a lot of places to stay around the festival, but if you buy your **Car Camping Pass** with your ticket in the presale, your planning is done. Camping is the authentic Coachella experience. And since the drugs usually haven't worn off by the last set, the campgrounds blow up with small carnival rides and even a Silent Disco after hours.

For those less interested in sleeping on a patch of grass and smelling like the sweat from that fat guy who kept bumping into you during The Black Keys (heathens!), hotels and house rentals are the next best bet. Hotels near the festival are listed on the official Web site, while houses for rent can be found on Craigslist. Old people in Palm Springs don't trust hippies, so be ready to sell your liver to afford the security deposit.

Getting to the festival isn't an issue for campers, but for those who opted out there's the official **Coachella Shuttle Pass**. Buy it with your ticket for the peace of mind that you'll be dropped off at 2:00 A.M. nowhere near your hotel. There's also a taxi line outside for those who want to watch other people get picked up without getting home themselves, but the best option is in the parking lot, where enterprising locals come and offer cheap rides to anyone brave enough to get in the car with them.

Once you're in the festival, the fun really begins. The merchandise tent is located front and center to the entrance, because nothing says "a weekend escape from the trials of capitalism" like paying $40 for a T-shirt. Past that are the food stalls selling everything from **Spicy Pie Pizza** to **Pink's Hot Dogs**. The **Beer Gardens** and VIP areas have some better options, but you'll be forced to eat and drink behind the fence.

The actual music is divided between the five main stages: **Main Stage, Outdoor Theatre, Gobi Tent, Mojave Tent,** and **Sahara Tent.** The latter sticks to the electronic acts and functions as a sequester for underage teens doing ecstasy for the first time and realizing, "Man, lights are pretty." There's a smaller stage called **The Do LaB** in the center of the grounds, headed every year by a performance group called Lucent Dossier Experience, which is basically Cirque du Soleil without the classy pretense that the entire audience isn't on shrooms.

Coachella is an art festival as well as a music festival, and it doesn't bother pandering to the beret-and-goatee crowd. Coachella is big and loud, and usually uses art as a playground. From the giant T. rex that eats empty water bottles to the giant bugs with pedals that make the wings flap, the art is fine-tuned to gleefully entertain people who've reduced their cognition to that of two-year-olds. The **Ferris Wheel** is the one constant and the most famous image of Coachella, though it makes a shitty meeting spot when everybody uses it as one.

It's a shame Coachella is only two weekends long, because each weekend is the best of the year. The sun, heat, palm trees, and distant mountains create a vista that would be beautiful even without the crazy hippies walking around on stilts built to look like flamingos.

NOTES FROM A VETERAN
The security around Coachella depends almost entirely on the mood of the security guard at the time. If you're sneaking something in, hide it well just in case you get the asshole that wants everything short of a cavity search.

VERDICT
Will stick in your memory no matter what substances it's been filtered through.

Colin Heinrich

3. Glastonbury

LOCATION: Glastonbury, United Kingdom
SEASON: The June weekend closest to summer solstice.
IDEAL CONDITIONS: Sunny and dry (good luck).
LODGING RECOMMENDATIONS: Camper van.
INGESTIBLES: Canned booze (possibly peed in), Brothers Cider, liberty caps from local cow dung, caffeine pills sold as ecstasy, tea and cake (The Crow's Nest), meat pies (Pieminister), anything you can smuggle.

Bigger isn't always better but in the case of Glastonbury, the world's largest open-air music fest, it is. Run by a dairy farmer and his daughter since 1970, it somehow stays true to its hippie roots despite an

Festival-goer smartly dressed in Wellingtons in anticipation of heavy mud conditions that will inevitably ensue. Photo by Dean Chapple.

101 Places to Get F*cked Up Before You Die

attendance of 177,500. Maybe it's the local yogis and mystics who descend each year to spread their chi. Maybe it's King Arthur smiling down from his hilly grave. Maybe as a former hangout of Jesus' uncle, it has good karma for all time. Whatever the case, prepare yourself for an alternate universe. Reality ends at the gate.

Start day one with a veggie breakfast in **Green Fields** £6 ($9 USD), the fest's new-age hub. Enjoy in a wind-powered yurt while scouring the festival paper for secret gigs. Everyone from Fatboy Slim to Radiohead has played here unbilled. The main stages in the venue's north end are where you'll find the big-name acts. U2, Stevie Wonder, Neil Young—they've all played the iconic **Pyramid Stage.** It may be tempting to park here for the day, but don't. Some of the best experiences are on the outskirts. In **Dance Village,** it's never too early for amphetamines. Stop at **Pussy Parlure,** a 1920s saloon where drag queens spin salsa and English maids tickle you with their feather dusters. Vaudeville is alive and kicking on the fest's eastern fringe with circus acts, tap dancers, comedians, and poets. It's the best place to see a roaming brass band of pink elephants or join a jazzercise class. At **The Park** you can scramble up a ribbon tower with teetering drunks. The crowds are lighter, which means more room to dance. There's also the famed **Rabbit Hole** where you wriggle through a tunnel to rave with Alice and the Queen of Hearts. The **Stone Circle** is a mini Stonehenge with a panoramic view of the festival. Retreat under a five-hundred-year-old king oak and watch the sunset, snog a stranger, or propose to your girlfriend (it happened to me). **The Lost Picture Show** (free) is a crumbling Cuban cinema with velvet throw cushions and tangy mojitos. If you want to party until breakfast, **Shangri-La** and the surrounding areas are after-hours central. Watch acrobats leap from a fire-breathing animatronic spider (**Arcadia**), sip vodka in a spaceship (seat belts required), or get down at a New York gay disco (mustache required). Once our friend went looking for us in what he thought was a club.

It was actually a "decontamination facility" where a panel determined he was toxic, put him in a biohazard suit, and sent him to the "New World" via an overpass called the Skywalk.

Some final pointers for Glastonbury:

- Plan early. Tickets sell out eight months in advance . . . in less than two hours.
- If you're camping, arrive early and in daylight. Nothing kills the festival spirit like trying to pitch a tent in the rainy dark while everyone around you has the time of their lives.
- Mud sliding might look fun in pictures but sticky, poo-colored trousers don't get you laid.
- "Love the farm, leave no trace" is the official policy so pick up your shit.

FUCKED UP FIRSTHAND

Sunday was strangely hot so my boyfriend and I took shelter in the intriguingly named "House of Fairy Tales." Inside, a pretty woman in a child-sized chair sang a song about magpies. We grabbed a few shakers and jammed along. Storybooks were strewn everywhere and as I opened one, Goldilocks wandered in and took a nap. Later, we saw a sword swallower, a knife thrower in red heels, and a live painter doing a spot-on portrait of Joe Strummer, upside down, in five minutes. We were sprayed with disinfectant by a SWAT team fighting swine flu.

VERDICT

Glastonbury's like a free pass: it's four days off from the world.

Becky Hutner

4. Carnaval Humahuaqueño*[1]

LOCATION: Jujuy Province, Argentina
SEASON: Usually takes place in February.
IDEAL CONDITIONS: Warm sunshine and brisk mountain air by day (nights get chilly).
LODGING RECOMMENDATIONS: Hostel Humahuaca or El Sol Hostel in Humahuaca; Casa los Molles or Hostel Malka in Tilcara.
INGESTIBLES: Beer, empanadas, humitas, milanesas, sweet alcoholic concoction (sometimes called vacuna), asado (roasted meat), wine, coca leaves, chicha (fermented corn drink).

It starts with a spray of *nieve,* which from a distance soars through the air in graceful, foamy arcs, and then lands, thick and sticky, everywhere. In the end, there is nothing about Carnaval Humahuaqueño that isn't a fog—from the memories to the chalky bursts of *talco* (talcum) powder. You come with friends or go it alone. Either way, it's not long before you're dancing in the street with grinning strangers who thrust communal drinks forward and rub *talco* in your face.

The scene is frenetic, carefree, blissfully messy. You'll find no beads or extravagant floats. Even the diablo costumes—vibrant patchworks festooned with bells, mirrors, hand-painted masks, and glittery horns—sport a homespun feel befitting Quebrada de Humahuaca, with its scorched mountains and dusty villages.

In Jujuy Province, native Andean traditions mix with Christianity, making Carnaval a celebration of fertility, *Pachamama* (Mother Earth), and, of course, *el diablo.* On the Saturday before Ash Wednesday, the *Desentierro* or "unearthing" the devil (a rag doll named *pujllay,* from the Quechua word "to play"), officially kicks off the festivities.

---

[1]* Watch for starred entries because they are top places to get f*cked up.

Once the devil descends, he mingles with the people and it's unclear (and does not matter) who is who. It's all fueled by copious amounts of beer and *chicha,* which is doled out on the street from giant jugs.

The celebrations of all valley towns bear the same hallmarks: bursts of water and *nieve* (baptism), flurries of *talco* (earth), the high, clear song of the quena flute against the bombo drum's deep and joyful boom. You float along, plastic cup of *chicha* in hand, as *nieve* streams past and street vendors fry up breaded beef *milanesas.* There is no "standing by." Those stopped near a passing parade are plucked from the edges and whisked into the fray.

Inside the *fortines* (forts), visitors are greeted with *vacuna,* a sweet alcoholic "vaccination" to ward off envy and sorrow, before feasting on roasted meat, cheese-coated corn, empanadas, and sweet, mealy *humitas.* All can attend with a small donation, but breakers of the fortinero rule (forget pain, commit to fun) "suffer" a *fusilamento,* "execution by firing squad," forced to drink wine in the center of the room until they feel the love.

Start your Carnaval in Humahuaca, whose main plaza teems with people dancing under the stark white **Iglesia de la Candelaria.** On the terraced steps of the **Monumento a los Héroes de la Independencia,** an imposing tribute to the men who fought in the War for Independence, fiesta-goers clump against stone walls while vendors hawk jewelry and woven fabrics. By night, the crowd here undulates to carnavalito music while the setting sun smudges the sky around blazing mountains.

In Tilcara, one can break to wander among the partially reconstructed ruins of the **Pucará,** a hilltop pre-Incan fortress. From this sun-drenched perch, against a backdrop of fiery mountains awash in punches of deep purple and rich sienna, the chaos below is muted. But back in town the parades meander and the drinks flow all day and night.

The Sunday following Ash Wednesday marks the end of the festival and an emotional parting ritual (*cacharpaya*) where the *pujl-lay* is reinterred. Revelers leave offerings of coca leaves, cigarettes, and *chicha*, and the diablos wail their farewells to the devil and Carnaval. Until next year . . .

NOTES FROM A VETERAN

Come prepared, or be careful. They say, "What happens at Carnaval stays at Carnaval," but nine months from now there will be many more residents in this region—we call them *hijos del diablo*.

VERDICT

They'll tell you not to go last minute. There will be no rooms. But there is always space. Be prepared to get dirty, in all forms of the word.

Suzanne Russo

5. Cervantino

LOCATION: Guanajuato, Mexico
SEASON: Early October.
IDEAL CONDITIONS: Clear skies, crowded.
LODGING RECOMMENDATIONS: Casa Zuniga, Alma del Sol, La Casa del Tío, Hostal del Campanero.
INGESTIBLES: Caguamas of Victoria, mezcal, Pacholas Guanajuatenses.

Guanajuato is a colonial city built atop several hills in central Mexico. It's a few hours from Guadalajara on the highway that leads to Mexico City and is known for panoramic views and prehispanic mummies. It's also a perfect UNESCO world heritage site to get completely freaking wasted at, especially during Cervantino, a forty-year-old festival celebrating the works of Spanish writer Miguel de Cervantes. During Cervantino, every theater, ballet, and music hall hosts world-class performances. Meanwhile the streets are filled with drunken morons. It makes for something between Art Basel and a Philadelphia Eagles tailgate, having little to do with Cervantes and more about a quixotic good time.

You'll have trouble finding a place to sleep, but it's okay; people leave their unsecured construction sites available for campers. Unlike other cities in this book, there's no need to explain places to go, because Guanajuato during Cervantino has the most parties per capita of any city in the world. Just share bottles of mezcal with everybody you meet, from the cowboy playing marimba to the mime following people around to the one-man Dead Kennedys cover band. Fall asleep in the middle of the park, wake up, and drink more.

In the morning you'll certainly need breakfast. Roam around until you find a restaurant that's been in operation for seventy years by an eighty-six-year-old woman sitting at the one table in the place. There you'll be confused about the difference between different Mexican *antojitos* (street food). You'll discover that a *sincronizada* is two tortillas that have cheese and ham in between them, and that they're pretty good.

Drink some coffee, and another round of beers, because you're doing this again, now.

NOTES FROM A VETERAN
We just paid a guy forty pesos to electrocute us. I dunno, it was kind of fun, a way to bring our group closer together.

VERDICT
Make Don Quixote proud.

Joshua Heller

6. La Tomatina

LOCATION: Buñol, Spain
SEASON: Last Wednesday of August.
IDEAL CONDITIONS: Sunny with 100 percent chance of tomato-pitation.
LODGING RECOMMENDATIONS: Buñol is tiny; you are better off finding lodging in Valencia, about forty minutes east.
INGESTIBLES: Just about every type of alcohol you can think of, but don't eat the tomatoes!

La Tomatina is the now famous celebration where forty-five thousand tourists, drunkards, and tomato soldiers descend on the tiny town of Buñol wearing swim goggles and crappy clothing purely in order to hurl tomatoes at one another. Officially there are restrictions mandating things such as you must squash all tomatoes before throwing; you cannot throw anything other than tomatoes; you may not rip T-shirts, et cetera. However, once the tomatoes enter the picture, anything goes. Expect that every piece of clothing you wear will be ruined, and that you will be smacked in the face by something other than a tomato. It's all part of the fun!

Festivities in the town run all week, but they really heat up Tuesday night, with multiple open air *discotecas* and bars cranking out tunes and booze into the morning hours. Don't go too crazy the night before—you'll want to head to the center street of town sometime around eight in the morning for two reasons: 1) around 9:00 A.M. it gets so packed you will have trouble getting anywhere near the center, and 2) the *palo jabón.*

The *palo jabón* is a twenty foot tall "*palo*" (stick) greased with "*jabón*" (soap) and lard, topped with a giant juicy ham. For the next few hours, hundreds of determined festival-goers repeatedly assault the pole in dogged attempts to dislodge the ham from the top. Of course, even with multiple people attempting the climb every second of every minute, the amount of grease used makes it nigh impossible to get anywhere near the top. The key to success is to use your fellow climbers as hand- and footholds, since nobody gets purchase on the pole itself. However, everyone wants the ham for themselves, which means everyone sabotages one another's efforts, and sometimes they take to violently shaking the pole from side to side until the ham flies off to a thunderous roar of approval.

Afterward, a cannon goes off, and you can see the trucks—huge flatbeds loaded with tomatoes—coming from a mile away, moving about a foot a minute through the sea of people. Every twenty feet or so the trucks dump a big pile of tomatoes on the ground, which is quickly fallen upon by the surrounding hoards in a scene of utter pandemonium. Tomatoes, tomato bits, shirts, and anything else you can think of whiz through the air. Nobody stays on their feet as the ranks behind you push forward, and invariably the pile becomes full of sopping red smiling people writhing over one another and trying to get up.

After one hour flat of this madness, the second cannon shot sounds and all is theoretically over. Tomato bits continue to fly (albeit with less gusto) as the mass of red slowly traipses outward toward the nearby river or the civic center's showers. The residents of Buñol happily pull out their hoses, sinks, and buckets to help wash the crowd, with water pouring freely from every balcony and garage in the city onto the bloodred crowd below.

You've never been so happy to see an ancient Spanish woman wielding a hose in one hand and a cigarette in the other.

FUCKED UP FIRSTHAND
Our chartered bus pulled up to the outskirts of Buñol somewhere around 4:00 A.M. and discharged us unceremoniously in front of a makeshift street bar with nothing more than a time and place to meet in the afternoon, both of which turned out to be erroneous. I

wandered the streets with some newfound Irish drinking buddies until we decided to try to rest before the madness.

Later I got to the center right as the streets started filling up from every direction. We watched the *palo jabón* until the shot finally sounded, and eagerly watched the trucks make their way to us through the crowd, preceded by waves of slung tomato pulp. The next sixty minutes remain a blur of red, projectiles, and glee, followed by a quick wash in a stranger's garage and a weary trek back to the misplaced bus. One of my new friends lost both her shoes in the pandemonium, so I graciously offered her my Tevas and hiked back across the blazing asphalt in some pieces of discarded cardboard.

VERDICT
Life-affirming.

Corey Breier

7. Boryeong Mud Festival

LOCATION: Boryeong, South Korea
SEASON: Two weeks in July, hot for sure.
IDEAL CONDITIONS: Sensual muddiness with your cocktail protected via Ziploc bag.
LODGING RECOMMENDATIONS: Book early, accommodations fill up months ahead. Cheaper than joining a tour group is heading back to Seoul that night.
INGESTIBLES: Soju, beer, Korean barbecue, mud.

Originally a marketing promo for the mineral-rich mud of the region, the Boryeong Mud Festival has become an internationally famous party/excuse for getting drunk and playing in mud all day long. While Koreans know how to drink (it's not an accident that the top-selling spirit worldwide for the past eleven years—Jinro soju—is Korean), the Boryeong Mud Festival is more of a celebration of expat drinking and Koreans are outnumbered two to one by American military personnel, English teachers, and perpetual "gap yah" types.

For the equivalent of $5 USD, you get access to a carnival of mud specially trucked into Daecheon Beach. Horseplay and mud wrestling are expected in the giant pools; muddy slides are provided, and you can have buckets of mud tossed onto you in mud prison. You can paint yourself in colored mud or relax in the mud massage zone if the other options are too rowdy. There is a mudflat obstacle marathon and mudflat skiing for the athletically inclined as well as other activities (Mr. Mud contest, puppets, carnival games). The waterproof wristband allows for unlimited reentry into the mud zone. At the end, the wristband can also be traded in for a free cosmetic sample.

Outside the mud zone, beachside convenience stores are coated in muddy hand- and footprints. Tents along the beach provide food and drinks. Fried chicken, seafood, and Korean barbecue are your major options. Drinks are plentiful, with a focus on soju, beer, and cocktails. Given the no-glass rule on the beach, cocktails are served in heavy-duty Ziploc bags on a string that you hang around your neck for hands-free imbibing.

Daecheon Beach itself is a respite from the muddy crowds, where you can still listen to the music while swimming, tanning, or napping. At night, there are concerts and fireworks scheduled to continue the party. If the schedule for the night you're there isn't interesting (*read:* if it's the mud skin-care show), save on accommodation and head back to Seoul on the bus.

Hints:

- Beer and soju are cheaper than water.
- Shower facilities are cheap and worth using if you want to be allowed on any form of transportation afterward.

- Lockers are readily available to keep your worldly possessions safe and mud-free.
- It's still possible to get a sunburn while covered in mud.

NOTES FROM A VETERAN
It's really hard not to enjoy frolicking in giant vats of mud.

VERDICT
Mineral-rich.

Suze Morris

8. Saint Patrick's Day

LOCATION: Dublin, Ireland
SEASON: Mid-March.
IDEAL CONDITIONS: Apexes of Irish drinking culture are reached during Saint Patrick's Day and Halloween, but the alcoholic wrath of the locals can be unleashed at random on a rainy Tuesday night or before, during, and after any bank holiday.
LODGING RECOMMENDATIONS: Abigail's and The Generator hostels.
INGESTIBLES: Deep-fried Mars bars and nearly everything else from the chippers around town. Dutch Gold, Guinness, whiskey, Buckfast, Irish breakfast.

If there were a school to learn how to get fucked up, the headmaster would be Irish. The average Irishman can drink up to two six-packs of Dutch Gold on a quiet Tuesday night while staying in watching a movie, just for the exercise. I learned this and a few other things in Dublin during my college days.

To raid Dublin Irish-style on Saint Patrick's the trick is simple: start early. Make sure to stock up on disreputable Dutch Gold, whiskey, or Buckfast—the fortified wine invented by Benedictine monks—so you can wake up to intoxicant libations.

Brazilian kids fully representing in Dublin for Saint Patrick's. Photo by Scott Sporleder.

Drink a "few cans" (between five to twenty-five liters of beer to the average Irish) while you have your Irish breakfast and stagger to the bus stop. After showcasing your best drunken and disorderly behavior on the double decker, thank the driver as you stumble off, like a true gentleman, and go see the parade.

In the city center you will be spoiled for choice. There are over a thousand pubs in Dublin, each with its own distinctive stench, so don't be scared to get creative. Most of them will be packed on Saint Patrick's Day, so it is up to you to elbow your way in.

Behind every door you will find hordes of drunks in green attire with clover antennae, top hats, ginger beards, and unbelievable drinking stamina. The **Temple Bar** area is where you can set the gears in motion. There you will find a cluster of bars with standouts **The Mezz**, where you will find live music, and **The Foggy Dew**, home to the most diverse patrons in Dublin, also with live music on selected days.

If you are looking for an old-fashioned statement of Irish drinking culture, **The Celt,** not too far from O'Connell Street, is the place for you: old Irishmen singing ballads, pictures of Michael Collins hanging on the walls, and live traditional sessions accompanying your perfectly poured pints of Guinness. Meanwhile at **Fibber Magees** you can howl the notes of "Too Drunk to Fuck" by the Dead Kennedys, surrounded by society's unwanted during karaoke nights.

If instead live music is really your thing head to **Whelan's** on Wexford Street, the hub of Dublin's indie music scene. The **Wexford Street** area also has many other options, such as **Flannery's**, good for pulling, and **The Village.** The dark side of the clubbing scene, often involving chemicals and dubstep can be found at **Twisted Pepper.** Finally, to avoid bar hopping, a solid choice is **The Globe,** which starts off like a pub and turns into a late-night disco. No matter how you do it, if it's Saint Patrick's Day you're entering a surreally drunk world, with no restriction on age, gender, or nationality.

NOTES FROM A VETERAN
Go to **Copper Face Jacks** if you want to meet some genuine Irish farmers and then probably end up fighting them.

VERDICT
Surviving drinking elbow to elbow with an Irishman on Paddy's Day will award a thousand or more fucked-up points.

Pietro Buzzanca

9. Full Moon Party

LOCATION: Koh Phangan, Thailand
SEASON: November through January or May through July.
IDEAL CONDITIONS: Warm and sunny, sporadic lightning storms to keep it exciting.

LODGING RECOMMENDATIONS: Anywhere in the village, just off the beach—Yan's Dormitory n Bar, Dancing Elephant, etc.
INGESTIBLES: Buckets, Chang beer, more mind-altering substances than you can shake a hallucinated stick at.

You're here for the Full Moon Party. So is everybody else. They've come for the past eighteen years, waxing and waning with the lunar cycle. Full moon, half moon, black moon—there's never a break in Koh Phangan's culture of debauchery. Five thousand to ten thousand people flock to the island for the parties every month. Koh Phangan is littered with hostels, but it's a big island and the Full Moon Party takes place almost entirely on the southern peninsula of Haad Rin. The best hostels are close enough to walk, but far enough away to avoid too much noise and the occasional drunken ransack. Luckily, many of these hostels offer online booking ahead of time.

Within Haad Rin Village, there's **Yan's Dormitory n Bar**. At 500 baht ($16 USD) per night, it's cheap for the island and comes with complimentary food, laundry, and the coolest proprietor this side of an insane asylum. Nearby is the **Dancing Elephant Hostel**, another cheap alternative that focuses on organizing events. These and others line a "Hostel Row" and at night they merge into one giant party. For more private accommodation, **Seaview Bungalows** are right on the beach with quick access to the cliff-side bars, and many have their own hammocks for lazy people-watching. **Paradise Bungalows** is where the Full Moon Party started way back when, and it still maintains that same atmosphere and enthusiasm. These bungalows have more privacy and amenities, but usually cost significantly more than the hostels, ranging from 600 to 2,000 baht ($20 to $67 USD) per night based on size and proximity.

The best food on the island comes from the small, local Thai restaurants with names you can't read. Try **Maddy's Kitchen** on Hostel Row. Portions are always heaping, and a plate of pad Thai won't run you more than $2 USD. Farang cuisines are readily available to the less-devoted traveler. **Mama's Schnitzel** has a nice atmosphere with a quiet upper seating area when you need some late-night drunchies before bed. **Om Ganesh** is a bit of a trek, but offers some amazing Indian food, and **Monnalisa** and **The Shell** restaurant even have some pretty decent Italian.

The actual Full Moon Party takes place on **Haad Rin Nok Beach** on the east side of the peninsula, and everything can be found within a few hundred yards. The center of Haad Rin Nok, and probably the center of the Full Moon Party in general, is **Cactus Bar.** Its fire shows, music, and beautiful foreigners help make it one of the first stops on the beach for new arrivals. Just down the beach is **Drop In Bar,** another staple. Drop In Bar also features fire jump rope and a fire slide that anybody can take part in. The bar sells burn cream for the drunker patrons.

In the nights leading up to the full moon, the best parties drift away from Haad Rin Nok. **Coral Bungalows** hosts an incredible pool party where buckets and balloons of nitrous are the weapons of choice, though the pool is hardly sanitary by the end. The **Sramanora Waterfall Party** and the **Jungle Experience** take place farther inland. These can be difficult to get to, but it's free admission and there's nothing like a laser show projected on a jungle waterfall.

When it's time to take it easy, head down the beach to **Mellow Mountain** and **Kangaroo Bar.** These cliff-top bars have some sort of agreement with the police, and the menu has everything from joints to mushroom shakes, making it the perfect place to chill for a few hours and watch the party going on below from a distance.

The bars are where the party happens, but drinks there are expensive and trite. The real spirit of the Full Moon Party comes from the bucket stands. Buckets are pails containing around ten shots of liquor topped off with Thai Red Bull (crack, essentially) and Coke. Stands offer different kinds of liquor, but usually fill the bucket with

SangSom rum regardless of the order. Stands line the beach and streets with such eloquent names as "Fuck My Bucket" and "Jack Sparrow Fuck Bucket." The stands inland tend to be a bit cheaper (around $5 USD), but the beach stands set up earlier. If you talk to these early campers, they might stamp your hand, entitling you to discounts later.

There are, of course, other things to do on the island besides party: scuba dive, ride a Jet Ski, ride a banana boat. Hell, go visit the main bulk of the island and ride an elephant. However, Koh Phangan tends to have a premium charge added to activities compared to other islands.

Island culture is quick to understand. Every night is just as crazy as the Full Moon Party itself. Cigarettes are a backpacker's handshake. Swimsuits are the dress code. Sleeping is not recommended. Swimming in the water at night is disgusting. Remember, the whole beach is a party. Don't stay in one spot for too long, because there's something fun going on right next to you at all times.

FUCKED UP FIRSTHAND

Two days before the Full Moon Party, I met some Welsh girls on the beach, and we decided to check out the mushroom shakes up at Mellow Mountain. As it turned out, the girls were burlesque dancers who perform on stage with musical acts at festivals. A mountain of a man from one table over joined us, and this guy turned out to be a paratrooper on shore leave between missions. My expanded mind was in awe of the people I was meeting.

When the sun went down, we all went to the water to swim and catch phosphorescent shrimp that come out at night. That was when an apocalyptic lightning storm broke out. We ran for cover back up to Mellow Mountain, where we watched bolts tearing across the sky and striking in the water a few hundred yards away from us. The DJ picked up on the energy crackling through the air and started spinning house music, and the dozen or so people in the bar turned it into a dance party.

VERDICT
Burn cream.

Colin Heinrich

10. Holi

LOCATION: Holi, India
SEASON: Last full moon of the lunar month Phalguna, which usually falls in March.
IDEAL CONDITIONS: Semi-comatose on chocolate bhang cake.
LODGING RECOMMENDATIONS: Anywhere throwing a great party!
INGESTIBLES: Charras and bhang lassi.

From Ladakh to Kerala and Puducherry to Bengal, Holi is widely and enthusiastically celebrated across India. Actually, you don't just "celebrate" Holi. You "play" it. The general schtick is this: children and adults run around and spray, smear, sprinkle, and douse one another with colored powder and water.

It's also a nationwide excuse to imbibe cupfuls of *bhang lassi*—thick yogurt drinks laced with hash. It's an acquired taste, but they're strong and bring on a deep, lasting high.

Holi isn't a polite holiday. In some ways, this is good—playing Holi relaxes India's generally strict social norms. But it can also act as an excuse for what amounts to physical and sexual harassment. Take safety seriously—rape does occur, and in 2012 hundreds of people in Mumbai were hospitalized for exposure to poisoned color.

The combination of drugs and groping makes it a good idea to avoid the streets and play Holi among friends, in private. Usually this means a house party, but hotels, bars, and clubs will often throw their own private events. Companies like **MTV India** also host huge, outdoor parties in Bombay. Under the right circumstances, Holi looks like a gorgeous, otherworldly rave.

The best places to celebrate Holi are Bombay, where the biggest parties happen and it's easy to find drugs; Rajasthan in general, and specifically Jaisalmer, where colored powder is thrown up in the air to the sound of traditional ragas; Jaipur, where you can see the yearly elephant festival; Calcutta, where Holi is combined with Vasantotsav, the festival of spring, inaugurated by Rabindranath Tagore; or finally Mathura and Vrindivan, two villages about four hours from Delhi, where Lord Krishna is said to have been raised. Celebrations there are legendary. Avoid Kerala and Tamil Nadu, where celebrations are more subdued.

Things to remember:

- Wear clothes you don't care about ruining. Oil your hair and skin to protect them from staining.
- There are two types of Holi color: organic and chemical. Stick to the organic stuff, and make sure that's what your hosts are using.
- Bake and get baked! Holi is a time for everyone to rediscover his or her inner child. Don't bother showing up if you don't want to get wet, messy, colorful, and fucked up.

FUCKED UP FIRSTHAND

The key is to get into a rickshaw and have him drive fast—fast past the young guys smeared in fuchsia, turquoise, and saffron, leering with their hooded, probing eyes and crooked, smearing smiles. If we stop, I know that they'll crowd the rickshaw and rub their powdered hands across my breasts and thighs in the name of all things Holi. My old, pudgy driver will sigh and wave them away, world weary and apathetic.

My friends are sitting on the lawn of the Raheja mansion in Juhu, strewn about like blowsy spring blossoms. Someone knows someone who invited us here, to the second or fifth home of one of Mumbai's premier families. I'm hugged and kissed and smeared with color, handed a beer and a sludgy, green *bhang lassi*.

After the lassi, everything blends together. I forget all the worries of the morning, reeling easily from the lawn to some rooftop with a raucous rickshaw ride in between. A drunken stranger comes up and covers my head with pink powder, rubbing it in deep. It's not organic, and it never comes out. I've no choice but to dye my blond hair deep red, fall in love, and reinvent myself in Mumbai.

VERDICT
Revelatory.

Madeline Gressel

11. Koninginnedag

LOCATION: Amsterdam, the Netherlands
SEASON: April 29 and 30.
IDEAL CONDITIONS: Wake and bake.
LODGING RECOMMENDATIONS: Hotel Brian for budget, Stayokay Amsterdam Vondelpark for hostel.
INGESTIBLES: Beer—Heineken, Amstel, Grolsch, and Bavaria—marijuana, hashish, krokets from FEBO, broodjes (mini sandwiches) stroopwafels (syrup-filled waffles), crepes (Pannekoekenhuis Upstairs), Indonesian "rijstaffel" or rice table (Bojo).

Amsterdam has been contextualized as a rite of passage for every college student or backpacking schlepper traveling through Europe: hanging out on the Leidseplein at **The Bulldog** drinking Heineken, hallucinating on hash and scarfing down a fried *kroket* (croquette) out of a FEBO vending kiosk.

But the true mayhem is on the Queen's Birthday, Koninginnedag, celebrated every April 30. This is no day for drinking tea with your pinky in the air and waving to the Queen as she rides in a carriage through town. This is a serious shindig. The electricity and energy you feel in the air is not from the royals, but from the orange-clad ragers who flock to the Netherlands' capital to throw down. And really, the Dutch can't wait until the actual day, so they start celebrating April 29 on Koninginnenacht (Queen's Night).

Revelers gather throughout the city to watch parades, listen to live music, drink, dance, sing, sit on rooftops, and spread the orange love. **Dam Square,** which normally is a hangout for street performers, visitors, and pigeons, is a good place to start enjoying the festivities.

Leidseplein and **Rembrandtplein,** the regular headquarters for most of the nightlife, will have heaps of activity since the clubs and bars host parties and live music. Also head to the **Jordaan.** It's typically a more mellow part of Amsterdam (however, nothing is mellow on Koninginnedag). This area is also known for its brown cafés, such as **De Prins,** where you can get cheese fondue and a decent brew while you sit on a canal-side terrace. **Twee Prinsen** may look stuffy on the inside, but it has a young and lively scene.

You'll find plenty of live music on the streets, but if you'd rather go to a venue in the city center, try the ultra cool **Melkweg** or **Paradiso.** For atmosphere and jazz, go to **Alto** in Leidseplein. If your preference is more eclectic, hit **De Kroeg** for alternative, funk, soul, and punk.

If you want hash of course you're in luck. In Leidseplein or near it, you can check out The Bulldog or **De Dampkring.** (*Hint:* The Bulldog in the Red Light District is cooler than the more commercial one in Leidseplein.) Another haven is **The Other Side,** which attracts an LGBT crowd but is open to everyone.

The Red Light District always caters to the five senses. Coffee shop **De Oude Kerk** (The Old Church) plays reggae and offers hamburgers as well as other munchies. **Durty Nelly's** is an Irish pub that also has an adjoining hostel if you can't make it out.

If you want some Zen, go to **The Greenhouse**, which has three locations. At the main headquarters, old Indian wedding saris adorn the walls, and there's a mini fountain made out of bat dung in a tiny alcove.

A nap may be essential for rallying on Koninginnedag, especially if you began partying the night before. You may find a spot of grass (real grass) in Vondelpark on which to chill, but more than likely there will be live music and plenty of people watching to do.

General rules about Amsterdam:

- Koninginnedag is hard enough to pronounce (ask a local), but wait until you're well into the festivities.
- Brown cafés are not smoking coffee shops—they are really pubs or alternative dive bars, and they don't sell weed.
- Many "hash bars" don't sell booze since a coffee shop must be licensed to serve alcohol. Frankly, in most cases, the coffee shop products do the job on their own.
- You can wake and bake. Most coffee shops are open at about 10:00 A.M.
- Ironically, the Red Light District is relatively safe because of the police presence. However, watch out for pickpockets who target the wasted.

NOTES FROM A VETERAN
One of the biggest myths about Amsterdam is that pot is legal. Technically, it's not. For example, if you have more than five grams in public (thirty grams in private), you can still be fined. However, police do not crack down on the legal, regulated coffee shops and smokers.

VERDICT
Orange hats off to the Queen.

Steph Glaser

12. Oktoberfest

LOCATION: Munich, Germany

SEASON: Late September through the first weekend of October (yes, Oktoberfest starts in September).

IDEAL CONDITIONS: Sunny and slightly crisp. The beer drinking is mostly indoors though.

LODGING RECOMMENDATIONS: Hotel Nymphenburg for budget. Wombat City Hostel for a hostel. The Tent for quirky—sleep in a giant, dorm-style tent, with campfire evenings and thick wool blankets—like summer camp for travelers.

INGESTIBLES: Beer, sausages of all sorts, sauerkraut, pretzels, roast pork/duck/chicken, roast wild boar and game, fish on a stick, pastries.

In 1810, the citizens of Munich celebrated the wedding of a prince and a princess. I like to think of them sitting back in their horses

Chris Reijonen in the zone. Oktoberfest, Munich. Photo by Sarah Reijonen.

and carriages (or maybe stumbling home drunkenly on foot, who knows), saying "*Schiesse,* that was awesome. Let's do it again." So they did. Two hundred years later, Oktoberfest—or *die Wiesn* ("dee vees'n")—is the biggest festival in the world.

Sausages. Pretzels. Roast meat. Lots of hats. Midway rides. Heart-shaped gingerbread with sweet messages. Brass oom-pah-pah bands. Giant glass steins of the six brands of Munich beer. Welcome to the Wiesn. The Fest has fourteen beer tents—long wooden structures with different tones, clientele, food, decor, and beer variety. They go from about a hundred seats to over ten thousand, inside and out. But be warned: smaller tents and popular times can fill up fast. Reserve seats in advance online.

The **Hofbräu-Festzelt** does have plenty of English-speaking tourists. But it ranges. Make your way directly to "the pit" (standing-room-only section) to start partying really hard. Everyone's ready to make some international best buddies. But keep a close watch on your tighty-whities. Those scraps of fabric on the chubby, mustachioed angel hanging above the pit? Yep. Those are people's underwear, sometimes forcibly removed by other drunken revellers. Tradition has it that there's no underwear in the pit—if anyone asks, tell them you aren't wearing any.

In any tent, you'll hear a lot of traditional brass band music, plenty of toast calls (*Prost!*), and a few bizarre English-language songs that apparently now count as Bavarian folk songs. Beer is sold by the *maß* ("mass"): one whole liter of wheat beer in a glass stein. In some of the more drunken areas, such as Hofbräu's pit, you'll sometimes see people getting a bit overexcited with their toasts and smashing other people's steins. Sometimes it's accidental.

The **Löwenbräu-Festhalle, Augustiner-Festhalle,** and the **Hacker-Festzelt** are a few more examples of the big tents run by Munich breweries. Don't miss the giant animatronic lion waving a stein at the Löwenbräu entrance. Wait for it to roar and growl "Löwenbräu!" It's an experience. Especially if you've already had a *maß* or two.

Augustiner markets itself as friendly for the whole family, and uncorks its beer from wooden casks instead of the usual steel vats. **Hacker** is much of the same, but also has a rock band playing every evening if you need a break from the oom-pah.

The smaller tents often have quirky themes or foodie specialties. **Wildstuben** serves up roast wild boar and other game in a hunting lodge–like tent. Try **Hochreiters Haxnbraterei** for barbecue pork knuckles, or **Glöckle Wirt** for classy decor—oil paintings, antiques, and more.

Sick of beer? (*Why?*). Try the wine or cocktail tents. Or do like some Bavarian women and have a Radler (half beer, half lemon soda—they also call it a girlie beer). There's also Spezi, a German soda that's Coke mixed with orange soda. Not really recommended by this Canadian if you're already feeling a bit queasy though.

FUCKED UP FIRSTHAND

Hofbräu felt right. I beelined to "the pit" and met a table of Italians. Nice guys. Nearing the end of the day, I found myself wearing light-up devil horns and squeezed into a corner with Aussies, Americans, a South African, and two local Munich guys. "Motherfucking *prost*!" said motherfucking George W. Bush, as one of the locals had introduced himself as. That may have been the extent of their English. The motherfucking prosts kept coming, the table kept toasting, and the steins kept draining dry.

At the "very late" hour of 5:00 P.M. (long day drinking), the other travelers began pairing off and disappearing. It left me with the two Munichers, who decided to pursue other people's steins, smashing them with an aggressive "Motherfucking *prost*!" Then they smashed the wrong stein and high-tailed it out of there, but not before one of them wildly drank the dripping beer out of his own broken glass.

VERDICT

Guys in little leather shorts and girls with healthy racks squeezed into corseted dresses. Start practicing now: *Ein maß, bitte* ("eye'n mass, bit-uh"). One day, it'll get you a beautiful liter of beer.

Jessica Peter

13. Mardi Gras

LOCATION: New Orleans, Louisiana
SEASON: Mardi Gras, bro. Typically February through early March.
IDEAL CONDITIONS: Stuck to the beer-soaked floorboards of an outdoor bar, double-fisting your choice—local booze or a stranger's breasts.
LODGING RECOMMENDATIONS: It's not about how much you'll pay but acquiring lodging at all. Hotels and hostels sell out early, but last-minute travelers can share a pad with folks via Airbnb. Whatever you do, don't fall asleep on the street; you'll get pissed on.
INGESTIBLES: Sazerac (wicked cocktail of whiskey, bitters, and absinthe), Hand Grenade (alcoholic Ecto-Cooler that comes in a cool fucking grenade cup), beignets, alligator sausage, King Cake (the creepy, plastic baby you'll bite on is *supposed* to be baked in).

Mardifuckin'gras. Originally a celebration of feasting before fasting for Lent (aka "Fat Tuesday"), New Orleans' Mardi Gras takes partying to epic proportions. **Bourbon Street**, a strip of touristy bars and cheesy restaurants, is the best place in NOLA to see titties on the regular during Mardi Gras, and let's face it—that's the main reason people come to New Orleans in February. But even bead-toting, fake-boobie flashers get old after a while. Less crappy bars include **Lafitte's Blacksmith Shop**, which looks like a place you'd get bombed if life were a real version of the Oregon Trail. If you're sick of stepping in vomit, escape the Mardi Gras madness and tuck into nearby **Arnaud's French 75**, where guys in white tuxes will pour you fancy-pants cocktails through thick screens of cigar smoke.

When the parades are over and the po-po close down the streets around the **French Quarter**, you'll need to find some indoor spaces to continue getting schwasted. **Johnny White's Bar** is a less douchey version of Bourbon Street neighbor **Pat O'Brien's**; grab some booze from bartenders who are often as wasted as their customers. **Cajun Mikes Pub n' Grub** is open until 2:00 A.M. (or whenever people stop getting sloppy, which is sometimes well beyond that), with its delicious, cheap ass po' boys and $2 PBRs. Stave off a potential hangover with coffee and a beignet at **Café Du Monde**, which is usually filled with obese tourists during the day, but is pretty pleasant at 4:00 A.M. (open twenty-four hours a day, hollaaa!).

A hundred and twenty hours of party parades: The best thing to do is trip balls while watching the famous Mardi Gras parades, known for their elaborate floats and sometimes eccentric *krewes* (local organizations):

- **Krewe of Muses (Thursday):** hot chicks who throw girly things like sparkly shoes, jewelry, maybe birth control if you're lucky.
- **Krewe d'Etat (Friday):** floats that make fun of politics, political figures, and throw glowy skull necklaces.
- **Krewe of Endymion (Saturday):** float riders take the slogan "Throw Until It Hurts" to heart and pelt their audiences with all kinds of plastic crap—this shit is *cray*.
- **Krewe of Bacchus (Sunday):** this is the biggest of the party parades, packed with flamboyantly decorated floats, overindulgent costumes, and drunken celebrities dressed as crazy people.
- **Krewe of Orpheus (Monday):** was started by local Harry Connick Jr., but if you have to miss one then this newcomer is your safest bet.

FUCKED UP FIRSTHAND

Bells rang. Whistles blew. Lights flashed and an alarm wailed. The bartender threw a handful of ice into the air and passed a drink to Patrick. The drink was some kind of clear alcohol with bright red grenadine "bleeding" into the cup. Shoved into it was a rubber shark. Patrick downed the drink, removed the shark, and stuck it through the unzipped fly of his jeans.

Tropical Isle was like a washed-up Margaritaville: loud music, obnoxious-colored décor, and a trashy drink menu. It was the perfect place to start our "Drink All Day" day. A couple of girls stood at a sticky, high-top table nearby. I'm guessing they were local, from their matching booty shorts and tank tops emblazoned with the name of a restaurant down the street. They had "butter" faces (everything sexy "but her" face); still definitely fuckable.

Patrick sauntered over to the table, slurring, "Hey there."

"Nice shark." The blond chick eyed the exposed floppy rubber boner.

"I'll trade it for your underwear," Patrick replied with a drunken smile.

The blonde looked to her friend and shrugged. She disappeared past the breathalyzer in the corner of the bar where Patrick blew a 1.8 a few minutes ago, reemerging with a tiny, silken wad. She put it on the table, and ripped the shark out from Patrick's exposed crotch hole. "You have to give these back at the end of your drink," she said. "But you can keep the pann'ies."

VERDICT

The most glorious annual shitshow in America, Mardi Gras will be the best/worst decision of your life.

Katka Lapelosová

2: High Elevation

The most fucked-up job I ever had was working at a Tahoe ski resort as "parking lot." We were the guys who got there at 5:30 A.M. and skidded around in the resort's shittiest pickup with the heater cranked, some garbled classic rock station on the radio, and a fat bowl usually going. At different intervals we'd jump out, grab cones from the back, and set up long rows across the lots.

Later, as the cars started arriving, we were the ones out there waving flags and directing Tahoe vacationers into the parking places, moving cones for "secret spots" (an extra $20 for San Francisco regulars in the know). It was all hand signals and head nodding and you had to do it extremely high and well insulated in your goggles, headphones, and parka. If conditions were right there would be fresh snow falling, and as you tracked around in your snowboarding boots, the surface of the world was soft and quiet, the sun just breaking over the Sierra, and you were squarely within yourself—aware that "parking lot" was the lowest rung, looked down on by the lifties and the morons in rentals and the cafeteria, pretty much everyone on the mountain—but that you got the most riding time of anyone, and that's why you were there paying dues, that's why you'd learned all the glades and powder stashes, and as you waved in another car to the rhythm of the drum and bass in your headphones, it all felt like "yours" somehow.

You were Parking Lot Bro!

Everyone working on the mountain seemed to have his or her own little scam going (ticket-clipping being the oldest), and there was the predictable underground drug economy. At the time it seemed not only justifiable, a sweet pushback from the proletariat against the corporate machine, but something (as the exchange workers from

South America were in on it, too) you were almost proud of for its internationality.

Luckily I had sense enough to get out of there after a season. But in the ten years since I've always lived near mountains. I like the feeling and perspective of being up "at elevation"—say, riding an early chairlift at Eldora where you look back down through miles of Front Range blue sky and know that, had you made other choices, you could've been in Denver or "the flats" breathing a shit-brown cloud of pollution.

Of course not every place in this chapter is literally high altitude. Some, like Portland or Dawson, are actually low, but essentially nodes of adventure sports/mountain culture, places where people's stories from days out killing it at Mount Hood or completing multi-day floats down the Yukon River are then recirculated back into the local bars over pints of stout.

Overall, there's a wide range of places: Kathmandu, La Paz, Lukla, Machu Picchu, Anchorage, and others where the focus may not be on paddling or snowboarding or riding bikes. Which is right: sometimes all it takes is having a new scale, seeing mountains in the distance and feeling small.

When in doubt, go higher.

14. Whistler, British Columbia

SEASON: November through March (winter) or June through September (summer).
IDEAL CONDITIONS: A clear morning after a foot of fresh pow.
DAYTIME ACTIVITY: Shredding.
LODGING RECOMMENDATIONS: HI-Whistler Hostel, Sundial Boutique Hotel, Snowbird Whistler, or try Squamish or Pemberton for cheaper options.
INGESTIBLES: Poutine, sushi, smoked salmon, marijuana, Canadian whiskey.

Boarder at Whistler about to make the best of windblown pow conditions. Photo by Evan Gearing.

Between the peaks of Whistler and its counterpart Blackcomb, beneath the world's highest peak-to-peak gondola, and at the bottom of all those teetering chairlifts transporting humanity to crazy heights, lies picture-perfect Whistler Village. At night it transforms into a fucking hot mess of beautiful young people with goggle-tans, skin-tight jeans, and Volcom V-necks. Yes, families on vacation and wealthy couples in matching ski suits abound, but after dinner, most families scurry back to their overpriced hotel rooms before the village transforms into a playground for rambunctious twenty-somethings celebrating life, or youth, or finally pulling off that 720 stalefish.

But first, it's preferable to start your day shredding up (or hiking down, if it's summer) these world-class slopes. Look around: this is about as good as life can get. Then take a nap, or join the après crowd. The village is small. You can crawl from bar to bar in under ten minutes on pedestrian-only cobblestone pathways, which become an inebriated paradise for stumbling after too many "Sticky Canadians" (a shot of 151 rum and maple syrup).

Assuming you're spending all your dollars on your lift tickets, accommodation, and booze, eat on the cheap. It's the West Coast: that means sushi. If that's not your thing, hit up **Fat Tony's** (pizza), **Zog's Dogs** (gourmet hot dogs), or try these bars that have somewhat affordable eats: **El Furniture Warehouse** and **21 Steps Kitchen and Bar**.

The happy-hour epicenter for the chill, straight-off-the-hill crowd is **Garibaldi Lift Co.** Also popular is the **Dubh Linn Gate**, an Irish pub that was literally imported brick by brick from Dublin. Fucking hard-core. They have the biggest selection of beers, and the biggest pours: twenty ounces versus the more common sixteen ounces found elsewhere. It fills early because of its large patio and adjacent location to the gondolas, and stays full late because of its live Irish and local music.

Another fixture is **Amsterdam Café Pub.** This is a good place to grab some drinks (or food, if you haven't yet) before you head to dance at **Maxx Fish Lounge.** This is more of a top-forty/party anthem–style club, but for dancing in Whistler it's the best option. For the grindier, hoodie-and-skate-shoe crowd, there is **Tommy Africa's.** The kitschy décor, cover charge, mandatory coat check, and meat market might be a turnoff at first, but it generally gets packed on weekends, and '80s nights.

Other places of note: **Crystal Lounge,** which has cheap wings, drink specials, and karaoke nights to boot; **Citta's Bistro,** a local hangout that is pronounced "Cheetah" (don't look like a tourist) has live music in the summertime; **Black's Pub,** if you require more beer and less dancing; and **Three Below,** which can have killer drink specials, such as four shots for $14 USD or $5.75 USD doubles.

Once you're right drunk, danced to sweaty oblivion, and gloriously alive, be careful getting back to your room. Not only is there ice to be wary of, but many a drunk tourist has passed out in the snow and received a slew of frosty injuries.

Tips for Whistler:

- Drinking age is nineteen years old.
- No drinking in public (especially strict within the village).
- "Family Friendly" hours end after dinnertime.

NOTES FROM A LOCAL
Our motto in Whistler is to "live life like you're always on vacation." We stand by it. We don't need coffee or drugs. We've got Whistler and Blackcomb, fresh snow, fresh air, and the best view in the world.

VERDICT
Once you make that final bend on Highway 99, you'll understand.

Kate Siobhan

15. Anchorage, Alaska

SEASON: The months surrounding either solstice (June 21 or December 21); autumn equinox is pretty mellow; spring equinox is the annual Fur Rendezvous Festival.
IDEAL CONDITIONS: Nearly twenty-four hours of daylight in summer; winters are surprisingly mild.
DAYTIME ACTIVITY: Paddling on Prince William Sound, hiking in the Chugach.
LODGING RECOMMENDATIONS: Alaska Backpackers Inn.
INGESTIBLES: Microbrews, wine, local concoctions (ask your bartender for a "duck fart"), the holy trinity of seafood (salmon, king crab, halibut), reindeer sausages with cola-carmelized onions.

Don't let the "big city" of Anchorage (population: three hundred thousand) deter you from the fact that it's still the true gateway to

The Last Frontier. While it is Alaska's largest settlement, in summer months the scent of moose musk rolls down 4th, and in the winter it's host to the Running of the Reindeer, the arctic version of Spain's infamous bull-scamper. Anchorage is a world-class stay-buzzed destination, and even if the mosquitoes suck you dry, they'll be drunk, too.

If you visit in summertime, get out of the bars and into the wild (no broken bus or *Fuck the Free World* attitude needed) with a few sixers or growlers in your backpack: Drinking under twenty-four-hour daylight in June is best experienced outside. The microbreweries per capita here rival those anywhere, and their attached restaurants will keep you happily topped up on grub.

Grab beer to go courtesy of **Broken Tooth Brewing** (found at **Moose's Tooth** and **Bear's Tooth** restaurants) or **Midnight Sun Brewing** to prepare your palate for some Far North brews. If you're feeling classy, **Glacier Brewhouse** has exotic imports, such as a two-year-old Ukrainian eisbock.

More adventurous types should visit in winter. The bars are strung far enough apart that the first words you'll say upon entering them are "*Shitshitshitit'scoldlikewitch'stits!*" **Humpy's Great Alaskan Alehouse** lives up to its namesake with a few dozen handles on the premises (local, domestic, and import), and across the way is the **Sub Zero Micro Lounge** with a few more exotic taps for your discerning palate—usually some good live music, too.

The infamous **Darwin's Theory** holds the coveted reputation as "best dive bar" in a state that is chock-full of dive bars. If you want strip club sleaze without actually going to a strip club, the über-silver **Platinum Jaxx** is enough of a glitterfuck to do you in for a while. And if ever Alaska were to package an "authentic Alaskan bar" in the way the Irish have done their pubs, you'll love both **Pioneer Bar** and **F Street Station**. Speaking of Irish pubs, Anchorage's own Celtic sons can be found at **McGinley's**. This is one of the better staging grounds for the aforementioned Running of the Reindeer.

Save **Chilkoot Charlie's** in midtown for your last stop before heading home. After the metal detector entry and getting your security picture taken, make nice with the armed bouncers and saunter over to one of over a half-dozen sub-bars inside this dimly lit den with no windows and few exits. You can order a tequila sunrise if you want, but you'll probably feel a little out of place. You could be asked to remove your hood if you're wearing one—it's not quite the equivalent of wearing a football jersey or rosary beads in Belfast, but it's in the same vein of justified paranoia.

FUCKED UP FIRSTHAND

On every square inch of vertical surface around me was an array of fire hazard material piled on for ambiance: neon signage ("Bird Light" and "Birdweiser"), Christmas tinsel, and Big Spender certificates from past patrons who had "Spent the Equivalent of 1,000 Cents in One Night Here"—not to mention dozens of pairs of bras and panties, the result of fifteen years of drunk and horny women who, by the looks of it, bought their undergarments in bulk.

Across the room, a curvy sparkle-pop vixen in a white turtleneck and spray-on leggings ordered something fruity. Her arctic-bleached hair looked bioluminescenced in the dull light. The salty old dog beside her—probably an English pirate in a previous life—leaned in with a trademark Bird House pickup line: "Are you anywhere here?" He motioned to the wall with a circular motion, gesturing at the lingerie stapled to the sheetrock.

"No, and I could never be," she responded without flinching, a glint of weird sex in her eyes. "I don't wear underwear."

VERDICT

Besides 9.6-magnitude earthquakes, freak chinook winds, black ice, frostbite, can't-see-your-hands-in-front-of-your-face blizzards, not enough daylight, too much daylight, grizzly bears, black bears, mama moose, wolf packs, clouds of mosquitos that (literally) cast a shadow, a terrifying bore tide, avalanches, and Sarah Palin, there's no reason you *cheechakos* shouldn't already be here. And close the door on your way in.

Zak Erving

16. Salar de Uyuni, Bolivia

SEASON: For the classic optical-illusion pics, any month other than rainy season, which is November through March.
IDEAL CONDITIONS: A group of five like-minded companions (no more, no less—Jeep tours hold six).
LODGING RECOMMENDATIONS: Cheap places around Uyuni are impossible to miss. Tours come with base accommodation.
INGESTIBLES: The salt under your feet (literally), liquor you buy from shops before the road trip, llama pesto pizza from Minuteman Revolutionary Pizza.

Since there aren't too many drinking establishments around the great Bolivian Salt Flats, it's more important that you know how rather than where to party. For starters, when you embark on the typical three-day, two-night road trip around Salar de Uyuni, be absolutely positive that your driver is not drunk, especially around Carnaval (February). This sounds obvious, but it's harder than you think. Plan on an extra day or two in Uyuni as a buffer; strikes, weather, festivals, or hangovers prevent many travelers from departing on time (also harder than you think).

You can kill time and test your tolerance at **Extreme Fun Pub**, which has a sand-covered floor and crudely named cocktails in anatomically suggestive mugs. Bully your companions into taking "the challenge," where you must finish ten potent shots in a limited amount of time (bartender on-hand to assist with straw setup and lighting drinks on fire).

After you've realized you can't leave Uyuni for another day, head to **Minuteman Revolutionary Pizza**, where Chris from Boston and his Bolivian wife will offer you the kind of Western food you've taken for granted all your life. Bask in the little things (toilet paper, hooray!) before setting off on your Salt Flat adventure.

It's absolutely essential to purchase alcohol before your trip, as there's no place to buy it once you leave Uyuni. Try the souvenir shops, some of which have random selections of booze. Make sure you overdo it so you don't run out. Don't forget the *limónes*. And buy a bag of coca leaves for your driver, too.

Over the next few days you'll see hundreds of pink flamingos as well as psychedelic lagoons, geysers, snow-capped peaks, hot springs, and Salvador Dalí–like landscapes (particularly in the desert named after him). People usually end their tour at the Chilean border, but you can also ride back to Uyuni.

The obvious highlight is the four-thousand-square-mile Salt Flats, the world's largest. Scientists say it's the biggest reserve of lithium, geologists say it was a prehistoric lake, but alcoholics say it's just one gigantic tequila shot waiting to happen.

The little hotel here **Palacio de Sal** is, for those who are linguistically challenged, made of salt, but note that for sanitary reasons they don't allow you to lick the walls.

So here you go. Walk into the clean salt (away from where you park), get your group ready, hand the camera to your driver, rack up those tequila shots, and prep the slices of lime. Pour a splash of tequila on the ground to pay respect to *Pachamama* (Mother Earth).

NOTES FROM A LOCAL
Salar de Uyuni is a major stop on the Gringo Trail, so try to explore other parts of the Bolivian countryside, too, if you have time.

VERDICT
Salar de Uyuni is the manifestation of *Pachamama*'s awesomeness— and proof that she's an enabler.

Natalie Grant

17. Dawson City, Yukon, Canada*

SEASON: May through August (spring through summer).
IDEAL CONDITIONS: After spending weeks in the backcountry.
DAYTIME ACTIVITY: Paddling on the Yukon River.
LODGING RECOMMENDATIONS: Ranges from the very fancy (Bombay Peggy's, a beautifully restored converted brothel) to the relatively basic (The Bunkhouse, with communal showers, $40 USD a night) or the hostel across the river.
INGESTIBLES: Yukon microbrews, elk meat.

In 1896, George Carmack and his wife found gold in a creek near the Klondike River. In the next months and years, men left their wives, jobs, and ordinary lives, and underwent extreme hardship to

Singer-songwriter Brandon Isaak very much at home in the Yukon's Dawson City Music Fest. Photo by Zack Embree.

pursue elusive fortune in the famed Klondike Gold Rush. There has been nothing like it before or since. Dawson City is the settlement at the confluence of the Klondike and the Yukon rivers that was built by these miners. It was built, literally, by gold dust, a northern El Dorado that stands today as a testament to men, to will, and to desire.

All of this makes for rather a good time. The city today is a small settlement without paved roads or big box stores (save for the unfortunate behemoth of the **Westmark Hotel**, which partners with the Holland America line to bring cruise-goers in high summer). Old auction houses and brothels still stand, as does half of **Jack London's cabin** moved there from the woods. Parks Canada bandies about the phrase "living museum" a lot, and for once, it's relatively accurate.

Unsurprisingly, many of the fun things to do in Dawson are gold- and wilderness-related. If you're feeling kitschy, adventurous, or have read "To Build a Fire" recently, you can go pan for gold and may actually find some. Or you can paddle down the Yukon or wander **Tombstone Territorial Park**, which is almost surreal in its desolate beauty. Yukon is the only place in Canada where you can drive on a paved road beyond the Arctic Circle. You can climb the top of the hill above Dawson City and watch for the Aurora Borealis.

If you prefer your entertainment (relatively) urban, and would like to do some of the aforementioned getting fucked up, your options are similarly bountiful. Frankly, it's historically been all about the ladies. Hordes of ice-bound men often desire some fun and female company, and several enterprising ladies set up bars/dancehalls/casinos/other to that end.

Diamond Tooth Gertie's is a must-go—the oldest legal casino in Canada, founded by a woman who stuck a diamond between her two front teeth to become memorable during the gold-rush days.

There are slots and poker, of course, but there are also three live dancehall-girl shows a night, which are fun and impressive and funny and musical and filled with hot girls. **Bombay Peggie's** used to be a brothel and is now a great place to stay if you have a lot of money and a great place to get a martini even if you don't. **Klondike Kate's** has the best burgers in town and local beers. Owned by Europeans, **La Table** has fine dining.

Nightlife-wise, easily the cheapest and best beers in town are at **Midnight Sun Hotel**, which has a wide selection of Yukon Brewing beers on tap. (The Yukon is the only part of Canada where local microbrews outsell the big-name competitors, a heartening fulfillment of the old dictum "Think Globally, Drink Locally.") Other options are the **Sourdough Saloon,** or the **Eldorado Hotel,** or several others. In any case, the town is small, so finding out where the party is on any given night is laughably easy. This is essentially the whole theme of the Yukon: very few people, but quality far exceeds quantity.

FUCKED UP FIRSTHAND

Dawson City was an oasis after fourteen days of paddling the Yukon River. We drank microbrew in the park and listened to Quebecois gypsies sing about the Yukon wind, we read art books in the Yukon School of Visual Art's library, we ate absolutely stellar sandwiches at Cheechakos bake shop, and on the last night, we did do some of the aforementioned fucking up at a dance party/free concert organized by Dawson City's very own Free Store.

My alcohol tolerance was not so bombproof at that point, so my recollection of the night consists of fragments of strangely good acoustic covers of Yeah Yeah Yeahs songs and dancing with very pretty girls. Afterward, we went home to our little tent on the banks of the river, because in the Yukon you can pitch a tent on the banks of the river within city limits and no one cares.

VERDICT

A solitary oasis of civilization and central heating in one of the rawest and most beautiful wildernesses of the north, with good beer.

Tereza Jarnikova

18. Kathmandu, Nepal

SEASON: September through November (between monsoon season and winter).

IDEAL CONDITIONS: Drinking Raksi while contemplating Himalayas.

DAYTIME ACTIVITY: Go to Pashupatinath Temple or Swayambhunath Temple.

LODGING RECOMMENDATIONS: Hostels or cheap hotels in Thamel, like Alobar 1000. For slightly higher rates, Tings in Lazimpat is like a hostel for young families.

INGESTIBLES: Expensive beer and wine, local liquor (Raksi), momos (dumplings) to line the stomach, not to mention whispering offers of hash and opium.

Arriving in Kathmandu is like sending your senses to a new school in a fabled part of town where all the kids play games you've never heard of. Low-rise buildings of all shapes sprout out awkwardly like concrete crops planted at intervals over the past few years. Birkenstock soldiers of the tie-dye hippie squadron used to arrive in droves via the Magic Bus or magic carpet. They claimed a road called Freak Street and used to get *rangi-changi* (a brilliant word that means colorful in Nepali) on all sorts of concoctions.

Getting fucked up in Kathmandu is nothing new. You'll be offered everything under the smog-filtered sun, from hash to opium as soon as you get into **Thamel**. Getting fucked up is an all-you-can-eat buffet; just make sure your eyes aren't bigger than your stomach. Drop your things at the **Alobar** hostel and break the seal with a cold local beer. They're about $2 USD in the shops but they are hefty bottles. Everest is the light, crisp option while Gorkha has more of a full-bodied flavor (for the refined beer connoisseurs out there).

Before things get out of hand go to **Boudha Nat,** a temple with views of the far-off Himalayas. Dip into one of the dingy local bars in the area and ask for Raksi. It's a potent liquor made from millet or barley. Neck a couple of glasses of that and try to last the whole evening. Most bars are in Thamel so hail a taxi and bargain the driver down to a reasonable price. At tourist sites you're likely to receive a ludicrous first offer.

Sink to ground level and grab a drink around low-flying tables at **Electric Pagoda**. It's like a chill-out tent at a dance festival with good food and ambient music. Bop over to **Sam's Bar** with a marker and tag the wall with graffiti. **Fluid** is down an alleyway a few meters up the road—have a cocktail there to add to the *rangi-changi* contents in your bloodstream.

Check out the courtyard in **New Orleans.** You'll hear crappy cover bands wailing from rooftop bars everywhere so you need to be selective. **Purple Haze** is a capacious hangar of a venue with tributes to Hendrix and other rock and metal icons tattooed on white walls. As the traffic between your brain and mouth slows, skank across to **Phat Kath** and listen to some reggae then dart across to **Reggae Bar** (which doesn't play much reggae). Make your way to **House of Music** for some original live sounds. There are a few decisions you now have to make:

- Go home.
- Go to a horrendous sausage fest at **Fire Club** (aka Hell).
- Find a little booze store that'll let you drink behind the shutters for a while.

Choose the third option. Walk around the backstreets and soon enough you'll stumble upon a liquor store with the shutters half closed (kind of like your eyelids at this point) and old, wobbly feet visible through the gap. Pop your head in and no doubt you'll be welcomed in to sit on rickety stools and have meaningful conversations rife with gesticulation and exaggerated human connections between you and the grandpa rocking next to you.

NOTES FROM A LOCAL
Start early because most of the bars will start winding down as midnight approaches.

VERDICT
Rangi-changi.

Dikson

19. La Paz, Bolivia

SEASON: April through October (fall through spring).
IDEAL CONDITIONS: After acclimatizing for a couple of days (yes, twelve-thousand-foot altitude means you get drunk faster).
DAYTIME ACTIVITY: Cycling down Death Road.
LODGING RECOMMENDATIONS: Either the Wild Rover Hostel (unofficially the highest Irish bar in the world) or Loki Hostel. By the end of the night you'll probably have had drinks at both and already forgotten which one you're actually checked into anyway.
INGESTIBLES: Paceña (local beer), Roskoff (vodka), San Pedro (psychedelic cactus), and coca tea in the morning to help you see straight.

By the time you reach La Paz—no doubt after a cramped, overnight bus ride delayed by protests of unknown origin—you will already feel spent. But the party has only begun, my friend. So shake it off.

Getting shafted out of its coastline by Chile, Bolivia then festered in the international community's mind as having nothing but drugs and poverty, which is exactly the dumb myth that thankfully keeps tourist hordes away. There may be rampant drug use, but mostly by idiot backpackers like us.

Wild Rover Hostel on Calle Comercio and **Loki Hostel** on Calle Loayza both have weekly rotations of themed parties. Smear UV paint on your ears or wear nothing but toilet paper to blend in, and dancing on the bar is nonnegotiable. Before you start ranting about hostels, just don't. The poor bastard serving you drinks said the same thing when he first arrived here for a three-day trip. That was six months ago.

Head down Calle Loayza and act cool as you pass the bored, heavily armed policemen with riot shields, then hit the main thoroughfare: El Prado, or Avenida 16 de Julio. Reggae-themed **TTKOS** on nearby Calle México will get you dancing, sweaty, and hammered in ten minutes. It's in a basement (cave?) and decked out with Che Guevara art. Wooden bowls filled with cocktails come with a half-dozen straws for your table to share. Tuesdays are best.

Mongo's on Hermanos Manchego has great food; the small dance floor is always packed, and the sprawling layout has corners and hallways to ditch the clinger that won't leave you alone. Behind a few gates on Avenida Arce is **Traffic** (not to be confused with **Target,** on 6 de Agosto), and farther down is **Pa'Goza,** all with decent music. The English pub **Oliver's Travels** throws some wild costume parties; the **Adventure Brew Hostel** has beer on tap (gasp!) and a killer view from the roof deck.

If it's Monday, no choice but **Blue House**—open until dawn, guarded by bouncers with saintlike tolerance, and filled with alpaca-clad travelers. If avoiding gringos, try the deceitfully named **Hard Rock Cafe** on Calle Illampu (not the obligatory collection of celebrity guitar porn—just a loud, packed club), or the far better choice of dancing to Cumbia at **Malegria** on Pasaje Medinacelli. Note that almost all bars will have indoor smoking.

At sunrise, just one place remains open: the elusive cocaine bar known as **Route 36.** Putting its location here is pointless, as it moves every few months. It's actually not elusive, mind-blowing, or adventurous; it's a dingy, awkward lounge with shifty-looking backpackers failing to look casual while ordering bad-quality, overpriced cocaine from the waiter. That said, it's a fine place to chill out and chat until 10:00 A.M., even just with beer. Taxis often take you there if you ask, but do so at your own risk. No locals allowed, either. A better option may be to read *Marching Powder* by Rusty Young and Thomas McFadden and scare yourself away.

An infinitely cooler secret bar is the real secret bar, which may be the absolute best bar this writer has ever been to. Ever. *Hint:* it's in Sopocachi. Good luck.

FUCKED UP FIRSTHAND

Still alive! I've biked (all right, coasted) down the World's Most Dangerous Road, aka the North Yungas Road, aka the Death Road. Or "that thing everybody does in La Paz." After bundling up and starting at 15,400 feet, I'm dismounting at 3,600 feet and sweating bullets in shorts and a tank, surrounded by absurdly colored butterflies and chanting monkeys. It's the Amazon basin. How the hell?

Before our group heads back up to La Paz in the van (loose term), we stop to buy a half-dozen Paceñas each—the bike guides get one from everyone as a tip for being badass. Seats are limited; I offer to sit in the nook by the sliding door with my buddy. We toast, chug, giggle, reminisce, toast again. The van hits a bump. The sliding door opens.

A 3,300-foot sheer drop is inches from my toes, a thread of a river far below. And silence. The door latches shut again. Either the fifth beer has gotten to us, or we genuinely don't care.

VERDICT

Many strong souls have caved when it was time to leave, and ended up overstaying visas.

Natalie Grant

20. Portland, Oregon

SEASON: May through October, especially July, August, and September, festivals season.

IDEAL CONDITIONS: Mild summer, somewhere between 70 degrees Fahrenheit (21 degrees Celsius) and 85 degrees Fahrenheit (32 degrees Celsius) with occasional hot spells.

DAYTIME ACTIVITY: Head up to Mount Hood for year-round snowfield play.

LODGING RECOMMENDATIONS: Nines Hotel, Ace Hotel for upscale; Jupiter Hotel for midrange; Northwest Portland Hostel, Portland Hostel for on the cheap.

INGESTIBLES: Craft beer, local wines and spirits, coffee, marijuana, cocaine, an array of cafés, restaurants, and food carts spread across the city.

It's right what Fred Armisen said in the first episode of *Portlandia*: Portland is where twentysomethings go to retire, and the dream of the nineties is still alive here. But at the same time, there is so much change and turnover in Portland that one can't get bored of the place.

When you want cocktails and don't feel like changing out of your flannel, head to one of two places: **Dig a Pony (DAP)** or **The Sweet Hereafter**. The bar staff at DAP is easy on the eyes and are eclectic DJs. Downtown, start at **Valentine's**, a well-known hookup haven where Portland's art and musician crowds gather. Order the Seanz Kafka, a ginger-infused bourbon cocktail with Becherovka, lemon juice, and kombucha on ice. If you feel like seeing skin and possibly have some strange encounters, check **Magic Garden**. With its solitary pole, it must be the smallest strip joint in the city but a couple of drinks at this Chinatown lounge can lead to anything, often snorting lines off a mirror in some dark, red-walled loft.

On the eastside, mustachioed long-haired men and female counterparts clad in vintage loafers, skinny jeans, and black leather head to popular pickup spots **Rontoms** and **Rotture** for shitty but strong cocktails. The former boasts a large patio and Ping-Pong tables, while the latter doubles as a sweaty dance club where regional DJs spin foreign electronica and remixed indie hits. **Holocene**, however, with its industrial aesthetic, bright lights, and international nights, is the best choice for ass shaking. Before heading to either of these places, you might want to fuel up at **East End** a notorious bar with cheap, tall pours.

If it's dives you like, try **My Father's Place** and **Dot's Café**. MFP, as the locals call it, is old-school southeast, where the grandfathers of today's hipsters would have gone for a drink. There are still a few regulars who hang at the bar, but it's mostly a prefunking dive for pinball and Buck Hunter lovers who like to chase their whiskey with $1 jello shots. Dot's is known for its beer, burgers, and velvet nude paintings. Any night of the week is good to go at the **Horse Brass Pub**. It has hundreds of beers to choose from, including hard-to-find labels from around the world, and all-important dartboards.

After you close down the bars, shore things up with a late-night snack. The food cart pod at **SE 12th and Hawthorne** is perfect: crepes, fried pies, pizza and *poutine* (French fries with gravy and curds). If you're downtown, hit up **Lúc Lác**, a Vietnamese café open until 4:00 A.M. and serving a variety of cheap plates perfect for sharing and getting that stale boozy taste out of your mouth. A cheaper and more traditional option is the **Original Hotcake House**. Open twenty-four hours, it's everyone's famous bad-decision greasy spoon. At either of these places it's possible to find someone to buy pot from, which would help with some shut-eye so you can do it all over again the next day. Because that's how Portland does it.

Things to remember about Portland:

- If you're a liquor drinker, keep in mind that a lot of bars' bottom shelf stuff is a step up from what you'd normally get.

- Don't stay in one place all night. Portlanders move around, the scenes change.
- We're bike-friendly, but cycling and drinking is a DUI, and cops enforce it. Don't make that mistake.
- We're not Seattle.

FUCKED UP FIRSTHAND

It was a Thursday in August. It was also our second house party since Monday. Friends from around town and out of town showed up in their cutoff denim shorts, T-shirts, and wayfarers. There were two barbecues blazing in the driveway, two refrigerators full of High Life long necks and Pabst tall boys.

Around sundown a random couple asked if they could smoke me out as thanks for letting them inside the party. I obliged. But whatever they'd laced that pot with didn't sit right with me. As the minutes passed, my vision became foggier, my mood darker. I was told the next day by a friend that I'd gone up to the bar, demanded a bottle of whiskey, and then walked out of the house, not to be seen again until that morning.

It turned out that I'd walked to a small indie club we sometimes frequented on weekends. I had the stamp on my hand to prove I'd been there, but couldn't remember what I'd done. That night, along with some friends, I went back. The doorman greeted me with, "There he is!" and proceeded to give me a large one-armed hug. "You killed it last night." To this day I still don't know what happened.

VERDICT

More affordable than Seattle and San Francisco, almost like Brooklyn without the pretentiousness.

Christopher J. Miller

21. Machu Picchu, Peru

SEASON: July and August.
IDEAL CONDITIONS: Not rainy or foggy.
DAYTIME ACTIVITY: Vibing on ancient trails.
LODGING RECOMMENDATIONS: Aguas Calientes, a nearby town, has a plethora of overpriced accommodation available.
INGESTIBLES: Cusqueña beer.

Despite being proudly Australian I do not advocate staggering drunkenly around these amazing ruins slurring things like, "Fucking big walls, hey, mate . . ." before running off for a leak behind an ancient wall and generally acting like, well, an Aussie abroad. I do, however, think it is quite reasonable (absolutely necessary) to celebrate after trekking through Machu Picchu. If you cannot wait until after the

"I do not advocate staggering drunkenly around these amazing ruins slurring things like, 'Fucking big walls, hey, mate . . .'" Photo by Collins Paris.

ruins there is but one option: **Wiñay Wayna Camp** is the final camp-site on the four-day Camino Inca or Inca Trail, perched high above the Urubamba River. When the fog clears the views are astounding. Near the camping area is a large restaurant with a balcony bursting with plastic tables, overflowing ashtrays, and smelly trekkers. The excited mood on the balcony is not a party vibe so much as a look-where-we-are buzz as everyone who drinks here will be trekking at 5:00 A.M. to see the sun rise over Machu Picchu. To stock the restaurant locals carry food and alcohol up incredibly steep switchbacks; by buying a brew you are keeping these people employed.

The only alcoholic drink available is deliciously cool Cusqueña beer. A 10 soles ($3.80 USD) token is bought from a cashier then exchanged for a beer at the bar.

Following three tough days of alcohol-free trekking, drinking one beer at 8,000 feet feels like five at sea level. And after three days of gritty porridge and fatty chicken stew it is brill to be served all-you-can-eat sausages, rice, noodles, pork, stuffed peppers . . . you name it, and some hapless soul has lugged it up here for you.

The next day, catch a bus to Aguas Calientes, or Machu Picchu Town. There are numerous accommodation options but due to the ease of train transit to Cusco, most budget-conscious tourists only stay one night. The train ride back to Cusco is one of the most scenic in the world and serves plenty of beer.

FUCKED UP FIRSTHAND

After a mind-blowing, we spent the five-hour wait in Aguas Calientes sitting on a sunny balcony and gulping down lilliputian "Crazy sale! 4 for 1" cocktails. An hour later the table was filled with empty drinks and three very drunk gate-crashers.

When I finally jumped on the train I felt beyond relief to find a working, relatively clean toilet. This state reached near euphoria when I returned to find Chad grinning and handing me a fresh beer.

VERDICT

An almost cartoonishly intense place that should be experienced at least once whether drunk or sober.

Ben West

22. Lukla (Mount Everest), Nepal

SEASON: October through November.
IDEAL CONDITIONS: Foggy.
DAYTIME ACTIVITY: Acclimatizing, glissading.
LODGING RECOMMENDATIONS: Numbur Lodge is right near the airport, Everest Summit Lodge claims to have hot water and western toilets.
INGESTIBLES: Yak Donalds, Raski.

Lukla is the gateway to the Khumbu Valley; every person visiting

Sagarmatha is the Nepali name for Mount Everest. View via fifteen-seater, turboprop plane on a Himalayan mountain tour. Photo by Tim Kelley.

or leaving Mount Everest must pass through this small town. Smelly socks, yak wool hats, and Everest Lager are the order of the day. Peak trekking (drinking) season is October through November whereas Christmas sees many Australians flock to the region.

The first drinking options are at either the **Numbur** or **Everest Summit** lodges. Both hostels sell cheap Everest Lager and are close to the airport. After buying some brews, go to the end of the runway where you can enjoy the view while drinking and swinging your legs practically over landing planes.

When the fog rolls in, Lukla quickly fills with stranded trekkers waiting to fly; this is when the party kicks off. The cobbled main street offers a plethora of drinking options with every generic, rocky-walled hostel selling beer. The standout bar, aptly named **The Irish Pub**, sports Guinness posters, family shields, and framed blessings, such as "May the road rise to meet your feet" on every wall, and it's not until you see a shaggy yak amble past that you're transported back to Nepal.

If Irish bars fail to excite, the next option is to grab your headlamp—there are no streetlights in Lukla—and follow your ears. Simply walk around until you hear the sounds of merriment. Walk into said establishment, introduce yourself, and before long you will be surrounded with like-minded imbibers drinking Everest Lager or Raski, an earthy tasting sludge made from either millet, rice, or whatever the locals can ferment. Raski has an evil milky glow and a matching taste and aftereffects.

Hangovers, however, are well catered for in Lukla with something resembling coffee available from Starbucks (not a true franchise . . . some ingenious soul just copied the sign) and greasy yak burgers flipped at Yak Donalds.

NOTES FROM A LOCAL

Lukla's airport is the most dangerous in the world. The sole runway has a twelve-degree incline, short length, and ends with a sheer cliff.

VERDICT

Stoke levels will be high as you're partying days away from the nearest paved road.

Ben West

23. Salta, Argentina

SEASON: December (early summer).
IDEAL CONDITIONS: Warm weather, lots of drinks.
DAYTIME ACTIVITY: Visit El Cerro de Los Siete Colores.
LODGING RECOMMENDATIONS: Exxes Hostel, Kkala Boutique Hotel, Hotel del Antiguo Convento.
INGESTIBLES: Salta beer, mate, local wine, milanesas for days.

Salta, in the northern part of Argentina, is a good destination to stop and get totally fucking wasted as you're traveling around South America. As soon as you get to the bus station you'll be accosted by five to seven hostel peddlers, each one-upping the next trying to convince you that their hostel is the best. You should choose the one willing to drive you there for free.

Head to a **Juventud Antoniana** or a **Central Norte** football game. Sit in and get drunk with the crowd. If you've been traveling around Argentina you may have already gotten the taste for Quilmes (pronounced Kill·mees), but you'll probably equally like the local but uncreatively titled Salta beer. Or if wine is more your thing you should check out a locally produced Torrontés varietal. Drink this in your room or wherever you see fit.

You're probably hungry now, so you should head to **El Palacio de la Pizza** because their pizza is actually delicious. Now that you know what to drink you have to find out where to drink it. Head down to the bohemian La Balcarce neighborhood and pop by as many places as you can fit in a day.

See if anything is cracking at **La Casa de Cultura** or head to one of Salta's many *peñas* or folk pubs. Places like **La Casona del Molino** showcase traditional Argentine music and provide a good starting point for a wild evening.

If you've gotten sufficiently twisted, head over to a *boliche* or disco, such as **Club XXI** or **Metropoli**, where you'll be with the masses dancing to electronic music and Spanish pop. The next day you'll be completely hungover, but it's not that big of a deal: you have to take an eighteen-hour bus ride to Mendoza, so there's time to recover.

FUCKED UP FIRSTHAND

After pounding through several liters of Quilmes, I walked to a club with a fifty-five-year-old park ranger I'd just met. He told me about visiting ninety-five countries, chasing grizzlies through the Canadian bush, swimming across the English Channel, and breaking himself out of an Angolan jail cell.

I wondered if I'd ever be able to tell stories as wild as his. Most of mine had to do with getting drunk and trying to hit on girls. Stories that were fun but didn't impress old men.

When he came back from the bar, he filled my glass with whiskey, and said, "Drink up." After slamming his drink back down, he promptly walked over to a circle of women half his age. Within five minutes one of them was gnawing his face.

VERDICT

The north of Argentina is overlooked.

Joshua Heller

24. Vancouver, British Columbia

SEASON: June through September (summer).
IDEAL CONDITIONS: After a weeklong wilderness trip to Whistler or on Vancouver Island.
DAYTIME ACTIVITY: Hang out in Stanley Park.

LODGING RECOMMENDATIONS: The Cambie Hostel (if you never want to sleep), Hostelling International, or better yet use Airbnb to get an apartment in the city. For a proper hotel experience, St. Regis or The Burrard.

INGESTIBLES: Marijuana, local microbrew, smoked salmon, poutine, and anything from a food truck.

If it's summertime, pack up your shit in the afternoon and get to **Wreck Beach** by the university. You'll have to teeter down about three thousand stairs (remember that for coming back up) but it's worth it. This is a stunning, secluded beach true to its hippie roots, a haven for nudists, musicians, free thinkers, and marijuana enthusiasts. Clothing is optional, partake or be respectful.

Why start here? Because die-hard Wreckers stroll up and down the beach selling nearly anything you could want while you suntan all those pale bits—beer, margaritas, sangria, drug-laced baking, and boring items like water and fresh juice. Legal? No. A longstanding tradition? Yes. Come sunset, drummers, fire-twirlers, and hula-hoopers go off.

Now that you're tanned, relaxed, and hopefully tipsy, head into the city. Say good-bye to that filth known as Molson Canadian and say hello to locally crafted "artisan" beer. **Gastown** has endless options. To blend in, be ironic. For serious beer enthusiasts, the place to be is the **Alibi Room**. A double-sided menu will keep you busy for hours. Or try **Six Acres**, which has bottled beers from around the world and some games to play at your table. Other pubs of note: **The Pint**, **The Pourhouse**, and **Bitter Tasting Room**. Check local forums, post boards, and papers for **Cask Nights**—a fresh cask of beer opens up usually around 5:00 P.M., and when it's gone . . . it's gone.

That's just downtown. On Main Street is **The Whip** and **The Five Point**, while on Commercial Drive there is **St. Augustine's**, which has a two-page beer menu and bountiful TVs for viewing sports. There's also the **Charlatan**, and **BierCraft**, all worth a check. If you're into good beer and playing nerd games, hit up the **Storm Crow Tavern** on Commercial Drive or **Guilt & Co.** in Gastown.

For dancing, the touristy place is **Granville Street.** At nighttime, it's blocked off from cars and is dubbed "The Entertainment District." Cops abound and nightclubs spill into the sidewalk. High heels, micro-skirts, and fresh rounds of nineteen-year-olds are found in abundance. If you simply must, give **Venue** or **The Roxy** a shot. Better dancing option: uber-sweaty **Celebrities** on Davie Street—a gay dance bar. Expect drag queens, bachelorette parties, and some serious exercise. It's hetero-friendly and picks up at midnight. Another option, **Shine Nightclub** in Gastown, offers three rooms with different styles of dance music. For big-name DJs and brain-melting bass, hit up **Fortune Sound Club** in Chinatown.

For live music, the best venues include: **The Railway Club, The Media Room, The Blarney Stone,** and the famous **Commodore Ballroom,** which are all downtown; **The Biltmore Cabaret** and the **Electric Owl Social Club,** on Main Street; and the historic **Waldorf Hotel** near Commercial Drive. Pick up a *Georgia Straight* newspaper for live-music listings.

Always wrap up a night out in VanCity with pizza from **Numero Uno** or **Pizza Garden,** or fresh, die-in-your-fuchsia-pumps-right-now *poutine* from **Fritz European Fry House.** Remember: the skytrain stops around 1:00 A.M.—which is dumb as fuck since all bars and clubs are open til 2:00 or 3:00 A.M.—so plan to walk or take a taxi if it's going to be a late one.

Tips for Vancouver:

- While marijuana is decriminalized, other drugs are illegal, even if they're baked into an organic quinoa cookie or a fair-trade chocolate brownie—Wreck Beachers be warned.
- Drinking age is nineteen years old. Though in the Entertainment District, you'd swear it was fourteen.

- When it comes to Vancouver and dancing, always check the venue's Web site to see if it's a theme night (i.e., '80s, '90s, hip-hop, house, or otherwise). If you're going dancing, you're going to pay a cover, so it better be music you like to dance to.

NOTES FROM A LOCAL

A nickname for Van is "No-Fun Couver" but the people using that term are just too damn lazy to be at the right place, at the right time.

VERDICT

Not so amazing for top-forty party people, but just right for the kind of people you want to party with.

Kate Siobhan

25. Žilina, Slovakia

SEASON: Summer (June) brings the crowds, but winter (January) is charming as hell with snow-covered mountains and holiday festivals downtown.
IDEAL CONDITIONS: A rustic pub downing shots of moonshine and making out with locals impressed that you know all the words to the latest Rihanna song.
DAYTIME ACTIVITY: Hike up Lietavský hrad (Lietava castle).
LODGINGS: Hotel Galileo is inexpensive and comfortable. Penzion Anton is in a weird part of town, but a single room is less than $40 USD.
INGESTIBLES: Hruškovica (pear brandy), Černá Hora beer, Slivovica and Kofola (plum brandy mixed with a delicious Slovak soda), the Portuguese carrot (super big joint), bryndzové halušky (sort of a Slovak version of mac 'n cheese).

Located about two hours north of the country's capital, Žilina is a town influenced by its youthful population. Most of all, though,

Slovaks party hard. Don't let that scene in *Eurotrip* fool you—Slovakia is cool as fuck, and Slovaks know it. You think *you're* a hipster? You've clearly never been to Žilina.

Žilina's got some historical points of interest and local attractions, but the best place to be is **Stanica Žilina-Záriečie.** Transformed from a run-down train station into a baller cultural arts facility, something awesome is always happening at Stanica. There might be a sick-ass dance concert or a crazy post-modern play, rock concerts featuring international acts, or a gallery hosting an exhibit on photography under Communism. One of the best parts about Stanica is its in-house café and bar, which gets crazy on the weekends and after events. They sell so much booze that they even managed to build a second theater on their property, completely out of beer crates and bales of straw.

The party doesn't stop at Stanica though. **Jerry's Cocktail Bar** provides creative libations that will help your drunk ass get from Mariánske námestie (nicknamed "Square Square") to Andrej Hlinka námestie ("Round Square"). There you'll find **Emócia Gallery and Caffe Club,** a swanky favorite of the local youth.

A good place to drink shots of Hruškovica is at **Migrena Pub,** located close to the train station, or check out the eclectic **Army Pub** to sample some of Slovakia's tasty beer, farther into town. But where do you go when you get those late-night drunchies? **Slovak Pub,** that's where. This place doles out huge portions of Slovak foods like *vyprážaný syr s hranolkami* (a hunk of fried cheese served with French fries), and *bryndzové halušky* (potato dumplings covered in gooey sheep's cheese and topped with crispy, fried bacon) until midnight most nights.

Slovak dos and don'ts:

- *Do* try Slovak wine. Don't be a vino snob and sneer at the idea of Eastern European wine—it's alcohol, dumb-ass, and good stuff at that.

- *Don't* stop drinking. Only stop drinking if a Slovak stops drinking, which may be a long time, so it's advisable to build up a high alcohol tolerance prior to arrival.
- *Do* know how to hold your liquor. Slovaks drink a lot, but they don't get so sloppy they puke, even if they are at home. If you drink so much that you start vomiting all over the place, Slovaks will call you a "baby teenager" because only the underage kids get nasty when they drink so much.

FUCKED UP FIRSTHAND

"Pauza!" is Polish for "Take a break!" but at Stanica it means all the Slovaks in the bar take a break and head outside to smoke weed. The conference featuring design students from across Europe has just ended for the evening, and the party has begun. Upstairs a heavy metal band plays. In the gallery, students are freestyle graffiti-ing the walls. Outside, a fire pit burns brightly, commemorating Prague Spring, when Soviet tanks invaded the capital of Czechoslovakia in 1968. Tonight, people roast marshmallows over it as a salute to more than twenty years of Communism-free government in Slovakia.

It's definitely the right time for a *pauza*.

VERDICT

It's cool to say you've been to Bratislava, but your trashy ass will sound more indie when you claim to have partied Slovak-style in Žilina.

Katka Lapelosová

3: Under the Radar

The big lie of course is that you need to actually travel somewhere to "get fucked up" (what's wrong with the back porch?), or "experience culture" (how about the side of town where you've never walked?), or "gain perspective" (ever worked construction?). Those who've traveled long enough learn that the most original moments—the times that are actually *transporting*—are not usually even reached in "the destination" but in the interstices of travel, the unexpected stop-overs and wrong turns, the botched plans, and the missed connections that somehow lead you to places not quite found on any map.

Which makes this not so much a call to stay at home, but simply look beyond the Race to See Who Has Been to the Most Places, and recognize any place as worthy of better investigation. Something under the radar doesn't necessarily mean it can only be reached by Tyrolean traverse across an otherwise impassable gorge after a six-day, alpaca-supported approach trek. Sometimes it's as simple as finding what's right there but simply missed by most everyone else.

26. McMurdo Station, Antarctica

SEASON: October through March is viable. Almost pleasant in summer (December and January).

IDEAL CONDITIONS: Temperatures just below freezing, calm winds, with the cloudy skies that partially relieve the blinding twenty-four-hour-a-day sunshine.

DAYTIME ACTIVITY: Glacier exploration.

LODGING RECOMMENDATIONS: Dorm 210 or 211 for the best mix of location, privacy, and socialization. Dorms 206 through 209 if you have

Likely the heaviest transport vehicles you'll ever be drunk in. Photo by Nathan Peerbolt.

issues sharing a bathroom. Hotel California if you want to get off the beaten path.

INGESTIBLES: Assorted wines, cheap cans of New Zealand beer, basic liquors.

Antarctica is home to numerous scientific bases and field camps. They are scattered across a continent roughly the size of the United States, making any sort of pub crawl seem impossible without the use of helicopters, dog sleds, or ice axes. However, as many participants with the U.S. Antarctic Program (USAP) can attest, hopping between the bars at McMurdo Station is entirely possible for any intrepid traveler with a genuine desire to get shit-faced.

Gallagher's Pub is the first stop for any FiNGy (Fucking New Guy), and is a combination of bar, restaurant, and dance club. This is the place for live bands and karaoke, or to see a circle of men dance around a lone, sought-after female. Go to **Burger Bar** on Sunday and Wednesday nights to eat the best (and only) hamburger money can buy. Darts, air hockey, and 2002 Golden Tee are available—all free of charge.

A short stumble from Gallagher's lies **Southern Exposure**, which until recently was the only smoking establishment in U.S.-inhabited Antarctica. Although its air has cleared in recent years, Southern still has the feeling and clientele of old-school Antarctica and is still the go-to bar when no other events are happening on station.

If you're looking for a more refined, caffeinated experience, head to the **Coffee House**. This Quonset hut–style building has some of the best baristas south of the equator. Here, you can sip on a hot, powdered-milk latte, and also enjoy some of McMurdo's "finest" wines. The Coffee House hosts open-mic night on Thursdays, and is the most cultured of all the USAP's drinking establishments. If you can get a date at McMurdo, this is the place to take them.

But the true adventure seekers, and drinkers, trek the two miles to New Zealand's **Scott Base**. The pub at Scott Base is small, but well-appointed, and boasts a spectacular view of The Royal Society Mountain Range across McMurdo Sound. Every Thursday they host "American Night," which is generally the only time Americans are welcomed to Scott Base without a personal invitation.

But even with this surprising addition to the hostelries of Mc-Murdo, the parties around station give the most opportunity for serious revelry. Halloween is the first major party of the season, and when many people choose their "ice wife." McMurdo also boasts Antarctic versions of other stateside festivities such as **Freezing Man**, a popular destination for McMurdo's eclectic elite.

The most infamous of all Antarctic festivals, however, is **Ice Stock**—the continent's largest (and only) outdoor music festival. Numerous bands, groupies, and one-man acts practice all season for the chance to play on the outdoor stage. Chili cook-offs, Frisbee tosses, and flash mobs are common occurrences on this popular New Year's Eve event.

Finally, remember these general rules about partying at the bottom of the world:

- Don't order anything you wouldn't drink without the usual garnishes (i.e., lemons, limes, olives, cherries, etc.). They don't exist.
- Beer Kozie's are used to keep your hands warm. Not to keep your beer cold.
- Bartenders in Antarctica, like everywhere else in the United States, only make money through tips.

FUCKED UP FIRSTHAND

"The odds are good that the goods are odd," said a drunken electrician after his fourth shot of Cuervo Gold. I sat next to him at the day bar, on Thanksgiving, after we had just completed the annual 5K Turkey Trot. It was my first season on the ice, and had just learned a valuable lesson on how (not) to free-ball while running in the cold. Although his maxim was in reference to the women around station, I would come to realize this statement is true for most things at the bottom of the world.

It was only after a *few* more drinks that a group of us left Southern and ventured onto the ice toward the "Ob-Tube." The light disappeared as we crawled down the turquoise metal Observation Tube, which was slid into the ocean through a hole in the ice. Much time was spent wiping our breath off the frozen glass, only to see the blooming ocean floor through the green glow of the sea ice's underbelly. It was only upon realizing the uniqueness of this experience that we wondered how odd we must look to the plankton outside.

VERDICT

Although the bars at McMurdo close relatively early, late-night partiers scatter to a variety of dorms, lounges, and workstations to continue in the revelry. So, much like the Antarctic sun that is continually shining, so, too, are the parties continually winding.

Mark Walsh

27. Bucharest, Romania

SEASON: Last few weeks before the Romanian summer vacation mid-June through mid-September.
IDEAL CONDITIONS: A weekday with nobody around, except a group of friendly taggers who invite you to an impromptu poker tournament.
DAYTIME ACTIVITY: People watching on Calea Victoriei, a concert at the Romanian Athenaeum.
LODGING RECOMMENDATIONS: The Midland Hostel, Hostel Miorita, The Funky Chicken Hostel, Ramada Majestic.
INGESTIBLES: Plastic liters of Ciuc beer, local wine purchased at a grocery store and brought into a bar.

From a Middle Ages trade center to the capital of a Communist nation to its revolutionary rebirth, Bucharest is a city steeped in history, and a super-fun place to hang out and get drunk with people you just met. Stay at a hostel near the city center so that you can tour the sites, and then come back home to party. Head to the **Museum of the Romanian Peasant** to check out posters with Communist-era nutrition facts and an old windmill, artifacts almost like time machines.

Drink rounds of Ursus draft at the outdoor café in **Herăstrău Park**. Find a *terraza* to eat dinner at. Even fancy places will feel like a good deal. Eat local food, such as cured sausage and bean stew or schnitzel.

Meet punks and follow them to the old **Lipscani** neighborhood. These dilapidated blocks that were once the center of trade during the Middle Ages, left derelict by Communist plans for demolition, are today in the process of the same gentrification that happens in Brooklyn or Los Angeles: young people opening bars in abandoned buildings. Head to a liquor store and buy a 14 lei ($4 USD) bottle of wine. Then follow them to their friends' bar and play poker with them for a few hours.

Drink two-liter bottles of beer that were purchased around the block, brought upstairs, and passed around the barroom table. Be surprised when they're listening to recordings of familiar American radio broadcasts. Once the bar closes go with your newfound crew to drink beers at the **Cişmigiu Park** canal, part of the largest park and gardens in the city.

Wander back to the hostel and eat shawarma (pita sandwich), and maybe if you're drunk enough, piss on the Gucci store.

The next day visit the dictator Nicolae Ceauşescu's insanely gigantic palace. It's a neoclassical monstrosity that tries to mimic the grandeur of Versailles, only two hundred years later. Ceauşescu razed eighteenth-century neighborhoods and displaced hundreds of people to make room for his dream house, although he was overthrown and executed before the building was complete. Today the building houses Romanian parliament and real estate conventions.

You'll enter the wood-paneled Human Rights Hall, a room dominated by oak tables, flowers, and a massive chandelier. You'll correctly guess that naming this hall after "Human Rights" was a post-revolutionary edit.

For lunch, eat some tasty Lebanese cuisine at **El Bacha** or Romanian fare at **Taverna Sarbului**. Then head to the shopping center. This may sound counterintuitive to the seasoned traveler, but you have to explore the craziness of the **Cotroceni Mall**. This is a fancier place than any shopping center back home: high ceilings, luxury stores, an ice skating rink, a video arcade, a restaurant inside of a fake mountain, and a movie theater with a VIP section. Treat yourself to a VIP status at the movie theater. For about $15 USD you'll be offered a platter of sliced meat, pasta salad, bourekas (pastries), poppy-seed cake, Belgian endives, cookies, and possibly free drinks.

Free drinks is a good way to start another crazy night in Bucharest.

"It's okay, you aren't from here."—Security guards coming over to investigate commotion, then leaving when they realized I was a foreigner.

VERDICT

An underexplored EU capital you should get to before the EasyJet set takes it over.

Joshua Heller

28. Oxford, United Kingdom

SEASON: Year-round. May through October for warmest weather.
IDEAL CONDITIONS: May mornings listening to the choir sing at daybreak after you've been out all night.
DAYTIME ACTIVITY: Punting at the Cherwell Boathouse.
LODGING RECOMMENDATIONS: Bath Place Hotel or The Buttery for central location. YHA Oxford for hostel.
INGESTIBLES: Cask ale, cider, cocktails, Pimms, pies, chips, doner kebabs.

Oxford is famous for its architecture and university, but it's also, as writer Jan Morris puts it, "a notoriously bibulous city." The pub is where everything collides; it's the great democratizing force in a place so often stifled by its own heritage. The woman finishing her Laphroaig and sliding inelegantly to the floor might be the world's leading Tibetologist. A cashier at the Tesco around the corner, a novelist. And although most nights here are the same (cider-soaked and expensive), a curious sense of possibility always underpins a night out in Oxford.

Tourists mainly drink in the center of town. On hot summer nights, patrons of **The King's Arms** on Parks Road spill out onto the street, smoking cigarettes and knocking over pints. The nearby **Turf Tavern,** accessible via an alleyway that seems to lead nowhere, is supposedly where Bill Clinton "did not inhale" as a Rhodes Scholar in the 1960s. **The White Horse** on Broad Street was a haunt of fictional detective Inspector Morse, and **The Bear Inn** on Alfred Street has a collection of more than four thousand club ties.

In Jericho, have a burger with your pint at **The Rickety Press** on Cranham Street, a pie with your pint at **The Victoria** on Walton Street, or something vegetarian with your pint at **The Gardeners Arms** on Plantation Road. While you're in the neighborhood, stop by the **Rose and Crown,** on North Parade, where mobile phones and swearing are forbidden. When the pubs shut, order chips, cheese, and hummus from a kebab van (they're everywhere) to soak up the booze.

For a different version of Oxford, head east across Magdalen Bridge. **The Star** on Rectory Road is dark, dingy, and has pool tables. Eat on Cowley Road: try **Atomic Burger** for burgers, fries, and '80s nostalgia, **Mario's** for pizza, **Red Star** for cheap noodles, and **George & Delila** for ice cream. On Magdalen Road, **The Rusty Bicycle** is a favorite among locals, and **The Magdalen Arms** serves some of the best food in the city.

Most pubs close between 11:00 P.M. and midnight on weeknights, later on weekends. If you can avoid pissing off fickle owner Andy who guards the door, drink the rest of the night away at the **Hi-Lo** on Cowley Road; order a can of Red Stripe or a splash of Wray & Nephew's overproof rum and enjoy the reggae. Also open late is **Bar Aroma.** If you need a meal before staggering home, join the bedraggled hordes next door at **Bodrum Kebab House.**

The best cocktails are at **Raoul's** or **The Duke of Cambridge** in Jericho. **Kazbar,** on Cowley Road, does tapas and a decent mojito.

Overall, take advantage of any day without rain, and at night strike up a conversation with someone at the bar and see where you end up.

FUCKED UP FIRSTHAND

It was my first night in Oxford and we were at the Turf taking snapshots of the sign at the entrance: AN EDUCATION IN INTOXICATION.

It was a hot night, the sky, at ten o'clock was just darkening, and I stood outside, where a man offered me a cigarette. We got to chatting; he told me he knew how to fly planes and that once, playing hockey, he'd tackled Prince William. I told him that someday I was going to be the female Toby Ziegler, or write a great novel, or probably both. We moved on, to another pub, and then to another. We kissed outside of a bar called Baby Love and took a cab back to East Oxford, which was a little more run down, a little more lovable. We sat on his kitchen floor, drinking sloe gin and eating chocolate cake out of the fridge. Years later, we still live in that house.

VERDICT

Inhale.

Miranda Ward

29. Davis, California

SEASON: Beer pong season (year-round).
IDEAL CONDITIONS: Sandal weather (again, year-round).
DAYTIME ACTIVITY: Strolling the arboretum, Farmer's Market (Saturday and Wednesday).
LODGING RECOMMENDATIONS: Aggie Inn, Best Western, Econo Lodge, or someone's lawn.
INGESTIBLES: $6 Natural Ice or Light.

Davis is one of the last true college towns left in California. Most life in this town of fifty thousand revolves around the twenty-five thousand students at UC Davis. The campus is directly across the street from downtown. It's a fun place to get totally wasted for four years, or just one night.

Davis is fifteen miles from Sacramento, and an hour from the Bay Area along Interstate 80. It's also accessible by Amtrak, and thirty minutes from Sacramento International Airport.

Start the night off with a twelve pack of the shittiest beer you can imagine from **Fast & Easy** convenience store; for $6.50 you can buy twelve Natty-Lights and a Slim Jim. Now that you have your first coat of buzz on, you should probably eat something so that you can survive the next five hours of getting totally wasted. Head to dinner at **Sophia's** for some excellent Thai food, with occasional live music and trivia nights. Order a few drinks here and see what else is happening in town, maybe the lacrosse team is throwing an insane themed party, or if you've had enough drinks maybe you can crash a sorority mixer

Head to **Cafe Bernardo** for their notorious Wicky Wacky Woo, a cocktail where they ransack the entire liquor cabinet: vodka, gin, rum, tequila, triple sec, amaretto, orange juice, pineapple juice, cranberry juice, Bacardi 151-proof rum.

Now you are totally drunk. I don't know what happens next.

Cut to tomorrow morning, you are very hungover. Maybe you should try to find your way back to your bed. After you've regained your bearings and most of your consciousness you might want to take it easy exploring the **UC Davis** campus or eat at the **Coffee House (CoHo)**. Check out public art across campus, such as the famous **Egg Heads,** a sculpture series commissioned by Robert Arneson.

Once you're fully recovered you may be hankering for a burger. You have lots of options: **Sam's, Tommy J's, Burgers and Brew**, and **Redrum Burger**. Maybe you want something lighter and more organic. Head to the **Davis Food Co-op**. After you've created a base of food in your stomach it's time to start drinking again. Head to south Davis for the German-style brewery **Sudwerk**. After several *marzens, helles,* and *hefeweizens,* grab a cab or walk back to downtown for an evening out at classic college bar **Froggy's** (catch ultimate cover band Cold Shot) or to **G Street Pub,** a fun but dirty place to see live music and weird karaoke.

As the night evolves, consider the juxtaposition of world-class university education and beer-bonging a case of Natural Light.

NOTES FROM A LOCAL
Instead of being those shady fifth-years who hit on freshman girls at frat parties, we became the shady fifth-years who hit on first-year grad students at college bars.

VERDICT
Davis can be pretty boring if you aren't drunk. So most people in town are pretty drunk. Come drunk, stay drunk, and you'll love it.

Joshua Heller

30. Johannesburg, South Africa

SEASON: November through May (summer).
IDEAL CONDITIONS: Hot tarmac in the day, balmy nights in the City of Gold.
DAYTIME ACTIVITY: Apartheid Museum, Johannesburg Fort.
LODGING RECOMMENDATIONS: Look for a hostel or bed and breakfast in Melville.
INGESTIBLES: Castle lager on home turf, cheap cigarettes, pap (South Africa's corn meal), biltong (dried beef).

Jo'burg is South Africa's concrete jungle, a hive of people hustling. It's underground music spilling over onto the airwaves; it's the relics of Kwaito-influenced house music being reborn. It's Converse and skinny jeans. It's ghettos and skyscrapers. It's a throbbing city with a central area undergoing resurrection, as derelict rusty shells become magnets for artists and joy seekers. It definitely offers you the opportunity to get fucked up.

Look out for the **Word N Sound** poetry and live music events that happen at least every month. Far from a prim and proper poetry recital, this heaving megaphone for urban culture has a few members within its ranks who will drag you to a few places you otherwise wouldn't see.

Inspired, go to the **Braai Shack** in **Rosebank** for your pap and traditional eats. Wash it down with a local beer, Castle lager or Castle Lite. Alternatively, get stuck in and have a milk stout (kind of like Guinness), or millet-based home brew. If a *braai* (barbecue) isn't your thing, swan down to the **Neighbourgoods Market** in **Braamfontein** and mingle with Jozi's hipsters as they clash Nike sneakers with traditional printed cloth.

While the sun is still up, head to **Newtown**, a vibrant inner-city suburb. Stiffen your upper lip and check what's on at the **Market Theatre**. The **Bassline** weaves together a diverse live-music lineup throughout the year. As the sun threatens to sink behind skyscrapers, hop on a *kombi* or walk to **Arts on Main**. You could be here for a while, depending on what's going down.

On Sundays the rooftop of this downtown complex morphs into an end-of-weekend mashup with DJs and a city skyline for a backdrop. Keep an eye out for anything on a rooftop in Jo'burg. Another heavyweight is **The Beach**. Recline on a lounger with a view of **Mandela Bridge**. **The Warm Up** is a deep-house event on the first Saturday of every month that oscillates between the crowns of the Lister and Citilec buildings.

Greet the night with cocktails at **The Foundry**. After a live gig or DJ set in Newtown, cross over the city to **Melville**. Barhop as the shutters start coming down. Check out the reggae bar, **Kingston ON 4th**. Not sure whether you're hungry or tired, but certain that you're hammered, drag yourself to the moonlight eatery, **Catz Pyjamas** for a meal you will only recall the next day because of the stains on your jacket.

If it's Sunday, Kingston ON 4th runs **Trenchtown Rock Sundays**.

Vibe on dub and hide behind the smoke from the Caribbean *braai;* play a board game if your mental state permits, and toke on a bubbly hookah. The rooftop at Arts on Main could be the best way to see out the weekend and regain a sense of normality with a pacifying drink or two.

NOTES FROM A LOCAL
Don't believe the hype! Sure Jozi is renowned for high crime rates but there's much more to the city. It's a bursting hub of activity and new entertainment for those who want to see through the negatives.

VERDICT
Jump in.

Dikson

31. Harare, Zimbabwe

SEASON: Year-round.
IDEAL CONDITIONS: Even winter is warm. All you need in Zimbabwe is a clear sky.
DAYTIME ACTIVITY: Horseback riding in Hwange, wildlife sanctuaries.
LODGING RECOMMENDATIONS: Small World is Harare's suburban hostel and only a ten-minute taxi ride from downtown. This is the place to stay if you want to meet other travelers.
INGESTIBLES: Chibuku (millet-based home brew nicknamed Scud as a result of its ability to demolish sobriety), Bohlingers or Zambezi beer, sadza (maize meal) and stew.

Zimbabwe has fallen victim to bad press in the past decade, blowing its problems out of proportion. If you've chosen Harare as a host city for your drunken nights then pat yourself on the back, you've got a lot to look forward to. December and April are the best for partying, as the diaspora swarms back for either Christmas or the **Harare International Festival of the Arts (HIFA)**, one of the biggest festivals on the continent.

Your first excursion should be **KwaMereki**. It's a dusty car park on the outskirts of the city separated down the middle by *braai* (barbecue) stands and strong women stoking fires. Buy your beer and meat and take it to one of these ladies. I recommend Amai Gonyeti, which loosely translates to "Mother Truck." Nurse your quart of lager and wait for the maestro to bring you the *sadza*, vegetables, and meat (that you will consume ferociously). *Kombis* (minivans) are the main mode of public transport but they don't really operate at night, so you may want to bargain with a taxi driver to drive you around in the evening.

Go back into the city center for sundowners at **The Keg and Maiden**. The English-style pub overlooks the well-groomed national cricket pitch. Check what's on at **Book Café**. Open for over a decade and recently relocated to a new, more spacious home, this venue hosts some of the best international and local musicians and events in the country. Reggae nights draw a loyal crowd of Rastas and contingents of Scandinavian women. **Newlands** is five minutes away. Have a game of pool at **Bolero** then shuffle next door to **Red Bar** for a dance and a whiskey tonic. Make sure you don't wear a red shirt as blending in with the walls isn't a good look.

During HIFA (April/May) the center of Harare surges into life with music taking over the **Harare Gardens**. This week-long party thumps into the early hours every night with acts from around the world. It's less than $5 USD for a day pass and if you get the chance to go it's the Eden of Debauchery. Beware of the seven-day hangover that follows.

Look out for the **Funkalicious** club nights that bring in international DJs to different venues around the city. Go to **Half Bar**, a converted house with sofas that accommodate drunkards in need of a pit stop. Check out **Lime** in Borrowdale and hope that the UV lights shield your drooping features. When everything seems to be closing around you there is only one option left. In the backstreets of **Strathaven** there is a bar/club/beer hall that displays inebriated clientele like a modern art exhibit. Go to **Londoners** and make friends with one of the guys who is making absolutely no sense.

Unsure how you got home and hosting a determined headache, get a cooler box of beers and drive out to **Domboshawa**. This spiritual rock outside of Harare can cure the most vicious hangover. With the city on your left and the sunset glowing on the horizon, enjoy a postcard finish to a marathon night out.

NOTES FROM A LOCAL

In Harare you can experience such a diverse night out from swanky clubs to working mens' bottle stores. Be adventurous.

VERDICT

Get a driver, or jump in with locals, and traverse the city until sun up.

Dikson

32. Rotterdam, Holland

SEASON: June through August (summer).
IDEAL CONDITIONS: Long, windless, rainless festival nights.
DAYTIME ACTIVITY: Check out art at Kunsthal, or take pics of the Witte Huis.
LODGING RECOMMENDATIONS: Hostel ROOM Rotterdam for budget, Stayokay Rotterdam Cube Hostel for extra fucked-up-ness.
INGESTIBLES: Kopstoot (Dutch gin with lager), Belgian dark beers, cheap Albert Heijn–brand beer and wine, weed, hash, truffles (not the dessert), bram ladage patat (fries with mayonnaise), kapsalon, Turkish kebab and shawarma, herring.

Rotterdam is a multicultural working-class city not wanting anything to do with Amsterdam's glitzy red-light district and luxury and themed coffee shops overrun with tourists who can't handle their highs.

Begin your night mingling with artists on **Witte de Withstraat,** where you can enjoy *kopstoot* or a Dutch beer at a brown café such as **De Witte Aap** while listening to DJs spinning. Or chill in a coffee shop, where you'll be confronted with decisions you've never had the luxury of making. Which type of weed shall you buy? Amnesia Haze? Silver Pearl? Decisions, decisions. For a true Rotterdam-style smoking experience, smoke spliffs with tobacco and hash. Or for a psychedelic experience, purchase some truffles.

When your stomach begins growling, get your munchies at **Bazar,** a hotel with cheap eastern Turkish eats, or indulge in a greasy *kapsalon*, a dish consisting of fries with garlic sauce, cheese and salad on top, invented by a Rotterdam barber. Chat with the locals and maybe you'll get invited to a house party, where you can experience how Rotterdammers really get fucked up.

For a night of clubbing and hard-core partying, the **Nieuwe Binnenweg** area goes off, or head to the **Oude Haven** or **Westelijk Handelsterrein. Maassilo,** located near the Maas River, plays the best house and urban tunes, as well as the **Corso Rotterdam** and the **Thalia Lounge,** both housed in old cinemas. **Gay Palace,** a four-story club, is a favorite of the LGBT crowd.

As the sun rises, avoid taking expensive taxis. Instead, buy a stolen bike off a homeless guy at Central Station for about €10 ($13). You certainly won't be the only person swiveling along the bike lanes in this pedestrian-friendly city.

Some general rules about partying in Rotterdam:

- Smoking weed on the street is technically illegal, but there's little chance you'll get in trouble for doing it.
- That being said, surveillance cameras are practically on every street.
- Shrooms have been outlawed, but truffles are legal to buy at various coffee shops.

FUCKED UP FIRSTHAND

"We just left Bram's party to eat truffles and now we don't want to see any of them," Lana said as we all giggled. The room began wavering. Eric started laughing so hard that he fell over the couch's armrest and knocked over a painting. I stood in front of a mirror and watched my face transform into a cat and back.

Outside, we sat on a bench at the edge of the harbor. Eric pointed to a row of boats. "There are people living in those boats right now."

We spent the next ten minutes talking about people who live in boats. I slouched on the bench and closed my eyes, watching fluorescent shapes dance beneath my eyelids. I felt happy.

We walked back. When I finally crawled into bed next to Eric, wondering how truffles would affect our sex, he informed me: "My dick feels like rubber."

VERDICT

Anything you'd ever want.

Sarah Shaw

33. St. John's, Newfoundland, Canada

SEASON: May through September. Not winter. *Never* winter.

IDEAL CONDITIONS: Hot summer days, sans fog and drizzle.

DAYTIME ACTIVITY: Hike Signal Hill, keeping lookout for icebergs and whales.

LODGING RECOMMENDATIONS: A home from Couchsurfers.org. My sofa bed. St. John's should be experienced with the locals. Not a hostel.

INGESTIBLES: Screech Rum, all the native beers (Black Horse, aka "Pony Piss," Blue Star, Jockey Club, India), poutine with dressing (turkey stuffing and savory herbs), fish and chips, fried *toutons* (pancakes) with molasses, and a moose burger.

I've lived in St. John's for the past six years and I still get excited about taking people out for a night on the town. Only about 150,000 people live in the city proper, but there's a huge student population and lots of young professionals. We like to party, and we do it well.

If you're a newb, people will tell you to go to **George Street**. It's known for having the most pubs and clubs per capita than anywhere in North America. Start at **Lottie's Place**. It smells disgusting but there is no cover charge, ever, and they make cheap white Russians. Then go to **Trapper John's**, where you'll usually find a one-man band and young folks crowding the bar.

Newfoundland is considered the most Irish place outside of Ireland, and we're big on Irish/Newfoundland traditional music, or "trad," as we call it. **O'Reilly's Pub** usually has the best jigs 'n reels, but so does **Kelly's Pub** and **Shamrock City** (located just below George Street, on Water Street). My favorite places, however, are off-street. **The Republic** and **The Duke of Duckworth**, both located on Duckworth Street, are the best places to go for a casual pint and an older, more chilled crowd not looking to grind their junk on youngsters. The local music scene is also kick-ass, with tons of indie and alternative rock bands filling the venues. **The Rock House** on George features some of the best stuff, albeit at higher cover charges. But there is also **The Ship**, where the artsy-fartsy folk flock.

Come for the **George Street Festival**, at the end of July, when you're able to party on the street and watch live music. My personal favorite festival is the **Folk Festival**, however, held in Bannerman Park in early August. You'll find fewer douchebags there.

And finally, if you want to know what real Newfoundland is all about, go to the **Inn of Olde** in Quidi Vidi Village. The bar is literally located inside the owner Linda's home, and she'll weave you a tale of the St. John's of yesteryear if you just ask for it.

Tips for fitting in as a drunk in St. John's:

- Hold your liquor. We'll drink you under the table.
- Unlike most other Canadian provinces, bars are open until 3:00 A.M.
- If you can't understand the thick Newfoundland brogue, just nod and smile.

NOTES FROM A LOCAL
Three essentials you need for a party trip to St. John's: a poncho, a healthy liver, and a condom.

VERDICT
A small, isolated city on the edge of the Atlantic that is bitter cold most of the year is an excuse to drink. Blizzard happening outside? Drink! Hot summer's day? Midday drinking! (Or, as we call it, a Day Boil.)

Candice Walsh

34. Padova, Italy

SEASON: September and October (fall) or May and June (spring).
IDEAL CONDITIONS: Mild weather for outside drinking.
DAYTIME ACTIVITY: Tour the renaissance Palazzo del Bo, or visit the Planetario di Padova (planetarium).
LODGING RECOMMENDATIONS: Ostello Città di Padova for hostel; Casa del Pellegrino for budget; Albergo Verdi for a slight splurge.
INGESTIBLES: Wine, beer, and spritz, coffee (Café Missaglia), pizza (Pizza al Cubo), and gelato (Patagonia).

Southwest of Venice is Padova, a city known mostly for Saint Anthony, the Scrovegni Chapel, and *The Taming of the Shrew*. But beneath her palaces and porticos, Padova is one of Europe's best college towns.

The Università degli Studi di Padova (UNIPD) is one of the world's oldest universities and one of Italy's most prestigious. Padova isn't particularly glamorous, but her sixty-five thousand students make up for that in revelry.

The city center is a network of *piazze*, each unique. Back-to-back **Piazza dell'Erbe** and **Piazza della Frutta** are bustling and a bit offbeat. Neighboring **Piazza dei Signori** is family oriented. **Prato della Valle**, a park bordered by canals, is the largest piazza in Italy. By day, the bars lining these squares set out tables and serve coffee, aperitifs, and light fare. At night the tables disappear and the bars become little more than alcoholic street vendors.

Wednesday is the biggest drinking night, and the most popular beverage is the spritz, a regional favorite made from prosecco, sparkling water, and either Aperol or Campari. Order one of each and choose your favorite. Drinking starts after dinner, and by nine in **Erbe and Frutta**, there are so many people that you can't see the cobblestones. Expect to find philosophical discussion, impromptu concerts, dogs, drugs, and many cigarettes among the crowds. Mingle and go with the flow; it's easy to make new friends.

Thursday through Saturday, the piazzas are still options, but don't expect the same crowds. Fortunately, Padova has much more to offer. The **Cantina del Gufo** on Via Santa Lucia feels like an intimate WWII-era wine cellar. **Joyce's** on Via Euganea is an Irish-style pub where the quirky owner may encourage you to slam "autobooms." **St. John's Pub** on Via C. Moro features karaoke; by the end of the night people are dancing on chairs.

For live music, try **Café Pedrocchi** for jazz in a historical setting, or **Café au Livre**, a bookstore/bar. If you prefer DJs, there are *discoteche*, though understand that most are outside the city center and require a cab for transport.

Don't overlook UNIPD parties. To find these, befriend the students. Italians are generally welcoming to foreigners and very proud of where they come from, so try asking about Italy to break the ice. Once you make a friend and score a UNIPD invite, you'll have insider access to a legacy of almost eight hundred years of student life.

In Padova, keep in mind:

- Aperitifs are not the equivalent of happy hour. Have a drink or two and some snacks, but don't get sloshed. You still want to enjoy dinner, and there is always more drinking later.
- A spritz costs between €1 and €4 ($1.30 to $5 USD). You can also pick up a good bottle of Italian wine for €2 ($2.60 USD) at the grocery store and drink outside.
- Italians toast with *cin cin* "cheen cheen" or *salute* "sah-LOO-teh," and always with eye contact.

NOTES FROM A LOCAL
Listen for a song of "*dottore, dottore . . .*" and look for obscene posters and students in raunchy costumes. This is an old tradition at UNIPD; after graduating, students are subjected by their friends to large quantities of alcohol and good-humored humiliation.

VERDICT
Half a million young people in a city founded in Roman times equals la dolce vita.

Katelyn Santoro

35. Valparaíso, Chile*

SEASON: Warmest months are January and February. The coolest months are July and August.
IDEAL CONDITIONS: With your new novia/novio from Santiago.

Historic *ascensor* in Valparaíso. These were built in the late 1800s or early 1900s, and yes, Valpo is as steep as it looks. Photo by Kate Siobhan.

DAYTIME ACTIVITY: Stroll Paseo Gervasoni, ride the Ascensor Artilleria.

LODGING RECOMMENDATIONS: Valpackers Hostel, if you plan to sleep. Try CasaPuerto Hostel if you plan to rage.

INGESTIBLES: Completos (hot dogs topped with avocado, mayonnaise, ketchup, mustard, sometimes cheese, often chips), Pisco (grape brandy), Cristal and Escudo beers.

Valparaíso ("Valpo" to the locals), is located seventy miles north-west of Santiago and is one of the country's most important ports, filled with culture, history, the subject of more than a few poems and songs for its winding cobblestone and colorful buildings. It has a lot to offer, including the bars you're looking for, which stay open until 6:00 A.M. here. You have a long night ahead so you better get some dinner first.

Mastodonte on **Esmeralda Street** has a great fusion menu and delicious pizza. But don't they all? The real reason you should go is to drink house **Pirate Beer** out of one-liter bottles in a Jurassic-like ambience.

You can handle your liquor, right? Well, guess what? Here a mixed drink doesn't contain an ounce of liquor and some soda. A mixed drink is five to twelve ounces of liquor poured into a glass and served with a bottle of soda. Mix as you like. Two mixed drinks and you're not only feeling it, but you might be so in the bag that you're feeling up the Chilena who only asked you for a dance. She's not impressed with you or your wandering hands. Down, boy!

Now that you've eaten first head to **Plaza Anibal Pinto** where the clubs **Subterraneo** and **El Huevo** are both just around the block. **El Huevo** is the bar you planned to open when doing certain illicit substances as an undergrad that made your wildest dreams seem utterly attainable: . . . *and my bar, shall be five stories tall—five fucking stories!—and each floor shall have a different theme, and every night we'll have five live bands playing simultaneous music . . . and a basement filled with dark corners where the kids shall suck each other's faces . . . and people will drink beer out of giant five-liter tubes inspired from the neck of the giraffe (called* girafas).

Instead of going to rehab like you did, someone actually opened that bar and called it **El Huevo**. You're ambitious if you even make it past the first floor. But the rooftop is worth it, with scenic views of the city, a bar, and the sort of horniness that only happens when people drink beneath Southern Hemisphere constellations.

If for some reason you can't find everything you are looking for here, you can also try **La Sala** on **1054 Errazuriz**, which has everything **El Huevo** has but on a smaller scale.

After the bar scene you'll need to get some drunken completos. Even Anthony Bourdain agrees, **Sibarítico** is the place to get them. Since he featured the one in the neighboring town Viña del Mar on *No Reservations*, they've opened one in Valparaíso on Almirante Montt 51 Local 1, but it's recommendable that you hop in a micro (bus) and go to the one in Viña del Mar (5 Norte 167 near the **Casino** and **McDonalds**). A key component to any night out in Valparaíso is the twenty-minute bus ride to Viña (or if you start there, a ride to Valpo). It will involve lots of new friends, high speeds in a dubious vehicle, guitars, salesmen (who might be selling knives), and drinking on public transportation (which always makes you feel better).

NOTES FROM A LOCAL

We invented Pisco. Chile. Don't listen to anything that those lying sacks of Peruvian shit say. Chile, not Peru, is the birthplace of Pisco, which was first made in the town by the same name. . . . Technically, yes, that town used to be part of Peru, but is it our fault that our army is strong and theirs is made up of girly men?

VERDICT

Pablo Neruda described it best in his ode to Valparaíso: "*puerto loco.*"

Luke Maguire Armstrong

36. Chengdu, China

SEASON: May through October (late spring through fall).
IDEAL CONDITIONS: Mild weather, slightly overcast, tea time.
DAYTIME ACTIVITY: Absorb silence at Wenshu Yuan Monastery.
LODGING RECOMMENDATIONS: Sim's Cozy Garden Guesthouse, Shunxin Hostel, Shangri-la Hotel.
INGESTIBLES: Tsingtao, Chill (beer), baijiu (spirits), tea, and all the spicy fish and huajiao (pepper) you can manage.

Chengdu is a small "second tier" city (which means it has all the comforts of an international city with a lower cost of living than, say, Beijing or Shanghai) in southwestern China. It's known nationally as the place to go to relax, play mahjong, and eat spicy food.

Most foreigners end up in Chengdu by accident, traveling through on their way to cooler sounding places such as Nepal, Tibet, or Jiuzhai valley. Or they come for the panda sanctuary or the monkeys on Emei Mountain. If they're lucky, they might decide to go out for the night and find out that Chengdu is actually a 24/7 party.

If you like foreign style bars, **Jellyfish**, **Le Café Paname**, and **Buzz**, in the Blue Caribbean center on Kehua Road (Beilu) are infamous as places for foreigners and Chinese to interracially hook up. Sit stoned on the steps and watch hilariously drunk Italians attempt to prove their manhood while shouting things like "Give me back my women!" (it happens more than you'd think) or join in the giant orgy that is Jellyfish on a Saturday night.

Ladies' night on Saturday has enough free drinks that even Elliott Smith could drown his sorrows, not that he'd notice with all the women slipping around in bandage dresses and six-inch heels. Drinks average 35RMB ($5.60 USD) with absinthe costing around $8 USD. **The Spot** has the best burgers in town, while **Grandma's Kitchen** has awesome pie. There are plenty of quiet coffee shops and tea houses if you just want to relax. Come 6:00 to 8:00 P.M. if you want a spicy, local-style dinner (basically every restaurant in this center will have you spitting fire). The party really gets started around 11:00 P.M. Don't forget to end your night with some unbelievable *shao kao* (Chinese barbecue) at **He's Barbecue**.

For Chinese-style clubs, check out the **Lan Kwai Fong** complex, but you better come with money. If you go there alone be prepared to leech: smile widely and talk happily to the people who invite you to drink and toast you. If you speak any Chinese you will not want for drinks. If you come with a group, the standard operating procedures is to buy a table (this includes a bottle of liquor, a fruit tray, and some tissues), and toast one another and random passersby until everyone is wasted. Then jump on the tiny stage and dance until someone gets hurt. You can and should negotiate a price before paying for the table.

To chill out, **Jah Bar**, near "The boat" (a giant restaurant, inside a building shaped like a boat) on Linjiang Xi Lu, and **Lan Town** (in Jiuyanqiao), a laid-back tea house by day and bar by night, are great places to go if your idea of a party involves ingestibles (special cookies anyone?), snacks, and just hanging out. Closer to the boat on Linjiang Xi Lu you will find street vendors selling fried rice, fruit on sticks, and the best fried *jiaozi* (dumplings) in the city.

Other things to do in Chengdu:

- Try an infamous "KTV" party, which might sound nerdy (sit in a weirdly decorated room and sing while eating fruit) but invariably ends comically.
- Get a massage at one of the hundreds of neighborhood parlors (avoid the red-lit ones unless you want a happy ending).
- Have a party at the **Wowo!** There are no bottle laws and no specific time to close or finish selling drinks, so bars stay open until the party is over. But if that gets a bit old, just head over to the local convenience store and buy all the *baijiu* and beer you can handle.

NOTES FROM A LOCAL
The spring Zebra Festival is the quintessential Chengdu event. It's an outdoor music festival held in East Music Park where you can find all the best of Chengdu: happy, relaxed people, tea, spicy snacks, and awesome music.

VERDICT
In a country known for its strictness, Chengdu is chill.

Cheryl Vazquez

37. Ghent, Belgium

SEASON: Second half of July through September (summer).
IDEAL CONDITIONS: Sunny. It rarely gets humid here.
DAYTIME ACTIVITY: Check architecture at Graslei and Korenlei, as well as Saint Bavo's Cathedral and Saint Michael's Bridge.
LODGING RECOMMENDATIONS: Hostel Uppelink and Hostel Draecke, Ecohostel Andromeda for boat hostel.
INGESTIBLES: Uberdon (purple candy cone), frieten met stoverij sauce (fries with mayo and meat sauce), beer.

Ghent is too funky for mass tourism. You won't find a Starbucks or McDonald's on every corner. Gentenaars party with style, so act like a local and you will have no problem finding a good time. Locals bring first-timers to **T Velootje**, the strangest and scruffiest bar in town. The **White Cat** is a medieval cellar with pink walls and ceiling. The bar **Het Onverwacht Geluk** means "unexpected pleasure." Enter **Hot Club de Gand** through the small alley for free-swinging music and an upstairs terrace.

Dreupelkot makes *jenever*, a grain and malt liquor. **Spijker** was a thirteenth-century leprosy shelter turned grain warehouse. If you're looking for the compulsory Irish pub, check **The Cellar**. **Club Central** has cocktails and the occasional '80s party. By now you will want to nosh out on some **Jozef** traditional baked fries

Now resume mission: **Vlasmarkt** is known as Party Square. **AAP** bar has funky DJs. Check **Kinky Star** or **Charlatan** for live shows. If Vlasmarkt is too crowded, try the party corner with three bars: **Los Perros Calientes**—a beer bar with lounge pillows—**Minor Swing**, and **Misterioso** for jazz and live bands.

The **Overpoortstraat** is the student area and has thirty-two bars. It will be jumping off Tuesday through Thursday. The ceiling at

Molotov is covered with dolls and Duvels are only €2,2 ($2.90 USD). **Geus Van Gent** has a pool table and comfortable sofas. If you're into metal or punk, check **Frontline/Steegske**.

In the second half of July, the **Ghent Festival** (Gentse Feesten) kicks off for ten days. The downtown area closes and street performers line the sidewalks, with free concerts and performances in all the squares. The crowd reaches blowout levels and eventually you'll want to take a moment for yourself. Head over to **Graslei**, the daytime drinking spot (beside the Great Butcher's Hall) overlooking the canal where people bring beer and sit on the cobblestones.

Rules of Ghent:

- Beer is affordable, and available at convenience stores, aka nightshops.
- Ghent has the most vegetarian restaurants per capita in Europe. Thursday is meat-free day.
- *Nie neute* means "don't complain."

NOTES FROM A LOCAL

If you haven't partied at the Vooruit (Ghent's most beautiful building), had fries at Jozef, or a Roomer at Marimain, then you just haven't been to Ghent.

VERDICT

A medieval city with an eclectic party scene fueled by some 13 percent alcohol beer.

Noah Pelletier

38. Portland, Maine

SEASON: You'd think any time but winter, but brutal winter nights bring out the crazy in a way you've never seen.

IDEAL CONDITIONS: Hanging with a regular.

DAYTIME ACTIVITY: Catch a Portland Sea Dogs game.

LODGING RECOMMENDATIONS: In a town without a Four Seasons or Ritz Carlton, even the Hampton Inn is baller.

INGESTIBLES: PBR tallboys, whiskey shots, man drinks.

I'd argue that no city has a dark side like Portland. To the lobster-loving tourist, this city seems like a wonderful place to explore, just before settling down for some sleepyweepies at 10:00 P.M. What happens after 10:00 P.M. ends marriages, spurs babies, and all but demands fist fights. Portland, especially in the winter, is sinister.

Make a quick start at **Amigo's** in order to put some happy Mexican food in your stomach and kick in a buzz. A pre-gaming pitcher of PBR will set you back less than ten bucks and every drink is served in a pint glass, ensuring a double in every order. It's a tailgate party with a sombrero. If you're looking for a classy second stop, look no further than **The Wine Bar** in the Old Port. It'll be nice to have a highfalutin moment before you get nuts with some vino. Martini lovers will be just as happy.

If you can eke into the tail end of happy hour, visit **The Thirsty Pig**, which has $2.50 Shipyard drafts. The homemade sausages are raved about, but you might want to steer clear of them if you're going hard tonight. Sausage burps aren't going to get you laid.

Novare Res Bier Café has a selection of drafts like a wonder of small breweries, names such as The Musketeers Imperial Stout, Oxbow Freestyle, and Rogue 15k. They're also damn proud of their selection of whiskey and tequila.

Oasis is where all of the college kids go to fight. It's often a spectacle of blood and vomit by the end of the night, kind of like *Gladiator* with ripped frat shirts instead of armor. Somebody here is getting pregnant tonight, and it's anyone's guess if she's keeping the baby. Can it be terrifying? Yes. Is it some of the best people watching in North America? Dude, totally.

Howie's Pub is a savage-hearted dive bar. Drink scotch on the rocks and you'll blend right in. Unfortunately you won't be able to understand many of the locals as the night goes on; after four drinks the Maine accent turns into gobble that can only be understood by police officers conducting sobriety tests.

Tip: You're having fun if . . . it's a "wicked pissah," you've test driven a BMW (Big Maine Woman), been drunk until chummin', or you've been questioned by a Statey.

The real trick with Portland is to attach yourself to a resident drinker, someone who can provide you with alternative venues if your night isn't flowing. It's that kind of town. You may end up in a cruddy hotel bar and have the best night of your year, or you may end up drinking at a random house party where a lot of people are going to the bathroom and returning with severe sniffles. Hitch the right partner and you'll end up wherever the devil is sending people that particular night.

FUCKED UP FIRSTHAND

In the late nineties I worked with a band called Rustic Overtones, who were and are one of the biggest rock bands to come out of Maine. My job was to get them played on the radio, but we all became fast friends and before I knew it I was making every excuse to take a prop plane from New York City to Portland, just so I could hang out with these beasts.

We would often go to Oasis to watch the Roid Monsters fight. Girls would stake their claim, then find another chick making out with their man. A catfight would ensue. I don't think I ever remember seeing a cop come in to deal with the anarchy. It might just be assumed that this is what Maine's breeders do on a Saturday night.

If you're not from the northeast, you can't fathom how cold it will be at night. Layer like crazy and don't be shy about wearing long underwear. It's sexy here.

Tom Gates

39. Reykjavik, Iceland

SEASON: March through October, but anytime is legit.

IDEAL CONDITIONS: Not rainy would be ideal, but unlikely. Wear a hood.

DAYTIME ACTIVITY: Reykjavik Century Museum or the Open-Air Folk Museum.

LODGING RECOMMENDATIONS: Reykjavik Backpackers is a great hostel where you can easily meet people.

INGESTIBLES: Icelandic beer such as Viking or Gull. For liquor, Icelandic schnapps such as Brennivin and Topaz (at least once).

Keith Malloy experimenting with post-surf hydration/hypothermia-avoidance methods in Iceland. Photo by Chris Burkard.

The place to be is **Laugavegur Street:** the best access to bars, shopping, restaurants, and the coolest graffiti. For a more tourist-oriented feel, you can stay in one of the hotels near the City Center, or choose one of the many centrally located hostels. **Reykjavik Backpackers** has a bar in the hostel lobby, where they host weekly trivia nights, open mic nights, and watch football games, and the staff "leads" a Friday and Saturday night bar crawl.

The weekend bar crawl, or *runtur*, is an event for tourists and locals alike. Starting at around 11:00 P.M., the usually quiet streets are filled with people drifting (and later, stumbling) from bar to bar. Keep in mind that Reykjavik is a city of 120,000 people, and it's entirely possible to see the people you meet on Friday night on your walk of shame Saturday morning. I learned the hard way.

Alcohol can be expensive in Iceland, so some people choose to drink before going out, or find a happy hour with a good deal. Many bars on Laugavegur have two-for-one beer and wine specials, such as **Dillon,** which has an excellent beer garden for a nice day. **Kaffibarinn** also has great specials, and a chill vibe that's perfect for starting the night off.

You can usually find a band playing at one of the many trendy bars, such as **Bar 11** or **Kaffi Rosenberg.** I stopped by **Q Bar,** the main gay bar in Reykjavik, and caught a great acoustic band completely by accident. If Icelandic indie rock doesn't appeal to you, there's always karaoke. The obvious choice is the Beatles-inspired **Ob-La-Di Ob-La-Da,** where you can sing your heart out to Queen even on a weeknight.

For the finale, don't forget to buy a round of Brennivin for your friends.

NOTES FROM A LOCAL

Factory is a place where you end up. They have three areas with music and usually there's a band playing upstairs. People go quite crazy there, dancing on tables.

VERDICT

Two words: Aurora Borealis.

Rachel Miller

40. Tiraspol, Transnistria

SEASON: May through October (summer through fall).
IDEAL CONDITIONS: National holidays.
DAYTIME ACTIVITY: Presidential Palace and the House of Soviets.
LODGING RECOMMENDATIONS: Tiraspol Hostel or Hotel Russia.
INGESTIBLES: Vodka, Staraia Kreposti (Transnistrian beer), Kvint cognac.

The biggest precondition for partying in Tiraspol is making sure you know how to get there first. Transnistria is a small sliver of a territory located between the Dniester River and Moldova's eastern border with Ukraine. It's only recognized by Abkhazia, Nagorno-Karabakh, and South Ossetia, three other breakaway territories, and many consider it to be the last remaining piece of the former Soviet Union. The easiest way to travel there is by train from either Odessa, Ukraine, or Chişinău, Moldova, though buses and taxis are also an option.

The best place to start any big night out in Tiraspol is on **October 25th Street**, the city's main drag. Everyone usually goes to **7 Пятницъ (7 Fridays)** first for pre-party food and beverages. A good meal and a drink costs only about $5 USD.

Once you have prepped for a night of heavy drinking, head to either **Plazma** or **Hotel Russia**. Plazma, the one that resembles a miniature and much tackier version of Caesars Palace, is two stories of Eastern European club debauchery. Think interactive crowd games and pole dancers. There is also a hot club in the basement of **Hotel Russia**—just down the road from the House of Soviets.

If you are feeling adventurous, you can stray from the main drag and hit up **Vintage,** Tiraspol's newest club at the time of this writing, which is located in the Balka district, or **Villa Rich** in the back of **Park Pobedy,** which is a bar/restaurant/bowling alley/beer garden (summer only).

Finish things off at **Club Cherry,** an all-night disco also found beside Park Pobedy. This place is for those who can't stop dancing or are intrigued to learn more about the "amateur strip nights" they occasionally host.

Some general rules about Tiraspol:

- The distillery for Kvint cognac is located here and tours are available.
- All discos have an entrance fee and "face control." Usually costs no more than $3 USD and getting through should not be a problem if you are dressed right and behaving yourself.
- Do not drink in public. It was outlawed by the new president.

NOTES FROM A LOCAL

You haven't really "done" Tiraspol unless you've had a welcome shot of local vodka at a shop, drank an entire bottle of Kvint cognac with locals at a disco, and been invited to their village dacha party to eat homemade food and drink homemade wine the next day.

VERDICT

Surprising amount of nightlife for a noncountry.

Larissa Olenicoff

4: Dirtbag

I've always traveled dirtbag[2] style. As a dirtbag you avoid hotels, you camp, you stay on people's couches. This way of traveling gives you intimate, possibly edifying (if temporary) windows into people's lives. Before Couchsurfing.org, you just found places to pitch your tent on points and beaches on the outskirts of town. You'd ask the local fishermen if it was cool. You learned that by yourself you were vulnerable. But if you were staying on "Don Pedro's" beach (and nine times out of ten he'd just invite you to stay with him, to sleep in his spare equipment shed), you were set. People might've fucked with you on your own, but nobody's fucking with "the gringo at Don Pedro's."

And so you get to know him and his family. You help them haul in the boats sometimes. You play with the kids. You learn the local words for fish, fruits, trees, police, drugs, winds, rivers, constellations, and alcohol. You learn nicknames of the kids and old men. You learn local ways for cooking rice, chopping firewood, spicing beans, pruning tomatoes. You learn how to live in close quarters with huge families where there's no indoor plumbing and it's not "dirtbagging" but just life.

You stay long enough to get a haircut, the women laughing, saying, "*Ay que guapo!*," whipping out the razor unexpectedly, shaving your beard and leaving a tight little mustache in the local style. You stay long enough to feel that some dues were paid, some progression made with the words and the wave or the mountain or wall or

---

[2] Slang originating from climbing community: describes people who travel/live as cheaply as possible, camping for extended periods or living out of vehicles to enable maximum dedication to the sport.

whatever the terrain objective might've been. You stay long enough so that when it's time to go the *familia* you'd stayed with is sad and you are, too.

Many of the "budget" places in this chapter (Nairobi, Mexico City, Kiev, Bangkok) necessitate a more urban approach to dirtbagging, but it's still possible. Others, like Antigua and Phuket, still seem good to go in the original "just show up with a hammock" style.

In the end maybe you want more "comfort," too; there's nothing wrong with that. But it's good to keep in mind what you might be missing, and that it's most often found just beyond wherever and whatever the travel industry wants you to spend money on.

41. Goa, India*

SEASON: November through March is high season. August through October is rainy and quiet, but magical. The week before New Year's is insanely packed.

IDEAL CONDITIONS: Sunny and breezy, not muggy.

DAYTIME ACTIVITY: Hit beaches Colva, Palolem, and Agonda.

LODGING RECOMMENDATIONS: For budget, the guesthouses along Morjim and Ashwem beaches are a perfect balance of happening and relaxed. For luxury, the Taj Holiday Village or The Marbella Guesthouse near Fort Aguada.

INGESTIBLES: You can find whatever. Booze in Goa is cheap.

At the end of the infamous Hippie Trail lies Goa, long synonymous with hippies and trance music. Though the Hippie Trail is now defunct, Goa lives on with its seemingly dissonant combination of mellow yogic living and night-long debauchery.

Goa is India's smallest state, a thirty-six-mile-long stretch south of Mumbai, dotted with beautiful beaches, small villages, and mangroves. Goa is divided into North and South. South Goa has some of the most beautiful beaches, but the area is generally geared to-

After 10-plus hours of trance you go to the beach and turn cartwheels. Photo by Krish Tipirneni.

ward relaxation and wellness. When you want to party, head north.

When night falls, you have a few options: you can head to Anjuna and Vagator for the all-night trance raves at **Hill Top, Shiva Valley,** and **Curlies;** hit the swankier top-forty clubs along North Goa: **Shanti** and **Club Fresh** in Morjim or hop from bar to bar in Calangute, where it's always busy and the drinks are cheap.

In an ingenious bid to circumvent local noise regulations, **Silent Noise** rages quietly in South Goa, where revelers wear wireless headphones pumping with music. Three DJs play simultaneously, competing to get the crowd to tune into their set.

Don't get fucked up on an empty stomach—Goa has some of the subcontinent's best food. Besides the oodles of delicious Goan food, check out **La Plage** on Ashwem beach, where you can stuff yourself silly on French fare, and **Thalassa** in Vagator, a Mediterranean restaurant that still ranks as one of my best meals in all of India, hands down. It's recommended you go stoned and try the feta-filled pastries and profiteroles.

At the height of Goa Season is **Sunburn Music Festival**, which always runs the week before New Year's. Sunburn attracts some of the biggest global names in electronic, trance, and house music (Paul van Dyk, Armin van Buuren, and Pete Tong)—as well as a major influx of party-goers from across the country. The festival is held over three days and across multiple stages. An amazing experience—if you're willing to deal with insane traffic, crowds, and jacked-up prices.

NOTES FROM A LOCAL
There are spiritual beaches here, and ghosts.

VERDICT
Seek and you shall find.

Madeline Gressel

42. Chişinău, Moldova

SEASON: May through June (early summer).
IDEAL CONDITIONS: A good buzz, some fellow travelers unfamiliar with Moldovan culture.
DAYTIME ACTIVITY: Visit Milestii Mici, the biggest wine collection in the world.
LODGING RECOMMENDATIONS: Chişinău Hostel, Flowers Hotel, Weekend Boutique Hotel.
INGESTIBLES: Plastic bottles of vodka, Moldovan wine, rum and cokes.

Chişinău is probably not the first place you'd think of when someone asks you to compile a list of "great cities to get wasted in." But this capital of the former Soviet Socialist Republic of Moldova definitely deserves an honorable mention. After all, according to the World Health Organization, Moldova is the drunkest nation on the planet, consuming an average of 18.2 liters of booze per person per year! You'll never outdrink a Moldovan . . . but you can try.

Spend your first morning downtown checking out the tourist sites. Don't miss the miniature **Arc de Triomphe** and the **National Museum of Archeology and History of Moldova**. After you feel like a cultural aesthete, take yourself out for brunch and an early afternoon drink at **Cactus Café**. They serve hearty American-style breakfasts in a Wild West decor. Try one of their excellent breakfast cocktails (I mean they don't call it that, but mojitos go really well with your bacon and cheddar omelette).

If you want to keep your buzz-a-going, head down the block to **Eli-Pili,** a speakeasy-themed bar and restaurant on the first floor of a huge Soviet apartment block. Have a few pints of Bere Chişinău while you try to make friends with the university-aged clientele.

Depending on your skill set as a drunkard, you might want to take a "party nap" before dinner, or continue drinking into the evening. Either way at some point you'll need dinner, which is the perfect excuse to try Moldova's wine selection. Head down to **Symposium** for fine dining, ordering bottles from the wineries of local favorites Purcari and Acorex. Just be aware that when the bill comes, it'll be written in Cyrillic and you won't necessarily know what you ordered.

It's time for downtown. **Lava Lounge** is where the young crowd goes, or head around the corner to **BoozTime** (where the os form an infinity sign). When you arrive you might notice that the clubgoers aren't dancing, but instead standing around watching tango dancers; later in the night the floor gets crowded (even later in the night the crowd disperses to allow strippers to do their thing).

The next day as you're reeling from your hangover, explore the very modern shopping center **MallDOVA,** (which has so thoroughly embraced the value of the pun). You can go to **Rock and Roll Bowling** or, if your stomach has settled from last night, head to the **5D**

Cinema for an indoor roller coaster. Get some beers and wursts at the German-themed **Bier Platz** or head to **Planet Sushi** for sushi and cocktails with names like Pear Flavored Breeze and Coco-Jambo.

Spend tonight club-hopping in the Rîşcani neighborhood. Head over to the posh **Star Track** for dance parties with scantily clad men and women. Or head downstairs to **Military Pub** where you can watch DJs spinning from inside of a Soviet tank, shooting sound waves into the wasted crowd. For the biggest international acts you've never heard of (unless you're up on Ukrainian pop) head to **Drive** where the wide array of cocktails will distract you from the fact that nobody wears shirts.

After a long night clubbing and drinking and drugging and dancing, you're probably very hungry. You could look for stands serving late-night local dishes, but who are you kidding? You're wasted; all you want is a cheeseburger. Head to the **McDonald's** where you can find burgers for breakfast, Kanye West music videos to dance to, and appropriate facilities to puke in.

NOTES FROM A LOCAL

Half of this country wants to be Russia and half wants to be Romania . . . the only thing we can agree on is that we love to make party!

VERDICT

If you happen to be anywhere between Bucharest and Odessa, drop in.

Joshua Heller

43. Antigua, Guatemala

SEASON: Temperate all-year long. Peaks in April, during Holy Week. Dry season: November through April. Rainy: May through October.

IDEAL CONDITIONS: With a mariachi band accompanying you from bar to bar.

DAYTIME ACTIVITY: Bodysurfing in Half Moon Bay.
LODGING RECOMMENDATIONS: Jungle Party Hostel for budget travelers.
The Terrace Hostel has dorm options and clean private rooms.
INGESTIBLES: Wine, local Gallo beer, mezcal (Café No Sé), mojitos,
Cuba Libres, and the usual assortment of bar liquors.

This former Spanish colonial capital was abandoned in 1773 when a massive earthquake shook it to the ground. Today, Antigua has reemerged as both the cultural and debauchery capital of the country. With around a hundred bars and restaurants within walking distance of **El Parque Central**, expect a rough night and pack some aspirin.

Open the mini fridge on the back wall of **Café No Sé** on 1ra Avenida Sur near Iglesia de San Francisco and descend into the candlelit mezcal bar littered with graying expats. The Joven Mezcal starts at $4 USD a shot. For dudes (*cabrones*), there's a two-shot minimum. And don't you dare let the bartender overhear you equate mezcal with tequila. They may both come from agave, but they're not the same. Those are fighting words here.

Head next door to **Angie Angie** for Latin-Caribbean food and $4 USD glasses of Argentinean wine in their cozy garden. Or try **Café Sky** next door. They have rooftop dining, $3 USD mojitos, and an extensive menu.

Most of the spring break–type raging happens at **Reilly's Irish Tavern**, where bartenders don't so much encourage as force patrons to dance on top of the bar with them. Arrive early if you don't want to wait in line forever. Monday is the expat-run trivia night, and Friday and Saturday the bar fills up with young Guatemalan professionals from Guatemala City hoping to "*mejorar la raza*" with a gringo.

At some point in the night, slip off to **Ocelot**, a jazz bar across from La Catedral offering live music nightly. They share a patio with three other worthwhile bars, including the **Whiskey Den**, which supports free trade initiatives, has a massive selection of whiskey, and the best $2 USD cup of coffee in maybe the whole damn world.

Across the patio from Whiskey Den is **Braulio's Place**, which serves up way-too-strong Cuba Libres. Exchange a few kind words with the owner, Braulio, and he may just pick up your tab.

Upstairs in the same complex is **Lava**, which has a menu of filling $5 USD hamburgers, plays loud music, and has sweet rooftop views.

For dancing salsa, check **La Sala**, a block off El Parque Central. The bar is filled with slick Don Juans who have mastered the art of getting into blond European girls' pants. Bear in mind, some hips do lie, and don't be shocked if they tell you they love you on the first date. *Es que . . . te amo!*

The Terrace's rooftop restaurant and bar on 3ra Calle Poniente has a rotating menu of cheap specials and an open fire around which you can smoke 'em if you got 'em.

On the other side of town, on the corner of 3rd Calle and 1ra Avenida, **El Muro** has gained notoriety for its "Human Rights Night," which usually happens every other Thursday and promotes the people's right to get trashed. On these nights everyone drinks well drinks for free until midnight. How this is a viable business plan is anyone's guess and how no one has died of blood alcohol poisoning still remains a mystery.

The party doesn't necessarily end with the enforced 1:00 A.M. closing time. Ask your bartender where the "after party" is. You'll also find plenty of Antigua's criminal element there, so use whatever judgment you have left.

If you have the beer munchies after last call, **Ronny's Tacos** on La Calle de Santa Lucia serves tallboy Gallo beers and tacos well into the night.

Starting at midnight, **Quetzalito**'s rusted van will appear a block north of Ronny's. Five dollars gets you a plate of debauch deliciousness and a beer. His coffee is instant, but at 2:00 A.M. people don't drink it for the flavor. He sets up stools in a circle and on a good night a colorful cast of local and international characters tends to congregate and overestimate their sobriety.

FUCKED UP FIRSTHAND

Once I realized that I could hire a mariachi band to follow my friends and me on an impromptu pub crawl around Antigua, it was less of a choice and more of a moral imperative.

VERDICT

Just try to drag your ass out of bed before noon.

Luke Maguire Armstrong

44. Kiev, Ukraine

SEASON: June through September, especially July and August.
IDEAL CONDITIONS: Dry summer heat, but not stifling hot.
DAYTIME ACTIVITY: Explore the Caves Monastery, built by Kiev monks in 1051.
LODGING RECOMMENDATIONS: The Hub Hostel at 66b Saksaganskogo Street for hostel, Olga Apartments for short-term apartment rentals.
INGESTIBLES: Vodka, shawarma, varenyky (dumpling), pierogi, shashlik (barbecue).

I've pounded craft brews in Portland, shot Chinese *baijiu* in Shanghai, and downed absinthe by the bottle in Amsterdam, but nowhere have I drank more—in both quantity and frequency—and been more fucked up than in Kiev. The Ukrainians, as you might have guessed, drink a lot of vodka. That's not surprising. What is, however, is that Ukrainians, despite their reputation for being cold, nonsmiling people, are extremely generous and genuinely interested in cultures outside their own. Twentysomethings, born in an independent Ukraine, are especially curious about life in the West.

Perhaps that's why they're so eager to get us drunk.

Start with **Khreschatyk Street,** Kiev's main drag, where gorgeous women teeter atop unimaginable stilettos and oligarchs cruise in their Bentleys and Rolls, music bellowing from streetlight-mounted speakers. Cafés, bars, and nightclubs abound, as do the possibilities of getting into some good old-fashioned trouble. People might approach you if they hear your Western accent, but don't be alarmed; chances are they just want to know where you're from and what you're doing in Kiev. If you're lucky, they'll show you around. Hopefully they'll take you to some of these places.

Arena Entertainment Complex at Baseina Street 2 is where the city's socialites, including the sons and daughters of some of the country's wealthiest oligarchs, go to get smashed. The complex is a sort of choose-your-own-drunken-adventure type place, with **Sky-Bar Nightclub and Restaurant** and **Decadence House Night Club** for those who want to bump and grind, **Patifon Karaoke Club** for wannabe Eurovision stars, and **Arena Sport Zone** for football fanatics. It's pricey, but worth at least a visit.

If it's a sun-soaked-style wrecking you want, hit up **Gidropark.** Built in 1968 for the fiftieth anniversary of the October Revolution, this is where speedo- and thong-clad beachgoers prefer to get tanked. Beaches, sports grounds, boat stations, street food stands, carnival rides, cafés, and restaurants offer a day's worth of entertainment. Despite rumors of Chernobyl-radiation-soaked soil being dumped upstream some years ago, people still swim and even fish there. On August days, when temperatures push 104 degrees Fahrenheit (40 degrees Celsius), you won't think twice about jumping in.

For a more mentally stimulating night out, I like to join the arty crowd of journalists, activists, designers, photographers, and thinkers who hang at **Kupidon** on Pushkinskaya Street 5. People talk and chug Lvivske white beers from the western Ukrainian city of Lviv late into the night at this basement café, surrounded by portraits of famed Ukrainian writer and artist Taras Shevchenko and other national heroes. There's plenty of traditional Eastern European stodge to choose from, like the "Suzirya" Soviet Sausages, which, according to the menu anyway, are delivered fresh daily by the Communist Party.

If it's the expat crowd you're looking to find, try **O'Brien's Irish Pub** at Mikhalivska Street 17A. Passers-through, ESL teachers, and business types pop in here for Guinness, Jameson, and the televised Western European football matches.

When in doubt, do what my good pal Igor calls "taking a walking beer." It's pretty self-explanatory, really. Buy a beer at a shop or kiosk and walk with it. Just be sure you have deep enough pockets to conceal the bottle, or find a dark alley or bench in an apartment yard where you can enjoy it. Technically, public drinking is illegal. But everyone still does it.

NOTES FROM A LOCAL
We drink more than you and our women are more beautiful.

VERDICT
Completely unpredictable . . . come prepared for anything.

Christopher J. Miller

45. Cairo, Egypt

SEASON: Most tolerable April through May or September through October (spring or fall). Avoid Ramadan (July through August) if you want easy booze access.
IDEAL CONDITIONS: A rooftop bar, puffing a water pipe, or sailing down the Nile with a bottle and a smoke.
DAYTIME ACTIVITY: Tour the Muhammad Ali Mosque (Citadel of Saladin), pyramids.

LODGING RECOMMENDATIONS: Stay downtown. Dahab Hostel (budget); Talisman Hotel de Charme (midrange "boutique"); Four Seasons Garden City (five-star splurge).

INGESTIBLES: Local Stella and Saqqara beers; shisha (water pipe normally used to smoke flavored tobacco); cheap hash and even cheaper weed; dollar street food for ballast—try fuul (mashed fava beans, best served with egg as hangover cure), and kushari (carbohydrate bomb—mix of different pastas, lentils, chick peas, fried onions, tomato sauce, chili).

Cairo is sprawling, crowded, polluted, noisy, and trembling with a frenzied energy that never, ever stops. You'll either love it or hate it. (You'll love it.) You may think Egypt is a "Muslim country" and that people don't drink. This is wrong; lots of people drink. Forget the generic upscale bars in the posh hotels and on Zamalek and explore the delicious dives of downtown.

El Fishawi, one of the most famous cafés in Cairo. Supposedly this place has stayed open twenty-four hours a day for more than two centuries. Photo by Holly Clark.

101 Places to Get F*cked Up Before You Die

Horreya Café (on Midan al-Falaki) is the go-to spot for many, a seething café with bean casings littering the floor and old men playing chess in their coffee-only section. The tiny **Stella Bar** around the corner on Huda Sha'rawi is quieter but often more crowded. The **Greek Club** above **Groppi** (from Mahmoud Bassiouni) is popular for food as well as beer (try the calamari), and opens its courtyard in the summer. **Le Grillon** (off Qasr al-Nil) also has food and a courtyard, and serves shisha, too.

Cairo at street level can feel like rattling around inside an exhaust pipe. Hotels **Happy City** (on Mohammad Farid) and the **Odeon Palace** ('Abd al-Hamid Sa'id Street) have rooftop bars where you can perfume your pseudo-fresh air with a pipe and look down on the mayhem below. Try **Shahrazad** (Alfi Bey Street) to experience the seedy—rather than cheesy—end of the belly dancing spectrum. Note how the fading Louis Farouk psychedelia is matched by the disinterested fluidity of the dancers.

Fueled by caffeine, nicotine, shouting, and the clack of backgammon or dominoes, café nightlife often outlasts the bars. Arabic coffee is thick, black, and sweet, and the tobacco smoked through shisha pipes is flavored with molasses and fruit. Apple is the best; honey produces less satisfying smoke but drills through your head. Wander the maze of alleys that make up the **Bursa** area downtown, or try to find a seat at **Tak'eeba** café next to the **Townhouse Gallery**.

For $10 to $15 USD you can rent a *felucca* (a traditional Egyptian sailing boat) for an hour and take your party on the longest river in the world. Opposite the **Grand Hyatt** is a good spot. The captain won't mind if you bring on food, drink, and any other ingestibles needed to enhance the sunset. Make sure you tip him directly at the end.

Remember:

- Egyptian culture is conservative, get "discreetly" wasted.
- People smoke *everywhere*. You're gonna have to suck it up.

- Toking is a national sport. It's largely tolerated but still illegal. *Be careful*.

NOTES FROM A LOCAL

Never go out before 9:00 P.M.; always arrive at least half an hour late; and if you make it through to the call to prayer, bonus—that's your cue to go find some breakfast.

VERDICT

Used to be known as *Umm al-Dunya,* the "Mother of the World," and still might be.

Nick Rowlands

46. Bangkok, Thailand

SEASON: Late November through mid-January.
IDEAL CONDITIONS: Overcast and breezy.
DAYTIME ACTIVITY: Tour the Bangkok Thonburi Khlongs.
LODGING RECOMMENDATIONS: Khaosan Baan Thai for hostel, Bangkok Loft Inn for budget.
INGESTIBLES: Vials of Red Bull, Chang beer, som tum (spicy green papaya salad), kai tod (charcoal-grilled chicken).

If you're a backpacker, go to Khao San. Take the **Chao Phraya Express Boat,** the cheapest and most scenic way of getting there. Enjoy people watching and live blues at **Adhere the 13th.** Relax on a train bench at Tak Sura. Bottles of Chang are 50 baht ($1.90 USD) at **Golf Bar.** Look for the sign that says COCKTAILS VERY STRONG: WE DO NOT CHECK ID CARD. Escape the maddening crowd in the **Sunset Bar and Garden Restaurant** courtyard. If you go to **Reggae Bar,** be wary of people offering medicinals.

Off Khao San, **Phra Nakorn Bar** is a mix of art and nightlife. **Volk Bar House** has $4 USD cocktails. **Telephone** is a popular gay bar.

Anywhere is an arena for intoxication if you have the skills. John Grossman on a Rocky Mountain beer surf.
Photo: Cody Forest Doucette.

ABOVE: Rare empty view of the Royal Mile, the Scots mile of road from Holyrood Palace to Edinburgh Castle. Photo by William McIntosh.

LEFT: Chris Reijonen living the "beer-drinker's dream" during inaugural trip to Munich for Oktoberfest. Photo by Sarah Reijonen.

OPPOSITE TOP: Mumbai is a trippy place, especially around Holi, when everyone is chugging. Photo by Parth Jhala.

OPPOSITE BOTTOM: A sadhu in Kathmandu's Durbar Square. Sadhus are wandering monks known for their ritualistic use of ganja. Photo by Mohan Duwal.

OPPOSITE TOP: Classic view of Machu Picchu with the peaks of Huayna Picchu clouded in. Photo by Collins Paris.

OPPOSITE BOTTOM: Plaza del Mayo in Buenos Aires: a 35,000-person celebration after San Lorenzo stadium—once claimed by the dictatorship—was returned to its people. Photo by Kate Siobhan.

ABOVE: Morning colors in Old Delhi. Photo by Abhishek Chandra.

TOP RIGHT: Holi is most famous in India, but goes off in other countries as well. Some entranced revelers in Singapore. Photo: Mithila Jariwala.

RIGHT: Thailand isn't all Full Moon Parties. Some solitude at Ko Pi Phi Lee. Photo by Scott Sporleder.

TOP LEFT: Candice Walsh along the Copper Coast of Ireland, soaking in the landscape from which her ancestors departed a few centuries ago. Photo by Scott Sporleader.

BOTTOM LEFT: There are hundreds of spots like these along the Pacific Coast of Central America and Mexico which, if you can just dig in for a few nights, you'll be revisiting them in your mind of the rest of your life. Photo: Chris Burkard.

The Central Business District, Marina Bay, and Singapore River precincts.
Lights from the Marina Bay Sands Integrated Resort. Photo: Mithila Jariwala.

Why Central America is so epic: This is all you need to have the best time of your life.
Photo: Chris Burkard.

Walking free: young monks in Bang Mot, Thung Khru, Bangkok. Photo by Anuchit Sundarakit.

In Thong Lor, beer enthusiasts go to **BREW Beer and Ciders**. On Wednesdays ladies drink free from 5:00 to 9:00 P.M. at **Witch's Tavern**. **Muse** has live bands downstairs and a chill-out club upstairs. The best place to watch the sunset is at **Sky Bar**.

In Royal Center Avenue, aka RCA, **808** has killer bass and a $17 USD cover that includes a drink. **Slim** usually doesn't have a cover, which might explain why it's so packed. If it's a weekday, go to **Route 66** where you should be able to get a table. **Cosmic Cafe** hosts an eclectic mix of bands from all over the world.

In Ekamai, **Sonic** is the indie rock club. **Escobar** is a cocktail bar that plays hip-hop and house. Pretty people go to **Nung Len Club**. Soak up some of that alcohol at **Baan Tawan Gai Yang** for reasonable prices.

Go-go bars are a staple in Bangkok. **Patpong** is the famous red-light district. You will mostly see tourists walking around ogling at (rather than indulging in) the sights. If you're the adventurous type, go to **Bar Bar**. Take a breather at **Red Parrot**. Hard-core sexpats go to **Nana Plaza** (Soi 4), which is basically a three-story epicenter of sleaze. **Soi Cowboy** (off Soi 21) is more laid-back sexy.

Walk over to Soi 11. There's a biergarten at **Old German Beerhouse**. The drinks really are cheap at **Cheap Charlie's**. Sunday is ladies' night at **Q Bar**. The local rooftop bar is **Nest**.

Rules of Bangkok:

- If you're unsure about a hostel, ask to see the room before you pay. Check to see if the air conditioner works.
- Khao San Road has some of the cheapest bars in town. Some stay open all night.
- Yaba, a type of speed, is widespread in Bangkok. Your tuk-tuk driver may be on it.

FUCKED UP FIRSTHAND

We were at a sidewalk bar in Khao San when my tour guide, Daniel, asked what I wanted to see.

"Something they don't show you in the guidebooks," I said.

A short tuk-tuk ride later we arrived at Patpong. I'd heard of the girlie shows here, and was about to protest when he said, "Don't worry. This isn't the Patpong you're thinking of." He was right. I glanced into the haze of smoke and strobe lights in one bar and saw that the men dancing on stage were covered, but an eye patch does have its limits. In Daniel's defense, the show he took me to was not mentioned in any guidebook. We grabbed some noodles at a street cart after the show. When Daniel asked where I wanted to go now, I said, "a regular bar."

We took a shortcut and were passing by an abandoned restaurant when a baby elephant appeared from the shadows. She was heading in the opposite direction, toward Patpong. I considered sticking my hand out, but didn't—mama elephant probably wasn't too far behind. But she wasn't. That baby elephant was embarking on a solo mission through Bangkok.

VERDICT
Just the right amount of "scary."

Noah Pelletier

47. Mexico City, Mexico

SEASON: March through May for best weather (spring, mild).
IDEAL CONDITIONS: Día de los Muertos (Day of the Dead) on November 1.
DAYTIME ACTIVITY: Visit Coyoacán and Frida Kahlo's Casa Azul, climb the ruins of Piramides de Teotihuacan.
LODGING RECOMMENDATIONS: Downtown Beds, the hostel side of Downtown Mexico.
INGESTIBLES: Mezcal, pulque, and tequila banderas, quesadilla de flor de calabaza (squash blossom quesadillas), mole, and chicharron de queso (cheese fried on a grill, folded into a tube and cooled), chocolate, churros, and café con leche.

There are more than twenty million people in Mexico City so if you can't find a party you need more help than this book can offer. In D.F. (*Distrito Federal*), "partying" is not a separate activity from eating, or sightseeing, or your daily commute. Clement weather, ubiquitous music, and an established drinking culture has created an easy and social street vibe, so don't be surprised if a conversation struck in the line for fresh-squeezed jugo ends up with you singing "*Cielito lindo*" with your new friends.

Start with a day on the **Touribus**, where you can explore the city's sixteen *delegaciones* (boroughs) with a hop-on, hop-off ticket and a six-pack. Chances are you're staying in **El Centro** or a neighboring colonia, so board at the **Zócalo** (the city's main square). To the north, you'll want to hop off and explore the wide-avenued, tree-lined colonias **Condesa**, **Roma**, and **Zona Rosa** on foot. Skip **Polanco** unless you've got the desire to hobnob with the super-rich. To the south, visit the artsy areas of **San Angel**. Walk to the **Jardin Centenario** for a glass of wine on a park-side patio, followed by a cup of coffee at **Café El Jarocho**.

Take a taxi to **Xochimilco**, timing it so you arrive with some daylight left. A note on taxis in D.F.: Make sure your driver is using a meter and keep an eye on the tariff—scams are fairly common. Your best bet is to find a taxi *sitio* (site).

Have your driver drop you off at **Xochimilco Park**. Visit any of the *quesadillarias* and order some squash blossom quesadillas on blue corn tortillas, to go. Grab your drink of choice at *la tienda* and take your picnic to the dock. This park sits on a system of waterways that dates back to Aztec times, and you can rent one of the hundreds of *trajineras* (brightly painted covered raft-style boats with seating for more than a dozen people). Negotiate your price. Once on the water, you will be able to purchase everything from candles to tacos to ice from the vendors that sail by.

When you've had your fill, take a taxi to **La Botica** in El Centro to sample mezcal from a half-dozen regions across the country. Order snacks from the bar and choose your music from a jukebox at this *mezcalería*.

Get yourself to any of the city's hundreds of cantinas, such as **La Mascota**, where drinks are cheap and the appetizers are free. Order a tequila *banderas* (a shot each of lime juice, tequila, and sangrita, which replicate the colors of the Mexican flag) and a beer chaser. Don't be shy: join those guys in the corner singing *corridos*. Watch for the hawker offering a go on his electroshock "game"; this may be the first time you'll be asked to test your *machismo* tonight, but it likely won't be the last. Pace yourself.

Best on a Friday or Saturday night, **Plaza Garibaldi** is the gathering place for mariachis who play live all night and into the morning. Buy a bottle of tequila and wander through the plaza where you can eat, hire mariachis, try your luck at midway games, and watch performers. This is also a good place to find a *pulqueria* where you can try *pulque,* a drink made of the fermented sap of the maguey plant.

NOTES FROM A LOCAL
You haven't partied in Mexico City until you've eaten tacos in an Aztec canal, shared a bottle of tequila with a mariachi band, and woken up just as it's falling dark and time to start all over again.

VERDICT
Importante.

Keph Senett

48. Nairobi, Kenya

SEASON: December through March.
IDEAL CONDITIONS: A city often described as having "perfect weather," 80 degrees (26 degrees Celsius) with little to no humidity.
DAYTIME ACTIVITY: Watch baby rhinos take a mud bath at Nairobi National Park.
LODGING RECOMMENDATIONS: YMCA for something cheap and clean, YWCA for longer stays, or a friend of a friend in the always rotating but accommodating nonprofit crowd.
INGESTIBLES: Tusker Lager, nyama choma (roast meat), beef samosas, mshikaki (shish kabobs), smokies (mini sausages), and mayai katchumbari (boiled eggs stuffed with tomato relish).

Dancing is an inextricable part of Kenyan culture and Nairobi seems to bring out the groove in even the most awkward of white boys. Nairobi's clubs are noisy, frenzied, sweaty caves, breathing and pulsing with thousands of young people who dance, drink, and laugh until the equatorial sun climbs up over the horizon.

In Kilimani you can lounge at **Casablanca** on traditional Swahili beds smoking *shisha*, catch up with a friend at the classy **Sailors'**, or go to **Tamasha** and enjoy great atmosphere and terrible service. **Westlands** is the clubbing center of Nairobi and if you're not sure exactly where to go, just show up at Mpaka Street and see where the music is loudest. **Havana** can be counted on for a crowd on Thursdays, **Galileo's** dance floor is usually packed, and **Tree House** throws themed parties that range from fun to unbearably cheesy. **K1** has great live jazz and **Gypsy's** is a popular expat spot and also a gay-friendly night out.

For a slightly grittier and cheaper good time, head into Nairobi's packed downtown clubs. **Tribeka** is great and Moi Avenue is packed with clubs such as **Jazz** that have hip-hop, reggae, and local beats blaring so loud you won't even notice the guy in the corner making lewd comments and fondling himself.

If dancing really isn't your thing, hit up a bar for a cold Tusker. Nairobi also has great brew pubs with seasonal selections of microbrews you can enjoy on crowded balconies. **Sierra Brasserie and Lounge** has cheap, delicious beer and bottles their most popular stuff. **Brew Bistro** has a killer buy-one get-one-free happy hour everyday from 4:00 to 6:00 P.M.

Don't forget the equally fun "locals" that dot the city. These are the neighborhood joints where no one bothers the sleeping guy in the corner, the floor is made of packed dirt, and cheap liquor is shared among friends. Just watch out for *changaa,* Kenya's potent moonshine that has been known to make people blind . . . not to mention defecate on themselves.

The best Nairobi cuisine is *nyama choma.* Huge strips of roasted goat and beef are served with hunks of *ugali* (maize meal) and *katchumbari* (pico de gallo) and a pile of salt to dunk everything in. Late night chicken-and-chips spots are ubiquitous and for some of the best drunk food around order *bhajia,* chunks of potato fried up with spices. Street vendors abound, but just take it from a girl who's had worms, be choosy about your source. The guy with sausages in a Tupperware container miles away from the nearest source of heat? That's a no.

Nairobi has a thriving art scene, and if you're lucky you could find a show with free drinks. Check out **Kuona Trust** and the **Go-Down Arts Centre.**

Don't miss **Blankets and Wine,** a monthly bohemian music festival, as well as **Safari Rallies** which are off-road car races that happen around the country.

Rules while in Nairobi:

- Do not wear khaki .This isn't a safari and there's nothing worse than being the *mzungu,* or white dude, on skyscraper-lined streets in head-to-toe safari gear.
- Do not carry valuables. While "Nairobbery's" reputation is blown out of proportion, pickpockets do abound.
- Do not fear Nairobi, but *do* respect it. *Don't* walk at night, *do* spring for cabs, and always be aware of your surroundings and your belongings.

NOTES FROM A LOCAL
Who do you think you are, Ernest Hemingway?

VERDICT
You can find transcendence chilling on Swahili beds smoking shisha.

Abigail Higgins

49. Phuket, Thailand

SEASON: May through September is drier and cooler, and more crowded.
IDEAL CONDITIONS: Dude cruise.
DAYTIME ACTIVITY: Check out the Sino-Portuguese wares of Old Phuket or snap some photos of Big Buddha.

Make the most of it. Full moon campfire/rocket launch in Phuket. Photo by Katie Scott Aiton.

LODGING RECOMMENDATIONS: Countless hotels from every price range. Pay by the month or the hour.
INGESTIBLES: Thai whiskey, pharmaceuticals, Asian beers.

Is it ironic that an island called Phuket seems entirely populated by prostitutes? We're not just talking about the go-go dancers in the windows and the hand-job factories lining the streets. It's also the tuk-tuk drivers, two-for-one suit tailors, DVD bootleggers, Thai boxing promoters, push-cart restaurateurs, cat-calling street bars, and everyone else in this beachy bar-town. All Patong seems hell-bent on furiously shaking their money-maker for you. Please come inside, have a look, just try, morning price, happy hour, happy ending, sucky sucky, come inside.

You should make the most of it.

The sooner you quit avoiding eye contact and start shaking your booty back, the sooner you can get busy getting sideways, wrongways, and everywhichotherways. Because Thailand loves that. At any given moment, fireworks will explode, strangers begin wrestling in the street, and sultry women magically materialize well within your personal space. Embrace the mischief . . . just be sure you know what you're embracing.

No question **Soi Bangla** is the epicenter. It's closed to traffic at night and riddled with lanes and alleys each offering various forms of sketchy entertainment, from gigantic super clubs like **Tiger Disco** and the swanky, upscale **Seduction.** Flamboyant ladyboys dance outside **Cocktails & Dreams** and Russian girls at **Moulin Rouge. The Night Station** is the biggest, best known, and raciest spot on Bangla, but one could probably spend weeks discovering their favorite nooks and crannies. (*Warning:* do not spend weeks here.)

Playschool A Go-Go, Exotica, and **Devil's Playground** are the hottest go-go bars, with scantily clad girls dancing on the bars and happy to spend time at your table for the ramped-up price of a lady drink.

Sai Kor Road hosts Thai boxing matches three nights a week, just upstairs from the wild **Tiger Complex** of bars and clubs. The intersection at Rat U Thit Road also hosts some top clubs, such as the Harley-themed **Nicky's Handlebar** and the tribute-band bar **Rock City. The Tai Pan Night Club** doesn't get started until late, but it's a full carnival of games, prizes, girls on poles, and a stage show you can't take your itchy eyes off of.

Then everywhere else you look, on and off Bangla, are dozens of tiny street-front bars with beautiful women calling for you to step inside. These "bar girls" love to engage in games like Connect Four or Jenga. Where things evolve from there is strictly between you and your new friend.

While the whole of Patong is paved in clubs, bars, and all-night massage parlors, there are a dozen other ways to fuck yourself up in Patong when you're not being creepy. Cobra farms. Go-Carts.

Firing ranges. Paintball wars. Sketchy bungee jumps. Elephant wrestling. WaveRunners and parasailing. Just sign the release form and hang on tight.

Remember the rules:

- Adam's apple, hairy lips, deep voice, and strong hands . . . yes, she used to be a man.
- Prostitution is not legal in Patong. Just so you know.
- You won't need a paddle for the "ping-pong" shows enthusiastically promoted on the street.
- Eye contact is an open invitation to well . . . whatever. It's an invitation.

NOTES FROM A LOCAL
The day you beat a bar girl at Connect Four is the day you've been in Patong too long.

FUCKED UP FIRSTHAND
At some point in the night I got it into my twisted brain that this whole town was just a snack bar designed by vampires to glamour us into complacent delirium then feed on us without recourse. With my Spidey-senses tingling, I stumbled from the club. Everyone there was staring up at the sky where an open circuit breaker was on fire, shooting sparks into the warm tropical mist and buzzing like a nest of electric bees. Just then an explosion of fireworks burst into the sky and suddenly the entire street went black.

Nobody panicked. Perhaps we were all too wasted to react. Perhaps we all knew it would come to this. From the darkness, a ladyboy appeared beside me and offered me a half-finished cocktail. He/she gave me a brisk package check and asked if I needed a massage.

VERDICT

Rent a beach chair and someone will bring you a coconut to wash down your Vicodin.

Nathan Myers

50. Suzhou, China

SEASON: Early spring.
IDEAL CONDITIONS: Before the mutant mosquitoes rise up from the canals to feast.
DAYTIME ACTIVITY: Visit the Buddhist monastery Hanshan Temple, or hike Tianping Mountain.
LODGING RECOMMENDATIONS: Nanlin Hotel Suzhou for hotel, Jinjiang Inn for budget.
INGESTIBLES: Baijiu (spirits), Tsingtao beer, mutton (Xinjiang Yakexi Restaurant), la mian (hand-pulled noodles), secondhand smoke.

Start at Shiquan Jie, aka "Bar Street," where the buildings are whitewashed, and the roofs have sweeping slopes and upturned eaves. There's also bars. Lots of them. Interspersed between blackmarket DVD stores, boutiques, and restaurants. Hit up **Jane's Pub Bar** or **The Pub Bar** for a beer and talk with some of the local expats. The neon sign outside of **The Drunken Clam** looks just like the one on the *Family Guy* cartoon and you can even order a quagmire. For something completely different, check **The Bookworm**, a two-story bookstore with an impressive food and drink menu.

Many expats live and party in Suzhou Industrial Park (SIP), which is east of the old town and distinguished by neon-lit, funky-designed buildings. **Black Mirage** is an American-owned bar that you have to enter through a Japanese restaurant and go upstairs. Order a San Miguel and a plate of Santel's Carolina ribs.

Blue Marlin has a decent happy hour (4:00 to 7:00 P.M.) and if you end up staying later there's a pool table and a resident band that plays every night. When the weather's nice or if a major sporting event is on head to the terrace at **Mr. Pizza.**

On Friday and Saturday nights there will be a crowd at **Rainbow Walk,** the complex overlooking Jinji Lake, where the fountains and light show kicks off at eight o'clock. Take in the sights with a margarita on the balcony at **Zapata's.** For a German microbrew, head to **Löwenburg. Pig and Whistle** has two-for-one beers until 8:00 P.M., and on Friday there's an all-you-can-eat barbecue.

Li Gong Di stretches across Jinji Lake. At night, you can watch the Suzhou Bird's Nest light up as you stroll the neon-lit arch bridges. The bars on the causeway are not particularly cheap, but don't let that deter you. **Pravda** is a swanky Euro-Russian club bar with nightly specials and a respectable dance floor. The band at **Harry's Forbidden Bar** is better than most, but for something more low-key, **Garbo's** has darts and a "Recession Drinks Menu" with cheap pints.

Things to keep in mind in Suzhou:

- Alcohol is dangerously cheap (a 0.5 liter of beer is less than a dollar).
- Taxis are inexpensive but be sure to have the address written in Chinese.
- A massage is an inexpensive and pleasant way to nurse a hangover.

NOTES FROM A LOCAL
For a blast from the past, check out Southern Commune 江南公社, a Communist-themed restaurant where the waitresses wear Mao-era outfits.

VERDICT
Suzhou is so much fun it should come with a warning label.

Noah Pelletier

5: Bar Crawl

Where the Appalachian Trail crosses the Susquehanna River, you'll find the old steel working town of Duncannon, Pennsylvania. And there's a hotel there that is (or at least was) famous among thru-hikers: The Doyle.

You can get almost anyone to agree that we're living through "times of change," but if you ask them to describe what's changing they'll pull out Hollywood-sized abstractions. "Climate" is changing. "Technology" is changing. "People" are changing. But the only real changes are those that affect small groups of people, unequivocally but often barely noticeably, at least at first.

I'll give an example: the day they installed a TV in The Doyle Hotel bar.

I grew up in the suburbs, and had only read or seen movies and TV shows about rooming houses and barflies, so the night I walked into The Doyle, it was as if I'd stepped into some fucked up, gritty version of *Cheers*. Here they were: barflies, almost all men, most of whom worked a single shift at the steel mill if they were lucky, but otherwise *lived* at the bar, each with his own stool as if it were a tiny sovereignty. Most wore baseball caps, hunting jackets, and each had a beer (the local "Iron City") in front of him at all times.

"Youz hiking?" a wiry bartender in a camouflage hat asked.

"Yessir." I set my pack down and tried to appear as if I'd grown up walking into rooming-house bars.

Over the next twenty-four hours I'd learn that: (a) many of these men actually did live here, and apparently went upstairs to pass out each night; (b) yet no matter how much they drank, they never appeared intoxicated; (c) drinking PBR was frowned upon as Pabst was supposedly "squeezing" the local breweries; and (d) the only thing they hated more than PBR were the "dumb-ass hunters" coming down from New York into their backwoods and "shooting at anything that moved."

"Youz lucky to be alive," they said, after I told them (it was mid-November, hunting season) about the hunters who'd literally been sitting on the Appalachian Trail with their rifles. They spoke as if the bar were a kind of headquarters, a safe haven, and I'd barely made it back from behind enemy lines.

But by far the most important thing I experienced was this unspoken mandate that *you kept the conversation going.* You listened and spoke. You added. These guys had taken joking, theorizing, and bullshitting to the level of art. You got the sense that as long as they could just keep talking, no local tragedy or personal shame—the ruined river, another plant closure, somebody running off with somebody else's wife—couldn't be disburdened and finally, laughed at.

I suspect that for those who live where pub culture still exists, none of this sounds out of the ordinary. I also suspect that for those born in the digital generation, this might sound all campy and sentimental. And yet I wonder: as rooming houses—where you could drink all day and night, then retire safely to your room—have died away in this country, where do genuine fuck-ups have their moments, what happens to all the lost conversation?

The next morning I took the creaking wooden staircase back down to the bar and it was as if no time had passed at all. The men sat—albeit somewhat quieter—with their breakfast beers. A bit of excitement then: the bartender came in with an ancient and heavy TV set. We watched him struggle with it, trying to hoist it up on a shelf, nobody helping but definitely giving barstool commentary: "A little more to the right!" "Shit, watch out, itz gonna tip!" "Naw, man, itz tilted!"

At one point the bartender couldn't fully position the TV with both arms, so he used his forehead to finally ram it into place.

"Aw, man, you got face-prints on it," somebody said.

After that he plugged it in and our faces stayed on it and the conversation went dead and you could feel something possibly changed in that little bar forever.

I'm afraid to know what The Doyle has become now. Places can only stay original for so long without fizzling or getting blown out. Either way, you can't take places for what they *were* but what they are.

That said, here are entire galaxies from Austin to Berlin to Glasgow to Halifax, from Brooklyn to Lisbon to Savannah to Belfast. There's lots of pub crawl country here. And for those needing bass music, foam clouds, and laser shows or whatever, we've got plenty of megaclubs, too, places where moments of transcendence may be possible, but you'll still have to accept that they occurred in a place called "The Dome."

51. Austin, Texas

SEASON: Year-round, baby!
IDEAL CONDITIONS: A spring or fall night when it actually gets below 70 degrees (21 degrees Celsius). Weekend. Bonus if there's a music festival in town.
DAYTIME ACTIVITY: Explore the Barton Creek Greenbelt.
LODGING RECOMMENDATIONS: Firehouse Hostel puts you in an ideal location for this binge. If you've got the scratch or a big group, check vacation rentals.
INGESTIBLES: Copious microbrews plus local vodka, as much street food as you can afford and stomach.

You're starting at Sixth Street, and no whining or "no shit, sherlocks." Let me finish. You're starting at the far eastern end of the street and walking west, drinking at as many places as you can and seeing how far you can make it. Consider it a challenge. A dare. Start early and get to the taproom at **Hops and Grain**. Thanks to Texas's legacy liquor laws, breweries aren't allowed to sell their product on premises . . . so these guys give it away (Friday 2:00 to 6:00 P.M.; Saturday 12:00 to 4:00 P.M.). With your five sample tickets, throw back a Pale Dog and whatever's in the "Greenhouse"—go nuts for the last three.

Nicely buzzed, start the trek west. If you've taken the challenge to heart and don't want to walk five minutes without a drink, **St Roch's** dive bar is just south of Sixth on Pedernales. One more long block gets you to **Hi Hat** for more micros and a decent wine list.

Once you're west of Chicon, you're in it. Grab a pint at **The Grackle's** "hipster jail"—their open-air but security-barred patio. This is also your first recommended food stop. The **East Side King** (**ESK**) trailer in the parking lot grills righteous East Asian–inspired takeaways. A couple hundred yards farther on, this combo is repeated with the dive bar **Liberty** and a second ESK with a different, Indian-leaning menu.

At Comal, you'll be tempted to deviate to **White Horse** or **Yellow Jacket Social Club** down the road to your left, but stick to the plan—you are nowhere close to being done. The next block of Sixth has biker-bar **Gypsy Lounge**, the hipster duo of **Hotel Vegas and Volstead**, followed by **The Brixton**. Stumbling yet?

Whatever else happens tonight, you have to stop at **Papi Tino's** for the city's best *Michelada* (beer mixed with lime, spices, and chili pepper). Sweet place for upscale Mexican if you've got the time and cash. If not, keep walking because you're about to enter the food-truck orgy zone clustered around bar and music venue **Cheer Up Charlie's**. Pizza, tacos, barbecue, sandwiches, vegan—the rotation changes, but the choice is always a tough one.

If you want to scrap this quest, see some music, and get shitty on prohibition-era cocktails, post up at **East Side Show Room**. If not, go for **Shangri-La,** last hipster outpost of East Sixth (and home to yet another East Side King trailer). Fuel up for the debauchery to come at **Pueblo Viejo's** trailer, probably the best tacos you'll see in Austin.

On the other side of I-35, you'll hit my last recommendable stop: **Easy Tiger**, with dozens of taps and Ping-Pong on the creekside patio. They bake, too. Just know that if you pick up some pastries "for breakfast tomorrow," that shit isn't going to work out.

West of Red River, you'll rejoin your fellow tourists and a liberal spewing of local college Greeks. This is "Dirty Sixth." Follow your incredibly drunk intuition and pass or enter doors at your choosing. That goes for music as well as booze. If the hairy bluesman burning up a Strat at **The Stage** pulls you in, all good. If you opt for **Coyote Ugly**, I *will* judge you.

It's a very long four blocks back to Firehouse Hostel—talking your crew into a drink at the downstairs lounge cleverly makes for a face-saving "Guys, I think I'm just gonna go upstairs and crash." If you want to continue the tour, O' brave soul, O' alcoholic, I'll leave you to wander the yuppie bars and farm-to-tables of West Sixth. Congratulations. You've no doubt pissed off a lot of locals.

FUCKED UP FIRSTHAND
The last time I did this little Sixth Street safari, I got hit up for $9 by a limo driver, overheard someone say they "needed to wash the blood off their hands," and was accosted by a homeless woman stumbling out of a liquor store.

VERDICT
This is what you get with one street. Austin's rabbit hole of fucked-upness is deep.

Hal Amen

52. Belfast, Northern Ireland

SEASON: April through September (spring through fall).
IDEAL CONDITIONS: Sunshine or shivering, Belfasters are ready to drink.
DAYTIME ACTIVITY: Hike sections of the Ulster Way.
LODGING RECOMMENDATIONS: Vagabonds, Arnie's Backpackers, or—if you prefer your own room, All Seasons or Old Rectory.
INGESTIBLES: Guinness, Irish whiskey, traditional fish and chips, Irish stew.

Irish social intercourse means *craic*. Banter, chit-chat, storytelling, relentless conversation. When tales are shared over pints of the black stuff you discover that Belfasters are quick-witted, excellent fun, and—after lifetimes of political strife—resilient. Belfast has perhaps the greatest concentration of traditional pubs on earth, and while

Don't pretend you can keep up with local crews in Ireland, or half the other places in the book for that matter. Photo by Chris Burkard.

101 Places to Get F*cked Up Before You Die

old-style places are making way for brash bars, the city is full of classics, such as archetypal, gas-lit **Crown Liquor Saloon,** which is a national treasure. To see why, bag one of the snugs decorated with carved lions and griffins and settle in for Guinness served alongside hearty Irish stew.

Authentic pubs are often secreted down cobblestone "entries," so poke around for legendary spots, such as the **Duke of York,** which is a riot over weekends. Nearby, the **John Hewitt** is ironically named after a slow-drinking socialist poet—it isn't old, but serves locally brewed Headless Dog; try it. **Pottingers Entry** gives on to **Morning Star,** offering the best pub grub in town—the chef-owner's Australian wife gets in kangaroo steaks. And **Whites Tavern** claims Belfast's first drinking licence—granted in 1630. Upstairs, its music room resembles a cheap 1950s lounge, and as with most worthwhile pubs, when it fills up, crowds and *craic* spill outside.

Bill Murray once played air guitar at **The Spaniard,** popular with barristers, bohemians, and everyone in between. Slightly bad-ass **Love & Death Inc** juxtaposes its grotty entrance with warm Belfast hospitality and motherfucking mean mai tais—sink a few before unleashing yourself on the dance floor.

In the modern, trying-to-be-glitzy bars, you'll find plenty of cock-foisting blokes and lasses in miniskirts and tan-can leather-orange complexions doing stiletto balancing acts. Sex and cocktails are core preoccupations among patrons at upmarket **Apartment**—dress the part and try your luck, or head for the hipster vibe at **The Cloth Ear,** or swanky **Café Vaudeville** in the hull of a former bank—you'll need alcohol to dull the pain of plodding commercial music, though.

Far more interesting is mingling with locals at **Errigle Inn** on Ormeau Road. Here, slink into a booze-fueled buzz in **The Oak Lounge,** populated by unnatural numbers of writers and hacks—the high-octane, expletive-ridden *craic* is pure Tarantino.

West Belfast's **The Felons** is hard-core republican drinking territory with cheap pints and brightly lit pool tables. It's aesthetically cheerless, but the number of drinkers in tracksuit pants signals authenticity. So much so that membership is only extended to regulars who've served at least a year and a day in prison.

While arty hangouts are clustered in Cathedral Quarter just north of center, university-dominated **Queens Quarter** is popping with low-price drinks specials aimed at students. Plenty of live music venues, too. Straddling **Katy Daly's**, where deals may include four drinks for $15 USD. **The Limelight** is where bands like Kaiser Chiefs and Scissor Sisters have cut their teeth.

The Stiff Kitten focuses on quality urban music—live acts and DJs. And there are regular concerts at the university's **Mandela Hall**. More intimate—and often intellectually stimulating—is **The Black Box**.

Pubs and bars will kick you onto the street by 1:00 A.M., so if you're set on a later night, get to a proper club. Biggest is Ibiza-inspired **El Divino**; best on Mondays is **Scratch**; and house monsters can air-fist at **Rain**. Or dance to diva anthems at **Kremlin**, Belfast's biggest gay club. More fun, though, is adjoining **Union Street**, where open-plan washrooms mean boys can pee without disconnecting from the dance floor.

Belfast is perennially festive, with lively outdoor events like **Belsonic** and the **Festival of Fools** in summer. The **Cathedral Quarter Arts Festival** includes killer parties, while **West Belfast's Féile an Phobail** is a staunch celebration of Irishness.

Festival or not, when there's sunshine, locals fill every inch of public lawn to soak up the rays. Grab beers from a nearby supermarket and join in.

NOTES FROM A LOCAL

True. Some pubs are either Protestant or Catholic. There's a long history of partisanship. Wounds take time to heal. The trick is to avoid taking sides; as an outsider you can drink where some locals would never dare.

VERDICT

Epic bravura contained within a compact metro.

Keith Bain

53. Madrid, Spain

SEASON: April through October.
IDEAL CONDITIONS: Warm nights and sunny days, which central Spain has in abundance.
DAYTIME ACTIVITY: Museum-ing at the Prado, Thyssen-Bornemisza.
LODGING RECOMMENDATIONS: Hostal Tribunal, Fuencarral Breogan Hostal, Hostal Nuria.
INGESTIBLES: Sangria, tinto de verano (red wine and lemon fanta), kalimocho (red wine and coca cola), tapas, hot ham water.

Spain's tanking economy and anarchic distaste for law enforcement have led to a rise in street parties known as *botellóns.* This pastime might be a favorite mainly among the young and broke, but it represents a vibe of Spanish nightlife that's as strong in the pubs as in the plazas—people-driven, friendly, and super laid-back.

The night doesn't start until eleven or twelve o'clock, so take time to fortify with tapas. A cheap and easy place to start is the chain **Cien Montaditos.** It's usually full of Spanish students and international *jóvenes* (young people), and is a great place to try *jamon serrano* or *tortilla española,* not to mention pints of tinto.

If it's your first night in town, stop in **Sol,** the center of town, the center of the Spanish road system, and the center of international tourist nightlife, as embodied by the monolithic **Club Joy Eslava.** Joy frequently hosts student nights and can feel like a college party during rush week, down to the top-forty anthems and occasional beer pong tournaments. If you're looking for chiller vibes, **Cuevas de Sésamo** is Sol's safe haven. Tucked romantically underground,

Sésamo is a quiet place to drink pitchers of delicious sangria and get inspired by the literary quotes on the walls.

A little farther north lies Chueca—Madrid's gay neighborhood. Start your night at the **Bar Nike** for carnival-sized cups of fancy kalimocho (with grenadine!). Nike tends to be wall-to-wall packed, so **Diurno** is a good alternative—the café/bar/video rental place has delicious mojitos and caipirinhas and free wi-fi. Clubs here come and go but **Delirio** can be relied on for attractive strangers and throwback disco jams from the *movida* (Madrid's hedonistic heyday). Ladies who love ladies will be happiest at **Fulanita de Tal** or **Escape**.

The hippest vibes in town though can be found in Malasaña. The neighborhood is full of cheap, unique bars, frequented by people with *superguay* (really cool) alt-life haircuts. **La Via Láctea** and **TupperWare** on San Vincente Ferrer specialize in kitsch décor and indie rock, which the DJs and crowds all love. Both have two floors—one for dancing, one for conversation. La Via Láctea is especially versatile, and if you're there early, it is quiet enough for a first date.

Most bars close at two, as does the metro, but the network of night buses or *buhos* (literally "owls") is extremely reliable. Clubs stay open for those who want to party all night, so you can dance until the metro starts again.

Kapital, in the museum district, is the biggest nightclub game in town: seven floors full of dance and lounge areas, and whether you're into house, soul, or Spanish hits, you'll find it here. **Pacha**, like Pachas around the world, is the place to go for deep house and trance and international DJs. **Sala el Sol** by Gran Via is both a concert spot that regularly gets acts from Dawes to Steve Aoki, and an all-night dance party.

In the afternoon, wake up and head to La Latina. Grab delicious veggie food from **Viva La Vida** to ease your hangover. Sit in the sun. Relax. Then order a caipirinha from **Delic** next door because life is short and *tienes que aprovecharlo* (you have to make the most of it).

The other night I went out to grab dinner with a friend in Goya and thought I was just going to be out for an hour. Suddenly, I found myself in the car of some Jordanian guy speeding toward Malasaña and we hopped from bar to bar until 6:00 A.M. This was all on a Wednesday.

VERDICT

Spain isn't only Barcelona.

Nina Mashurova

54. Brooklyn, New York

SEASON: Rooftop-party season.
IDEAL CONDITIONS: A day without humidity.
DAYTIME ACTIVITY: Walk the Brooklyn Heights Promenade.
LODGING RECOMMENDATIONS: Zip112 Hostel, Wythe Hotel, The New York Loft Hostel, NY Moore Hostel.
INGESTIBLES: $1 cans of Coors bodega beers.

Before we talk about North Brooklyn, let's just address the elephant in the room: hipsters. Yes, our contemporary notions of the American hipster is largely a by-product of Brooklyn (Williamsburg). But stop talking about it before you get onto the L train, because that doesn't even make sense anymore. If you're willing to overlook the increasing number of gentrifying condo-dwelling yuppies, entitled NYU students, and trust-fund art poseurs, you'll be able to find the working creative scene of artists and musicians who've made this such a desirable place.

Most life in North Brooklyn revolves around the L train, an easily accessible (if not totally crowded) line that you can take into Brooklyn from Union Square, Manhattan. Parts of Williamsburg and Bushwick are also accessible by the J train.

More light and space than you'll find in most New York–area bars, but these places exist if you have the scrill. Photo by Holly Clark.

After settling down in your tiny bedroom, walk down **Bedford Avenue** and shop in the vintage stores, and watch all the weirdos. After you've maxed out your credit card on second-hand clothes at **Beacon's Closet** on North 11th Street, you'll probably need a drink. Head over to the **Brooklyn Brewery** to drink some beers. Have dinner at **Diner** or **Moto** or **Pies 'n' Thighs,** or go über-cheap with a falafel from **Oasis**. See if there are any **Todd P** all-ages DIY shows or look for any warehouse loft dance parties.

Go for after-dinner drinks at **South 4th Bar** or **Maracuja,** or get drunk on the cheap at **The Levee**. See a show at **Brooklyn Bowl** or **The Music Hall of Williamsburg** or **The Knitting Factory**. Get funky at **Zebulon** or **Bembé**. Get twisted until 4:00 A.M. Then find the after-party.

In the morning, recover from your hangover at **Egg** . . . but if you need a Bloody Mary, head to **Enid's**. Spend the day chilling in

McCarren Park, and if you still want to drink, be discreet and pick up a to-go margarita at **Turkey's Nest.** Hang out through the afternoon or get your artisan on at **Smorgasburg,** a seasonal spin-off of local-centric Brooklyn Flea. Bike or walk along East River for an incredible view of Manhattan. On Saturdays in the summer East River Park has free outdoor concerts.

Moving on: have happy hour drinks at **Spuyten Duyvil,** then dine locally at **Dumont** for the best cheeseburgers you've ever stuffed into your face, or explore Bushwick for dinner at **Northeast Kingdom** or **Roberta's.** For ultra-cheap, pickup tacos go to the **Tortilla Factory** on **Jefferson.** See if anything is happening at the **3rd Ward** art space. Catch some punk shows at **Party Expo** or **Goodbye Blue Mondays.**

North Brooklyn is the perfect place to party all night long!

FUCKED UP FIRSTHAND

Ben had actually printed out a list of parties he wanted to go. We didn't know anybody at these places, but he said not to worry because we would be employing the power of his world-famous Dunkin Donuts Irish iced coffee. We walked into Dunkies for a thirty-two ounce iced coffee (light on the milk) and then walked next door to the liquor store to pick up a pint of whiskey.

We split the alcohol into our respective plastic cups and drank them as we walked between parties. We got drunker and more caffeinated as the night went on. I can't remember what happened, but it was *awesome.*

VERDICT

If you care about what the future of culture will look like in America you must visit Brooklyn.

Joshua Heller

55. Brussels, Belgium

SEASON: July through September.
IDEAL CONDITIONS: Sunny and warm. Doesn't happen often enough.
DAYTIME ACTIVITY: Walking around eating chocolate.
LODGING RECOMMENDATIONS: 2Go4, Jacques Brel, or Sleep Well for hostel.
INGESTIBLES: Trappist beers, waffles, gueuze (lambìc beer), carbonnades à la flamande (Flemish beef stew).

Belgium is to beer drinkers what candy stores are to kids. It's easy to let yourself get swept up in the selection here, so if you want to get the essence, start in the **Brown Bar Area**. There are six bars to hang out at, starting at **Monk** and ending at **Walvis**. Don't be afraid to ring the door buzzer at **Archiduc**, a 1930s jazz bar. **Mr. Wong** is the nightclub in Chinatown. Check out **Beursschouwburg** for a free S.H.O.W. (Shit Happens on Wednesday). **Madame Moustache** is the alternative bar-cum–freak show cabaret.

Saint-Gery is the square with trendy concept bars: **Mappa Mundo, Roi des Belges,** and **Zebra**. Watch the game at **Celtica,** which is claimed by some to have the cheapest beer in Brussels. **Booze 'n Blues** has old rock posters on the wall and soul music on the stereo.

The gay bars are on Kolenmarkt/Rue du Marché. If it's warm, go to the terrace at **Fontainas**. **Boys Boudoir** and **Baroque** for beer and bears. **Belgica** has Thursday specials. Ask for a Lambic at **Het Goudblommeke** in Papier, former hangout of Magritte and Hergé. Get lost in the windowless bar next door, **La Porte Noire**.

Delirium Café can get pretty intense on the weekends. Of course, that's what happens when your beer menu is the size of a phone book. If the selection seems overwhelming, ask your server for a suggestion. **Bier Circus** offers a slightly smaller beer selection and a more laid-back atmosphere. **À la Mort Subite** (sudden death) is a former dice shooter's bar. The Spanish community hangs out at **Ca-**

braliego. Don't ask why, but techno club **Blaes 208** has a second name, **Fuse,** on Saturdays. Check **Magasin 4** for punk and hardcore shows.

If it's sunny, meet some locals at the **Skatepark Place** at Rue de la Chapelle. Nonskaters will be hanging out here, too, drinking beer and doing their thing. The area next to the railways is a popular place for street art and graffiti.

Rules of Brussels:

- Do like the Belgians and eat first, then drink. *Ne fond leggen* means "Lay the base."
- Respect the alcohol content. Drink lower-percent beer first. Start too strong and everything else tastes weak.
- Don't steal the beer glass. Buy them for cheap at the flea market.
- Shop for Belgian chocolates and Trappist beer in the grocery store to save money.

FUCKED UP FIRSTHAND

The fireworks hadn't started yet. Museum Square was packed and teens were climbing statues for vantage points. A movie projector was aimed at a large, white wall. It was showing black and white footage of soldiers in funny hats setting up barbed wire entanglements, a savage tableau that would play throughout the fireworks display.

The celebration didn't feel right until 2:00 A.M. when I wound up at Delirium Café. I took one of the last seats at a horseshoe-shaped bench. I'd ordered my beer and was soon speaking with the wild-eyed boy beside me. There was no telling what he was saying, but I was prepared. I'd jotted down some phrases in a notepad.

"*Je ne parle pas Français,*" I said, "*mais j'ai parlé à un monstre marin*" (Meaning: I do not speak French, but I have talked to a sea monster"). This got him laughing. The wild-eyed boy introduced me to his friends. I brought in the New Year trading nonsense for beer.

VERDICT
Just show up.

Noah Pelletier

56. Cape Town, South Africa

SEASON: November through March (summer through fall).
IDEAL CONDITIONS: Sun reflecting off the ocean into your beer.
DAYTIME ACTIVITY: Beach blowout.
LODGING RECOMMENDATIONS: Long Street Backpackers.
INGESTIBLES: South African wines, cheeses, meat from the braai (barbecue).

Cape Town's terrain was created by an unfair god who thought other cities should learn what it means to be jealous. Most of your time will be wedged between green mountain faces and the convergence of two oceans. You can crack a beer anywhere with a view and feel nauseatingly smug.

You probably want to check out the beach first, and if you don't want more than twenty paces between you and a frost-jacketed glass of booze, go to **Camps Bay**. The restaurants that bask in the sun over the road from the beach are generally snazzy, upscale, and painted blindingly white. Go into **Café Caprice** for a beer or white wine. It's a minimalist setup with huge arches opening up the front so you can sit inside and still get sun. Another daytime option for classy fucked-uppery is going on the wine tasting tour in **Stellenbosch**. Hire a driver for the day and feign interest in each and every variety of grape. Before the sun goes down, check out the **IQ 2010 Sunset Cruise** for a swashbuckling swig or ten. It leaves from the **V&A Waterfront** every afternoon in the summer (November through March).

In the evening grab a drink at **Dizzy's Pub** in Camps Bay then plow toward **Long Street**. This is where feverish travelers and ghouls alike roam in search of music and hard liquor. Juggle your drinks on the terrace at **Long Street Backpackers** and see if you can recruit any reckless comrades for a burger at **Royale Eatery**. Directly above is **The Waiting Room:** a little club with big nights (live and DJ). As your tank fills go over to **Chez Ntemba** (just up from Long Street) for a thumping playlist from Congolese to house to hip-hop; always with the emphasis on gyration. On the main drag there are a few clubs jostling for late-night vampiric position. Try either **Joburg** or **Marvel**. The latter utilizes space by encouraging table-top dancing and is often the last place open in town.

If England has the Sunday roast then South Africa has the Chisa Nyama. These are places you can go and buy your meat to be thrown and flame grilled on a *braai* (barbecue). **Mzoli's** is a popular spot. Bring your own drinks and play tag with your scattered memories from last night. The polar opposite of this would be to keep your ears to the ground for any stomping Psy Trance parties that often happen on the outskirts of the city at ridiculously scenic outdoor pop-up venues. If you go on the second day of one of these parties don't be afraid of some of the haggard patrons slugging their way through their twenty-ninth hour of dancing.

NOTES FROM A LOCAL

There is a simple formula to *Kaapstad* (Cape Town): great people plus great hangout spots plus great people equals *supa memories*.

VERDICT

Majestic.

Dikson

57. Chicago, Illinois

SEASON: Severe winter weather is generally January through March—don't visit unless you are emotionally and physically prepared; otherwise May through September.

IDEAL CONDITIONS: Either a rooftop bar or at a baseball game, but choose your team carefully: you don't get a second chance.

DAYTIME ACTIVITY: Sailing on Lake Michigan.

LODGING RECOMMENDATIONS: Anywhere except near either airport if you can help it.

INGESTIBLES: Local microbrews, micheladas, Malort. If you're lucky, the tamale guy will stroll in with a mini-cooler full of the goods or a Jamaican food truck will be lingering outside your watering hole. Chicago-style hot dogs (without the ketchup).

Chicago is a world-class city with Midwest friendly. While your mind may conjure skyscrapers at first hearing the name, Chicago is a city of neighborhoods, each unique in personality. And you can get drunk in every single one of them.

Downtown. We call our downtown the Loop, for the loop that our elevated train (aka the "El") makes around the central business district. Head to the **Signature Room** at the John Hancock an hour before dusk on a clear night for the perfect downtown drink. Feel cultured and slightly less ashamed about your buzz on select jazz or salsa nights at the **Shedd Aquarium**, the **Museum of Contemporary Art**, or the **Art Institute of Chicago**. Buddy Guy's **Legends** in the South Loop is worth a late-night, cry-in-your-drink blues visit. And between **Reggie's** for rock and alternative and **The Shrine** for hip-hop, reggae, and soul, the South Loop has got a lot of musical ground covered.

Points North. In Wicker Park, at the intersection of North, Damen, and Milwaukee Avenues, lovingly known as "The Armpit" or "The Crotch," bars and late-night spots are everywhere. Check out whiskey-happy, Mexican-delish, and cash-only **Big Star** in a re-modeled gas station. Just a bit south, Division Street is dotted with dive bars, many of them tucked in the back of a liquor store front. Farther northwest along Milwaukee Avenue, Logan Square is becoming the new hip, artsy hood to hang and booze with well-crafted spirits at the **Whistler** and local brews at **Revolution**.

Points South. Pilsen is Chicago's chicano-dominated neighborhood. Margaritas? *¡Sí!* Some surprises you'll find are the stiff drinks and downright great Southern barbecue at **Honky Tonk**, the so-delicious-you-won't-believe-it's-local **Nightwood**, and the pinball-machine saloon **Simone's**. The cab ride to Bridgeport is worth it to drink well at **Maria's** and its neighbor, **Pleasant House**, which will bring your food to the bar.

In the summer there are three to five festivals every weekend, not including concert festivals such as Lollapalooza and Pitchfork . . . all serving booze. Chicago has twenty-six miles of beaches; get a drink at the resto-bars on Oak Street or North Avenue beaches. Alcohol isn't allowed at the beach, but plenty of people stash and carry discreetly. Overall everyone goes batshit crazy. Hours and hours of sunshine feel like love radiating down.

NOTES FROM A LOCAL
It's worth going out on a school night, better known as Industry Nights—Monday and Tuesday.

VERDICT
ChicaGO.

Sarahlynn Pablo

58. Düsseldorf, Germany

SEASON: August for warm weather, November through December for Christmas Markets, February for Karneval.

IDEAL CONDITIONS: Summer nights on a terrace, and sunny winter days.

DAYTIME ACTIVITY: Scope out the views from the Rhine Tower.

LODGING RECOMMENDATIONS: Park Inn for hotel, Backpackers-Dusseldorf for hostel.

INGESTIBLES: An 0.2 liter glass of alt beer, schweine-brötchen (pork knuckle sandwich) with sauerkraut, Killepitsch shots.

You can go to Düsseldorf any time of year and find people partying. The old town, or *altstadt,* has around three hundred bars within walking distance, more than anywhere else in Germany. They call it "the longest bar in the world," but really it's just bar after bar.

Do like the locals and take the U-Bahn to **Heinrich-Heine Allee.** If it's daytime and warm, head to **Uerige** and flag down one of the tray-toting servers. Everyone and their baby will be outside drinking €1,80 ($2.36 USD) altbiers and chain smoking because it's the best daytime drinking spot in town.

Punks and outcasts go to **Engel** bar where the music is good and loud, while hipsters frequent the clean, minimalistic **Brauerei Kürzer.** The Irish pub **Fatty's** has Guinness pints and narrow walls that encourage conversation. When you meet that special someone, take them to **Bar Cherie,** a French-themed café, and proceed to woo them by candlelight.

Order a *schweinshaxe,* or pork knuckle, from **Schweine Janes.** That should sober you up. For a digestif, head to **Killepitsch** and knock on the tiny walk-up window for a *schuss,* or liquor shot.

Düsseldorf isn't a club town, but the tight little dance floor at **Anaconda Lounge** will make you sweat. At **Schlösser Quartier Bohème** you can drink expensive mojitos while watching guys with their hair gelled like David Beckham and/or girls dress like Heidi Klum.

From November through December, booths are set up all over the downtown for the Christmas Markets. To keep warm, folks stand under heat lamps and drink *glühwein* (mulled wine). The mother of all parties is **Karneval**, when about a million fools dress up in costumes, drinking and shouting "*Helau*" (the local carnival greeting) in the streets.

A few notes:

- Beer is often the same price as bottled water, while wine and spirits can be quite pricey.
- You can ask for tap water, or *leitungswasser,* in bars and restaurants. Depending on the establishment, they will either: a) say yes, or b) say no. In either case, they will tease you for requesting "dish water" but, hey, it's free.
- You can still smoke in some bars, but most people step outside.

FUCKED UP FIRSTHAND

It was 11:00 A.M., and thousands were downtown wearing store-bought costumes that would fall apart come nightfall. I scraped my costume together at home: brown wig, aviator sunglasses, gaudy peach necktie, and trench coat. Underneath, I wore shorts, giving the illusion of *no pants.*

I met Nick and Wibke on Bolkerstrasse, the main drag. Nick was Snake from *Escape from L.A.,* and Wibke made an adorable lop-eared rabbit.

"What are you supposed to be?" she asked.

"I guess I'm a creep," I said.

A Jesus passed carrying a six-foot cross constructed of beer cans. His buddies followed behind, slugging beer and whipping him with rawhide. A group of Wibke's friends were partying outside a nearby restaurant. They had five cases of Beck's stockpiled beside a tree.

The girls were cows or hippies or tubes of mustard. The guys all wore silver astronaut suits. "What are you supposed to be?" asked one astronaut.

"They call me The Creep," I said. "Help me find a girl to cut off my tie."

Tradition demands that ties of all men get cut on the first day of Karneval. The astronaut immediately began stopping girls on the sidewalk.

"Do you have scissors? Hey, sexy, got any scissors?" The girls he approached were so gorgeous they looked bored. Then he stopped this blond vixen in fishnets. "Wanna cut my friend's tie?" She eyeballed me, then looked at him like he was something she'd scraped off her stiletto.

"Um, no," she said, and sauntered off.

Later, I learned about the second part to the tradition: After cutting the tie, the woman is supposed to kiss the man.

VERDICT
Three hundred bars within walking distance. 'Nuff said.

Noah Pelletier

59. Glasgow, Scotland*

SEASON: April through September.
IDEAL CONDITIONS: Summer days stretching out over the city.
DAYTIME ACTIVITY: Hiking on the West Highland Way (accessible via train).
LODGING RECOMMENDATIONS: Euro Hostel for budget or The Charing Cross Guest House.
INGESTIBLES: Whiskey, local food with wacky names like Forfar Bridies and Stovied Tatties, organic ales and lagers.

Glasgow was a heaving center of industry during the eighteenth and nineteenth centuries, with its population being one of the first in Europe to pass the million mark. Some high-caliber fucked-uppery took place in smoggy bars stuffed down cobbled alleyways throughout the city, calloused hands clasping murky ales after sweating it out in shipyards and warehouses. Today, relics of the old city merge with the twenty-first-century offerings of trendy, underground, and avoidable mainstream bars and clubs.

The best way to see the landscape take shape is to cut through the flatter terrain of Northern England into the escarpments of Scotland. Out of the train and into the city center, pad around your new hunting ground, sniffing out possible venues for the evening's liver bombarding. Scour around for the Merchant City area. The staff at **Guy's** can rustle up some Haggis and other Scottish plates or go to **Sapporo Teppanyaki** between 12:00 and 2:00 P.M. for noodle soup. **Oran Mor** hosts A Play, a Pie, and a Pint, an event where you, surprisingly, watch a play, eat a pie, and drink a pint all in a converted church.

Wine tasting's depraved evil cousin is the whiskey tasting tour. Venture out to **Auchentoshan Distillery** and try not to drown in a cask. When you get back to the city center you'll probably smell like an alcoholic, which is perfect. You'll notice that the names of some of the areas are the same as in London, like the **West End:** go there. The **Ubiquitous Chip** on Ashton Lane will happily welcome you under its roof with an impressive wine list and cozy vibe. The interior is filled with live art and they have a pub within a pub, called **The Wee Pub,** where they specialize in cocktails. Check out **The 78** for organic beer and vegan food. **Vodka Wodka** is on the same road. Explore **Kelvingrove Park** and the **Botanical Gardens** in the late-summer light with a hip flask fixed securely to your midriff.

Glasgow has birthed and hosted big music acts, so you have to see what's bubbling up in the venues. Scope **Nice 'n' Sleazy** on Sauchiehall Street, rifling through the jukebox and putting on something epic, like Fleetwood Mac. Plummet into the blacked-out basement and watch one of the hopeful bands. While you're in the area, check out **Brunswick Cellars,** and later, as things get fuzzy around the edges, squint and see if you can make out the sign of **Sub Club** on Jamaica Street. Wear a sober face at the door that you immediately loosen inside when the bass hits. Get a kebab for the way home and be sure to leave a wake of saucy lather on your shirt.

With a raging hangover skulking around your head and belly, tighten your boots and head up to the **Necropolis** with a can of cheap lager. Sweat out some of the night's shameful moments, and get a bird's-eye view of the city.

NOTES FROM A LOCAL
You plus whiskey equals Scotland.

VERDICT
Yae canne avoid 'avin a reet blast in Glasgeeeey.

Dikson

60. Halifax, Nova Scotia, Canada

SEASON: April through September (spring and summer). Winters aren't bad, but the party boats only operate seasonally.
IDEAL CONDITIONS: On a party boat.
DAYTIME ACTIVITY: Surfing, flaking out on the green at Citadel Hill.
LODGING RECOMMENDATIONS: With a Couchsurfer.org host, downtown near the harbor front.
INGESTIBLES: Alexander Keith's beer (don't ever say you dislike Keith's), Garrison's beer, lobster that's cheaper than beef, garlic fingers with donair sauce, sushi.

Halifax is Atlantic Canada's biggest city, but even if you're from out of town you're likely to run into the same person twice in one evening. And like most good East Coast cities, its peeps party hard. There are more than five major universities and colleges in Halifax, and for a city with a population of about four hundred thousand, that's a lot of drunken students. If it's warm, take Spring Garden Road ("Skin Garden Road") and pop into **The Fickle Frog** to see what the drink special is—sometimes it's a $5 USD Caesar. They do great pizzas.

Thursday nights: Power Hour at **The Split Crow**, 9:00 to 10:00 P.M. for cheap Molson. Line your stomach first with nachos at **The Economy Shoe Shop** on Argyle Street, or watch live music at **The Seahorse Tavern** (located just under The Economy Shoe Shop). Argyle Street has some of the best pubs and clubs: **The Loose Cannon** for Scottish tunes and a laid-back evening, or **The Bitter End** for fancy martinis and girls in shiny dresses.

For the most part, you don't have to walk far for bar hopping. Check out the **Pogue Fado** for good ol' fashioned Irish tunes, or **Maxwell's Plum** for huge tower beers and deep-fried pepperoni. Swing by **Your Father's Moustache**, just because the name is so awesome (and the greasy breakfast is fab). **The Alehouse** is all about grinding after hours, especially for Navy boys (and, consequently, me).

There are several party boats to hop aboard during summer months, including **Murphy's Party Cruises** and **Halifax Harbour Cruises**. You'll get a DJ and a dance floor on the deck of a tall-ship. Why not? If you can make it, come for the Alexander Keith's Birthday Party, on October 5. Alexander Keith was a popular Canadian brewer who started his brewery in 1820. He was kind of a big deal around Halifax, being the mayor three times and a member of the Legislative Council for thirty years. Almost two hundred years later, his beer still makes up every one in three sold in Nova Scotia. Every year on his birthday, the Waterfront hosts a big exclusive bash where girls hand out green antlers.

Keys to Halifax:

- If you want a late night out, be prepared to spend some money.
- Bar hopping is easy and encouraged.
- Beware Navy boys wanting to show you their "ship."

NOTES FROM A LOCAL

Don't stab anyone.

VERDICT

Almost suspiciously friendly.

Candice Walsh

61. Long Island, New York

SEASON: Summer. This place can be a ghost town between Labor Day and Memorial Day.

IDEAL CONDITIONS: A balmy summer eve, half naked in the back of a stretch limousine with Moët champagne cascading down your tits.

DAYTIME ACTIVITY: Check Montauk.

LODGING RECOMMENDATIONS: Beach rentals are popular but sell out quickly. Seedy hotels are available and cost way less when you stuff eight of your most intoxicated friends into one room. Best bet? Find a celebrity, seduce them, and spend the night at their mansion.

INGESTIBLES: Local wine by day, Blue Point Blueberry Beer by night, bagels after 1:00 A.M. and $22 Montauk lobster rolls.

Like the swallows of Capistrano, native New Yorkers flee the stench-filled streets of Manhattan each summer for fresh air in the Hamptons. Don't let the socialites fool you however; the East End of Long Island may seem swanky on TV and in movies, but it's really trashy as fuck.

Trendy vineyards dotted around Long Island's East End make it the ideal place to pretend like you're a Napa Valley wine snob. Really though, Long Islanders turn the formal art of wine tasting into a binge drinking free-for-all at places like **Martha Clara Vineyards, Baiting Hollow Farm,** and the **Jamesport Vineyard/Oyster Bar.** Those little flights of booze are deceiving—seventeen "tastes" later and your friends will stumble upon you lying facedown in the middle of a vineyard row at **Pindar,** Long Island's largest winery.

In the Hamptons, the biggest shit show happens at the **Boardy Barn**. This place is only open on Sundays between 2:00 and 8:00 P.M., and charges a $20 cover fee, but college kids with fake IDs still flock to this outdoor bar in search of $2 beers and summer love. Don't let the two-hour queue to get in deter you—pre-gaming in line is half the fun before entering a giant pigpen of sluts and guido douchebags.

Nassau County has a few towns that are "sleepy" by guidebook standards, but any Long Islander will turn your idea of suburban perfection into a total trashville drunkfest. **Floral Park** closes its streets for a town-wide, pedestrian party to celebrate the Belmont Stakes (see the race yourself at nearby Belmont Park). Join locals at bars like **J Fallon's Taproom** and **Jack Duggan's Pub,** open from the early morning until the last person pukes into their jockey cap.

The Irish population of **Rockville Centre** loves drinking so much that they even throw their own Saint Patrick's Parade a full week after the actual holiday. The historic event gets extra sloppy with the overwhelming amount of freckle-faced, ginger-haired townies gulping down green beer from red SOLO cups. Both cities are an easy thirty-minute ride by train from the City.

If you want instant drunken gratification instead of a "drink-all-day" tour, your best alternative is a ride on the infamous Long Island Rail Road (LIRR) "drunk train." Leaving from New York City's Penn Station between 2:30 and 4:30 A.M., you'll discover the Island's biggest lushes heading home from a raucous night in the city.

What you'll encounter on the LIRR drunk train:

- Exhibitionist porn from smashed couples hooking up between the seats.
- Vomit. Lots and lots of vomit.
- Screeching banshee women with too much makeup reeking of hairspray.
- Forty-ounce cans of beer stuffed into paper sacks guzzled by folks who can't admit the party's over.

FUCKED UP FIRSTHAND

The plan was to get Ann Marie drunk before her "big day" but really, it was a mutual goal for all of us to get inebriated and raunchy. Don't judge us—who wouldn't want to get bombed and hit on celebrities at swanky Hamptons' nightclubs? Except, I'd never been wine tasting before. Is it like "tasting" raw cake batter before you bake it, to make sure it doesn't suck? How could wine suck? It's just fancy alcohol. . . .

I was expecting a little medicine cup holding a pitiable amount of booze but behold, I was given a glass filled up halfway—for each tasting. Skeptical about the whole process, I shot down the first sample—that's how you "taste" wine, right? I didn't know the difference between "aromatic, oaky flavor" and "hints of apricot and summer air." With my extreme lack of wine-tasting etiquette, I demanded my second glass. I was shitfaced by my fourth.

Winery patrons didn't seem to mind our raucous laughter, rude phallic jewelry, or skinned knees from stumbling through vineyards filled with little grapes. Locally made Merlot? Sure. A "meritage of Zinfandel and Cabernet Sauvignon?" Whatever, I'm fucking drunk and it looks pretty. Do I want to buy a bottle? Hells yeah, I do! Give me five. I started uncorking on the ride home.

VERDICT

Residents do a fine job of taking the "class" out of "upper-class."

Katka Lapelosová

62. Lisbon, Portugal

SEASON: May through September, especially June.
IDEAL CONDITIONS: Smoking and taking in the view at a sun-soaked Miradouro (viewpoint).
DAYTIME ACTIVITY: Surfing Guincho Beach.

Always a better *onda* at monuments to people who were more poet than soldier. Statue for Luís de Camões in Lisbon. Photo by Dalton Campbell.

LODGING RECOMMENDATIONS: Oasis Backpackers' Mansion, someplace within five minutes of three major drinking districts: Bairro Alto, Bica, and Cais do Sodré.

INGESTIBLES: Sangria, beer, wine, aguardente, amarguinhas, caipirinhas, ginjinhas, moscatel, port, and anything else. All perfectly fine to drink anywhere in the city.

Lisbon is one of the most photogenic cities in Europe and the views are even better through saturated beer goggles. Booze is cheap and drinking in the streets—day or night—is practically encouraged; and it ought to be, given that Lisbon has on average 260 days of sunshine each year. Combine this with some of the most liberal drug policies in all of Europe; summer festivals; nearby beaches with world-class waves; and tons of bars, taverns, and clubs (most with no cover charge) and you have one of the heaviest hitting cities in the world.

No joke, it's never too early for a drink in Lisbon. The local liquor, *ginjinha,* can be found in a number of hole-in-the-wall locales and it's not uncommon to see locals knocking back a few shots of this sweet cherry liquor on their way to work. Once you've started, it's easy to keep your buzz up; corner stores all over the city sell liters of beer for $1.50 USD and no one bats an eye at popping the top in the checkout line.

The **Bairro Alto** district of Lisbon is a center of Portuguese design by day and a street-party destination at night with nearly a hundred bars. The bars in Lisbon are small, so most of their offerings come in plastic cups; the idea is to wander the streets and finish your freshly prepared caipirinhas and mojitos on your way to the next watering hole. Before leaving the bar district and heading to any of Lisbon's all-night riverside clubs, stop by a clandestine bakery for something to soak up the booze.

After you've warmed up in the bars, the clubs and discos along the Tejo River stay open until 6:00 A.M., some with after-parties until 10:00 A.M. **Lux,** being the most famous club in the country, draws impressive international DJs and live bands at prices that, frankly, make the rest of Europe look shamefully bloated and overpriced. The club district of **Cais do Sodré** used to be Lisbon's red-light district—a marketplace for prostitutes and hard drugs—and keeps its decadent history alive at **Pensão Amor**—a former brothel turned bar and lounge with an erotic library and bookstore, as well as regular pole-dancing shows.

Once the sun begins to rise and you're looking for something to ease you into bed, a joint at sunrise might just be the best option. While Portugal's across-the-board decriminalization of drugs doesn't exactly make them legal, it means being discreet with a small amount is generally accepted. You'll smell the hashish and marijuana wafting through the air at all the city's Miraduros (viewpoints) and parks.

In June, Lisbon goes ballistic. The month-long festival of **Santo António** is permanently linked now to all-day barbecues, free live music, cheap beer and local homemade liquors, and never-ending street parties in every available public space. The old traditional neighborhoods of **Alfama, Bica,** and **Mouraria** are the highlights. During the rest of the summer months, free concerts in Lisbon's expansive parks bring the people out for afternoons and sunsets with live jazz music and DJ sets of hip-hop and soul. Bring a few bottles of wine and pass out to some good tunes while sunbathing and realizing how fucking lucky you are.

NOTES FROM A LOCAL

A night in Bairro Alto with twenty-five bucks is all you'll need to wake up in a tree at 6:30 A.M. with your car keys up your ass.

VERDICT

If you can't handle it, just go to Spain like everyone else.

Dalton Campbell

63. Los Angeles, California

SEASON: Whenever the rest of the country is in the midst of a deep freeze.
IDEAL CONDITIONS: Post-chill pre–heat wave.
DAYTIME ACTIVITY: Mulholland Drive running/walking, Venice Beach hanging.
LODGING RECOMMENDATIONS: El Tres, Baxter 5, The W Downtown.
INGESTIBLES: Twelve-pack of Tecate, vintage cans of Four Loko, the dankest medications from the local cannabis dispensary.

Los Angeles is a sprawling metropolis that lifelong Angelenos ever only visit a small portion of. Because L.A. is so car-centric, it makes getting wasted throughout the city a daunting process. In lieu of getting a DUI, or having to convince your friend to be the designated driver, we'd recommend that you pick a neighborhood and stay put. You could join the crowds getting drunk on the beach at the Venice boardwalk, or spend time raging with ex–hair bands on the **Sunset Strip,** or in the gay clubs of **West Hollywood.** But if you want a more unique experience, head east of Western to the bohemian neighborhoods of **Los Feliz, Silver Lake,** and **Echo Park.**

Start your night in Los Feliz. Have a few glasses of wine at **Covell** on Hollywood. When the need for food hits, walk across the street to **Umami** for gourmet burgers and craft brews. Grab some margaritas and artisan mezcal at **El Chavito.** Keep the party moving next door at one of America's longest running tropical drinks bar, **Tiki-Ti.**

By now you're probably wasted, which means you're drunk enough to walk over to the **Drawing Room** and hang out with B-movie actors who've been drinking since the bar opened at 6:00 A.M. Increasingly tipsy, you might need to cool it down with some beers and chicken wings across the street at **Ye Rustic Inn.** Meet some people for an after-party, or head back to your hotel room.

Start the next day at the farm-to-table brunch spot **Local.** They don't have booze, so if the hair of the dog is calling to you drink specialty mimosas at **Dusty's.** L.A. is a city wrapped around rural. Pretend you're in the middle of the forest (despite the incredible metropolitan views) in one of L.A.'s great urban parks. Hike around **Griffith Park** and explore the **L.A. Zoo, Griffith Observatory,** and the **Gene Autry Museum** of southwestern culture. And since you're in the area you might as well get a pint at the newly minted **Golden Road Brewery** in an industrial tract between the concrete Los Angeles River and the Metrolink tracks.

After a few pints it seems like you've started another day of drinking. Might as well take in L.A.'s incredible weather with outdoor seating and craft cocktails at **Alcove's Big Bar,** balancing things out with some deep-fried shrimp and fish tacos at **Best Fish Tacos Ensenada.** Walk to Sunset Junction for shopping and people watching. If the line is not too long try the über-popular **Intelligentsia,** where coffee technicians use their java know-how to serve you up an optimal cup.

Walk the three miles or take the bus down Sunset Boulevard to Echo Park. Have a few more brews at **Mohawk Bend,** and if you're still hungry they've got a wide vegan-friendly menu with pizzas and sandwiches. For continental cuisine, head to the unexpected French restaurant **Taix.** You could also get incredible pizza at **Masa,** or exquisite contemporary American at **The Park.**

Now that dinner is out of the way, your next order of business is to get wasted. The most efficient way: $4 pints of PBR at the **Gold Room,** each beer served with a free shot of tequila. Keep drinking here, or head down the block to see what's up at **The Echo/Echoplex.** The venue hosts international touring indie acts and fun dance nights. If nothing is happening tonight, head to **The Short Stop** with smaller rooms and a DJ on most nights.

End your night here, or find out if locals know about any of downtown L.A.'s secret after-hours speakeasies.

NOTES FROM A LOCAL
I got wasted with Mexican cowboys, snorted Ritalin off a quarter, had a TV thrown at me, and sold a screenplay. Pretty eventful weekend.

VERDICT
This side of Los Angeles makes you throw every stereotype you've ever had about Los Angeles out the window (and replace it with new, equally unreasonable, yet very fun stereotypes).

Joshua Heller

64. Berlin, Germany

SEASON: Mid-summer (it'll still be rainy).
IDEAL CONDITIONS: A fair amount of caffeine or other stimulant to party consistently for forty-eight hours.
DAYTIME ACTIVITY: Pack a picnic and go to Grunewald.
LODGING RECOMMENDATIONS: Eastern Comfort Hostel Boat (Friedrichshain), Heart of Gold Hostel (Mitte), Baxpax (Kreuzberg), rent a flat on Airbnb.
INGESTIBLES: Vodka, Club-Mate, excessive amounts of currywurst.

Everyone has their own version of where to go totally fucking bonkers in Berlin, and each one of these prescriptions is 100 percent accurate. No matter how early you arrive in town, you'll hear the thumping bassline of a familiar track. You'll soon realize that it's 8:00 A.M. and they're playing an extended remix of the theme song from *Ferris Bueller*. This is Berlin.

After settling down, meander through Alexanderplatz toward the TV Tower and join a **Fat Tire Bike Tour** around the city. They cover tourist must-sees, such as the **Checkpoint Charlie, Brandenburg Gate,** and the **Reichstag**. If the weather is right travel back down to Görlitzer Park and drink beers in the crater and make new friends. Rogue bartenders often walk around with cheap cocktails for sale.

Dinner: hit the otherworldly Turkish steakhouse **Hasir Ocakbasi**. Get some speakeasy cocktails at **Würgeengel** or some beers at **Luzia**. If you feel the party urges but don't want to head to the club just yet, check **West Germany** or some of the smaller clubs above the Kaiser's grocery store at Kottbusser Tor. Go for drinks at **Soju House**, a DJ bar accessible through a secret door in the back of Korean drunk-food haven **Angry Chicken**.

Now that it's sufficiently late you should head to the real clubs.

Everyone will convince you to go to **Berghain,** but you only have a 40 percent chance of getting in. So you might stand outside for two hours only to be turned away. If you want to avoid red tape, head to the old rail depot converted into clubs near Warschauer Strasse. **Cassiopeia** always has something going on, and if that line is too long you're around the corner from **RAW Tempel** and **Astra.**

But if you weren't edgy enough to get into Berghain and minimal techno is still what you want to dance to, check **WaterGate** or **Arena.** You'll still wait in line, but you'll probably get in. If you can't stand EDM, **Magnet Club** has an indie rock night and there's soul at **Festsaal** or **Lido.**

Everybody in Berlin will talk about how amazing **Bar 25** was before it closed. If you want to get an idea of what they're talking about, try its reincarnation **Kater Holzig,** a former factory converted into dance floors. Its outdoor gardens are a perfect place to watch the sunrise over the Spree river.

Recover from the night inside the hospital turned art gallery, with brunch, at **3 Schwestern.** If it's Sunday you should travel up to the **MauerPark Flea Market** for knick-knacks, and the most rousing round of outdoor karaoke with six hundred of your closest friends.

Eat a late lunch at **Transit** for Asian fusion street food near Rosenthaler Platz. Then grab a few beers and espressos at **Mein Haus am See,** a fun bar with tiered couches.

Then do it all over again.

FUCKED UP FIRSTHAND

When we first arrived in Berlin, we posted a photo of ourselves drinking mimosas on the Eastern Comfort Boat Hostel. A Facebook friend saw it and suggested we meet up with her friends. A week later we were invited to her friend's dinner party. Trying to be respectful guests we brought a seven dollar bottle of wine. A butler opened the door and there was a formally dressed waitstaff serving high-end cocktails from a bar. After meeting the host, we hid our wine bottle behind a curtain. Over the course of an evening full of top-shelf liquor, we'd befriended everyone who was our age, and stumbled to a dance club near Rosenthaler Platz. The people we'd met that night became our main group of friends for our summer in Berlin.

VERDICT

This is the place in Europe to party for a month (or more) and not spend that much money.

Joshua Heller

65. Savannah, Georgia

SEASON: Fall to spring, especially Saint Patrick's Day.
IDEAL CONDITIONS: Plate full of seafood after a day at Tybee Island.
DAYTIME ACTIVITY: Taking gothic pictures around the city and Bonaventure Cemetery.
LODGING RECOMMENDATIONS: Bohemian Hotel for trendy/boutique; Thunderbird Inn for inexpensive/throwback.
INGESTIBLES: Green beer (Saint Patty's Day), microbrews, whiskey, po' boys, local crab and shrimp, and anything that can be battered and fried.

Savannah has the soul of an eccentric old woman, a very drunk one. She is a drinking town, period. Rambling through the twenty-two squares can be dazzling, especially if you're into history, ghost stories, and open containers. So, grab a traveler of whiskey and book a **Savannah Walks Pubs and Taverns Tour**. At just $16, you'll get spooked and be able to stay "in your cup" the whole evening. Many tours include **McDonough's Irish Pub,** the best place in town to get into trouble. Or stop in at **Lulu's Chocolate Bar** or **Jen's and Friends,** where you'll have your pick of three hundred martinis and two hundred beers. After that head up to Bay Street to the **Moon River Brewing Company**, known for their handcrafted Swamp Fox and Apparition Ale and a sizeable food menu.

No one comes to Savannah to do business, so slow down. Meander along the river on **Savannah's Belles Ferry,** a free ride. When you dock you can explore the shops along River Street, grab a Call a Cab from **Wet Willies,** and do some karaoke at the LGBT-friendly **Chuck's Bar.** Or try a **Savannah Slow Ride.** This spider-like bicycle utilizes the leg power of fifteen people to steer it through the streets of the city.

Vinnie Van Go-Go's and **Sweet Melissa's** are both solid bets for food, especially when sobering up. Their pizza slices are huge and the prices cheap. You'll be able to grab a late-night bite so you can keep drinking. Just don't forget to bring cash.

Finally, remember these general rules about Savannah:

- Don't wear heels on River Street, ladies. Tourists abound, so stick to tennis shoes, even if you go into a high-end restaurant.
- You can drink on the streets just about anywhere as long as your beverage is in a plastic cup.
- Don't get caught with your pants down. Drinking in the streets is fine, but you'll have to go into an establishment to use the restroom.

VERDICT

You might last into the wee hours of the morning and probably won't get robbed.

Blissom Booblé

6: Spendy

Upper-class connoisseurs are inherently disadvantaged. I'm talking about the boarding school kids who've already been to Europe ten times by their sophomore year of college, order sushi in fluent Japanese, and have opinions on *pâté de canard en croûte*, single malts, infinity pools, longboards, heli-ski operators, coho versus king salmon, and Tiesto versus Deadmau5. The ones who take annual fall trips to Cordoba, Argentina (wing shooting), late-winter ski trips in Chamonix, and a summer circuit that, depending on the year, includes Ibiza, Maui, diving excursions in the Sea of Cortez, and secret spots in Uruguay. The ones who know twenty-four different card games, play scratch golf, semi-pro-level tennis, and have pilots' licenses, scuba gear, wakeboarding boats, engraved whiskey flasks, dressage horses, and $10,000 carbon-frame downhill mountain bikes with, inexplicably, kickstands.

See, at some point they'll run into a roadblock of imagination. What other travel plan can they possibly make? Whereas those of us who grew up in culturally stunted suburban families—our once-a-year family vacations in places like Orlando or Tampa, splurges turning into the inevitable faux pas at some "world famous" steakhouse where somebody orders a $38 "Chef's Reserve" cut and then trips up the bow-tied waiter with: "Y'all have any sauce, you know like Heinz 57 or something?"—we've got nowhere to go but up.

The truth is, as a dirtbagger I have little business speaking on anything related to connoisseurism, except possibly snow and wave conditions, wild edibles, water potability, rice cooking, pancake consistency, backcountry shelters, and *vino tinto* (priced $12 a bottle and under).

So let's throw it over to the authors who know the local customs, like the vernacular for giving proper warning if you're about to vomit near people at an antebellum house in Charleston ("Pardon me kindly, sir/ma'am"), or the dress code in Mumbai ("leave the harem pants and flip-flops at home"), or prevailing attitudes toward public urination in Copenhagen ("You're going to see at least one male member midstream—try not to be too alarmed, and don't get caught in the backsplash"). And of course there are lots of recommendations for those wanting expensive caipirinhas in São Paolo, "Oslo's finest tiramisu," or private karaoke rooms (with bathtubs!) in Tokyo.

Shit, I'll leave this one to y'all.

66. Charleston, South Carolina*

SEASON: Anytime except summer, when school is out, the weather scalding hot, and the city full of obese tourists.

IDEAL CONDITIONS: Cocktail party in a historic mansion.

DAYTIME ACTIVITY: Smoking weed on the grave of John C. Calhoun, or one of many public fountains.

LODGING RECOMMENDATIONS: NotSo Hostel is a funky, youthful alternative to expensive bed and breakfasts.

INGESTIBLES: Firefly Sweet Tea Vodka, shrimp and grits, Tommy's Texas Cheese Fries. *Also note:* in Charleston you can split shots with friends (i.e.: "I'll take three Red Headed Sluts, split five ways").

Charleston's pastel-colored houses of bygone eras and its spookily polite residents make this Southern city seem a bit dated at first (check out the **Old Slave Market**, colorfully stripped of all its racist connotations and replaced with locally made handicrafts!). But a closer look reveals Charleston to be one of the biggest shitshow college towns in America. "Pardon me kindly, sir/ma'am," is a phrase often spoken before a local spews vomit across a wrought-iron gate from the 1800s.

Upper King Street is the best bar scene, where you'll find underage college girls in asscheek-clinging skirts accompanied by clean-cut young men wearing button-down shirts, Madras shorts, and boat shoes. Hit up **Closed for Business**, known for its beer selection, or try **The Belmont**, with bourgeois atmosphere and eclectic cocktails.

Lower King Street has some good spots, such as **Burns Alley**, a haunt for theater majors who can't afford to drink because they are poor-ass actors. The trashiest bar in Charleston is the **Upper Deck Tavern**, which was voted "Best Place to Watch Two Women Make Out" by the *Charleston City Paper*. You'll find frat douches and sorority girls at places like **King Street Grille**, the best sports bar to get sloppy at during college football games.

The most convincing reason to get shitfaced in Charleston is that Bill Murray owns a house there. He's often seen at **Tbonz Gill and Grille**, which pumps out locally brewed draught beer until 2:00 A.M. Partying with Mr. Murray is also possible while attending a **Charleston RiverDogs** minor-league baseball game. He owns part of the team and is sometimes spotted during Thirsty Thursday games, when booze can be had for $1.

East Bay offers swankier places, such as the **Vendue Inn**, where scantily clad cougars prowl the rooftop bar. If your trip to Charleston includes searching for a *Gone with the Wind*–style plantation-owning husband, check out the **Blind Tiger Pub** or **Southend Brewery**, stockpiled with khaki-pantsed business-types hunting for trophy wives.

Brunch in Charleston is quite upper-crust, but **AC's Bar and Grill** generously accommodates those who don't own a polo shirt or a set of pearls. Their weekly themed "Hangover Helper" menus include cheap-ass pitchers of booze and "champagne" specials (aka Miller High Life) paired with dishes like chicken and waffles or blueberry muffin French toast with root beer syrup.

Badass Charlestonian festivals:

- **Kulture Klash:** Gathering of graffiti artists, extreme hula-hoop dancers, burlesque acts, and more, usually held at a random parking lot or abandoned warehouse (October and April).
- **Charleston Fashion Week:** A week dedicated to gorgeous, self-absorbed locals complete with champagne fountains (March).
- **Piccolo Spoleto Festival:** Charleston's pride and joy, features live music, film screenings, international performers; sometimes brings in minor-league celebrities who just want to get trashed (end of May and early June).

FUCKED UP FIRSTHAND

It makes no sense to stay indoors. My friends and I study for an hour before dressing up in sequins and high heels to party hop through the Peninsula. I might have to make out with a frat dude to get a JELL-O shot, but it beats getting kicked out of a bar for using a fake ID.

We walk up Coming Street. From the start of Sorority Row, until the dodgy crack houses of Line Street, the sound of O.A.R. blasting from a Charleston Single House full of college kids is an open invitation to walk in off the street and join the party. We won't be turned away—Charlestonians are the nicest people I've ever met. The passing of a bong, the sharing of a greasy-ass pizza from Andolini's, or help holding people up during a keg stand are all ways Chucktowners show their generosity toward strangers.

I look at my phone. "Damn," I say to my friend as we trudge home with our shoes in our hands. "I'm going to be so hungover for class tomorrow."

"Yeah," she replies. "And it's only Tuesday."

VERDICT

An ounce more class.

Katka Lapelosová

67. London, United Kingdom

SEASON: Early summer.
IDEAL CONDITIONS: A jaunt in London Fields or Victoria Park.
DAYTIME ACTIVITY: Ride the London Eye to the sky, or take the Tube all around town until "mind the gap" becomes a phrase you never want to hear again in your life.
LODGING RECOMMENDATIONS: Stay with friends, or do Airbnb unless you really have the scratch to stay in a hotel.
INGESTIBLES: Rum, pints and pints, transatlantic jet lag, cocaine.

If you've never been to London before, go do the touristy shit. But there's other guides for that. You can easily get drunk at the **TGI Friday's** in Leicester Square and then take pictures with uncompro-

View of River Thames and downtown London from the London Eye, the world's tallest cantilevered observation Ferris wheel. Photo by Tasan Phatthong.

mising security guards for the queen, but frankly you'll have a better time just getting drunk wherever you are staying.

That transatlantic jet lag is the first layer of your "completely wasted lasagna." Add to that several after-work pints. Then a tequila shot because for some reason you talked about Mexico to a guy at the bar you'd never met before. By this point it doesn't matter where you go, but since this is a guide . . .

Jump on the classic 38 to **Dalston,** a West Indian and Turkish neighborhood that was in the midst of riots even though it is becoming slowly occupied by hipsters. The sociopolitical underpinnings of British society are interesting but who cares—you're supposed to be wasted.

Jump off the bus a few blocks before Kingsland Road at **The Duke of Wellington.** British pubs are always on corners; the light entering makes the space really pleasant for an afternoon. American bars are always dank places with few windows. Puritans escaped these publicly drunk Britons to force their descendants to drink in hidden rooms.

Head to **Dalston Jazz Bar,** and get wasted in this tiny room at the bottom of an apartment complex. Keep clubbing at **Dalston Superstore,** a superstore that was converted into a club when the hipsters arrived.

The next day, cure your hangover at **Bardens Bourdoir,** which you'll realize is the place you were looking for last night when you wanted to see that indie rock band from your neighborhood in Los Angeles. Today is another day, so head to **London Fields** and recover with more beers that'll turn into more beers that'll turn into more shots that'll turn into another crazy fucking night in London.

FUCKED UP FIRSTHAND

We're invited to a house party. In the front of the bus a man is wearing a pink tutu. Upstairs a girl with a buzzcut is wearing pink pants; she has a tattoo of a tooth on her neck. An autistic kid asks his foreign mom questions that she doesn't understand. This is our bus stop.

Beautiful bohemians are wasted after a day drinking wine in London Fields. They let me control the music on Spotify. I become a terrorist by attempting to sabotage their party by searching for my favorite worst songs. "Allstar." "Every Morning." "Butterfly." It doesn't work. They sing along. We dance to California party music for the rest of the evening.

VERDICT

Duh, this is either the most important city in the world or the second-most important city in the world.

Joshua Heller

68. Copenhagen, Denmark

SEASON: June through August—any time outside those months is unpleasantly cold.
IDEAL CONDITIONS: Drinking by the canal as summer dusk stretches into midnight.
DAYTIME ACTIVITY: Hit the Nørrebrogade flea market.
LODGING RECOMMENDATIONS: Somandshjemmet Bethel for budget, Generator for hostel (Scandinavian hostels are uniformly clean and secure).
INGESTIBLES: Beer (øl), schnapps (snaps) and akvavit (traditional grain liquor), pølse (hot dogs, dispensed from the pølsevogne that dot the city), black coffee.

The Danes are a hard-drinking people, consuming more booze per capita than famously alcoholic nations like Germany, Belgium, and Australia. You'll most likely be drinking beer, and it'll be Carlsberg or Tuborg (both owned by the same company). Prepare yourself for a shock—many visitors walk away from the bar thinking they've been short-changed, but you haven't been conned. It's just an expensive town to drink in.

The priciest drinks are along the touristy **Nyhavn,** a colorful canal lined with cafés. It's popular for good reason, so try to make at least one visit. Many of the cafés offer takeaway beers. It's hard to resist buying a one-liter (!!!) can of Carlsberg to consume while you look out over the harbor. (Drinking is legal in most public spaces in Copenhagen, so camp out along a canal if you need to save some kroner.) You may want to avoid Nyhavn venues like **Hong Kong**, a rough spot where the furniture is bolted to the floor. Hong Kong is a good example of a *værtshus*, a traditional pub where the rougher locals tend to gather. Don't be fooled by the lace curtains—the patrons of a *værtshus* are looking for a fight.

Danes have only taken to cocktails in the last decade or so, but they've taken to them like a Viking to pillaging. Best among the cocktail bars is the award-winning **Ruby,** situated across the canal from **Christiansborg,** the palace-turned-parliament of Copenhagen. This elegant and cozy space feels like a Victorian gentlemen's club. You can drink an expertly mixed classic, or a more modern variant, like the Ruby Daiquiri—rhubarb jam shaken with vanilla, lime, and Angostura rum.

Most of the bars catering to the fun-loving student and gay crowds are conveniently clumped around Studiestræde and Vestergade. **Cosy** is just what it says it is: a tiny room with a tiny dance floor, allowing you to get very close to brawny babes. **Masken** is similarly economical with space and drinks—you can get ten shots for 100DKK (about $18 USD). You can also pick up a cheap drink (and perhaps a Scandinavian student) at **Studenterhuset** (The Student House) on Købmagergade.

Although it's also a popular night spot, **Bang & Jensen** on Istedgade is the best place in town to recover the next morning. Tick a few boxes on an order form and you'll have a plate overflowing with cheese, jam, delicious Danish rye bread, pastries, and fresh fruit. Nearby **Dyrehaven** on Sønder Boulevard is equally pleasant, whether day or night.

The best plan in Copenhagen is no plan. Danes are fond of *hygge* (cozy) café-bars, often below street level. Pop your head into any one of these and you'll find room for no more than two dozen people, with eclectic furnishings and music choices. They're cheap, cheerful, and your best shot at having a chat with the usually tight-lipped Danes.

Keep these pointers in mind when partying in Copenhagen:

- Mind your manners: *tak* means both "please" and "thank you."
- Danes don't go out before midnight—the party won't really get started until 2:00 or 3:00 A.M.
- The Danes are pretty relaxed about nudity and, alarmingly, public urination. You're going to see at least one male member midstream—try not to be too alarmed, and don't get caught in the backsplash.

NOTES FROM A LOCAL
Young Danes spend their time in venues with nicknames like Klamydi-aslottet (The Chlamydia Palace) and Lydderen (The Whore)—anything but classy. After we all grow up, time is much better spent in places like K Bar, or listening to jazz at Den Hvide Lam (The White Lamb).

VERDICT
Underrated.

Liam Casey

69. Delhi, India

SEASON: October and November (after summer/before winter). Pleasant in-between weather.
IDEAL CONDITIONS: Still standing after closing down Shiro.
DAYTIME ACTIVITY: Check Humayun's Tomb, and walk through the Mughal Gardens while you're there.

LODGING RECOMMENDATIONS: South Delhi: better accommodation, higher prices ($85 to $120 USD a night). For hostels and budget go to North Delhi. **INGESTIBLES:** Kingfisher beer, mutton/chicken kebab varieties, Mughlai curries (Karim's in Gali Kababiyan), street food—dahi bhalla, chaat, golgappe, sweets—jalebi/gulab jamun, kulfi-falooda.

More popular for food and art, most people think that Delhiites don't party as much as their counterparts in Mumbai and Bengalooru. And then there are those who know better. Everything depends on how far your wallet will take you. You pay for what you get. Simple.

If money isn't an issue, **Lap** is for you. Extremely exclusive, members-only club. Glossy and very high profile. Cocktails start at $25 USD. Downside—difficult to get into unless you know a member. Or there is **Shiro**—great international and local music, amazing food (mostly Thai, Chinese, and Korean). Local Indian beer (varieties of Kingfisher) start at $12 USD. The upside is that Shiro is almost always the last nightclub to shut down in Delhi. **Skooters** is the latest addition to the party scene, medium-sized and priced like Shiro. Pick this one for an all-out dance club with a mixed-age crowd. All three are located next to one another in Samraat Hotel, Central Delhi. Cost for drinks and food are upward of $130 USD.

Other high-end clubs include **B-Bar** in Select Citywalk and **blue FROG** opposite Qutub Minar.

For more affordable fare, head to **Hauz Khas Village.** The entire strip is the best pub-hopping experience you'll get in Delhi. It's quieter, though, with a mix of terrace, basements, and funky floors. Hot picks are **The Living Room, Out Of The Box,** and **Raasta.** Beer starts at $6 USD and food is under $10 USD with a mix of Indian and Western snacky stuff. There are live bands on certain nights, check beforehand.

Or, go to **TC (Turquoise Cottage)** in Adchini for cheap booze and casual atmosphere. Music is Western and decent, and Kingfisher beer can be had for $4 USD. To go one up—better taste of rock and alcohol—choose **Cafe Morrison** in South Extension. It is pricey compared to TC's but Tuesday is ladies' night, and worth every bit. Long Island iced tea ($9 USD) and tandoori platter ($10 USD) come highly recommended.

Shalom in GK-1 offers two things: Sufi music nights on Wednesdays and the best mojitos in town. Food and drinks for two can run anywhere between $20 to $25 USD. Also, **Urban Pind** in GK-1 does expat nights on Thursdays (buy one, get one free drink for expats). Beer costs $4 USD for local brands and the Lebanese food is delectable.

Tip: Pre-game at the cheaper bars before you hit the popular joints, as they are usually expensive.

Also remember:

- Delhi is not at all safe for women at night. Go in groups and only to safe venues. Check up on clubs or bars before you go, especially the cheaper ones. Very important: be wary of overly friendly strangers.
- Entry is free, or between $5 and $6 USD on weekends. There's usually a cover charge for couples. Limited stag entry, depending on club. Check beforehand.
- Try to get in before 10:30 P.M. for popular clubs. Otherwise, you might have trouble unless you know someone.
- Shutdown time is between 11:30 P.M. and 1:00 A.M.
- Taxes are additional and there's more than one kind, so factor that in when budgeting for the night.

FUCKED UP FIRSTHAND

The lead singer of the band dedicated a song to the "pretty lady wearing white" in our group. I pretended in my head that he was referring to me. I knew I looked good in white and we'd been exchanging looks all evening. He was cute in a dark sort of way. He had a bad voice. On my third LIIT, I couldn't care less.

Later, the driver of the cab wasn't amused. He'd already asked me thrice to keep the window up. All I wanted to do was stick my drunken head out and feel the breeze on my face. He threatened to pull over.

The cops stopped us instead. Great timing. I jerked the car door open and threw up, missing the cop's shoes by a whisker. He looked disgusted.

VERDICT
Maybe think about Mumbai.

Priyanka Kher

70. Hong Kong, China

SEASON: All year-round.
IDEAL CONDITIONS: At the Lan Kwai Fong during a major holiday or sporting event.
DAYTIME ACTIVITY: Check view from Victoria Peak.
LODGING RECOMMENDATIONS: Cheap options are few. Hostels abound in TST Chungking Mansion, which is also home to Hong Kong's drug market. Airbnb is the best bet.
INGESTIBLES: Ketamine is king; stick to booze and avoid a nasty K-hole.

If you've come to Hong Kong seeking a languorous, hazy, rose-and-sepia-tinted Wong Kar-Wai dreamscape, think again. The Hong Kong of "Suzy Wong" is long gone, and in its place you'll find a fast-paced, clean, sophisticated city-state where British colonialism and Chinese imperialism linger in equal measure.

Hong Kong, like New York, consists of a central island linked to the mainland (as well as other islands). Hong Kong Island is where most of the Western expat and tourist action happens; Kowloon (on the mainland side of the Harbour) is denser, more Chinese, and arguably more "local."

Spendy

Drinking and going out are a massive part of Hong Kong life (though less among Cantonese than among their mainland Chinese and Western counterparts). The action is organized primarily in party zones—concentrated areas of bars, clubs, and late-night supper clubs.

On the Island, the major drinking locus is the famous (infamous?) **Lan Kwai Fong (LKF)**, a little, pedestrian cul-de-sac lined with innumerable bars trafficking in JELL-O shots, liquor, and *shisha*. People (British and Australian men) are friendly and raucous. Above LKF are Wyndham Street and the LKF Hotel, where many of Hong Kong's premier see-and-be-seen, bottle-serviced, super chi-chi clubs are, like **Tasmania Ballroom, Dragon-i, Azure, Prive, Solas,** and **Bisous** (the latter featuring a pretty impressive burlesque show). Unless you're "on the list," prepare to wait on line. If you want something a bit cooler, head to **Kee Club** or **Fly**. Both clubs import talented DJs to spin a mix of hip-hop, indie-electro, and dubstep to young and hip crowds who are there to actually dance.

The other main party zone on the Island is **Wan Chai,** famous for its "below-the-waist" culture, featuring hordes of Filipina and Thai escorts for hire. But don't be put off—Wan Chai epitomizes the relaxed, convivial British pub atmosphere that has been lost in the rest of Hong Kong and is worth enjoying. **Mes Amis** is a good place to start, then move on to **Typhoon, Delaney's,** or the less-reputable **Amazonia**.

Hong Kong has seen a recent, celebrated influx of speakeasy-style cocktail bars, the coolest of which is probably 001, distinguished only by an unmarked black door tucked behind a wet market. Inside you'll find a top-shelf range of Japanese whiskeys and cocktails, and a famed mac-and-cheese. **Lily and Bloom, Quinary, The Blck Brd,** and **The Pawn** are also highly regarded. The new kid on the block is **Honi Honi**, an outdoor tiki bar where drinks are served in coconuts and melons.

You'll also find exotic, artisanal cocktails atop some of Hong

Kong's best hotels, like **M Bar** at the Mandarin Oriental and **Café Gray** at the Upper House. Prices usually run upward of 120 HKD a drink (about $15 USD), but along with your drink, you get the opportunity to ogle Hong Kong's spectacular skyline. Same goes for **Wooloomooloo** in Wan Chai.

Hong Kong's shiny, high-heeled exterior can feel shallow and limiting. But if you're willing to venture off the beaten path a bit, a gritty counterculture exists, albeit a small one. The **Globe** is Hong Kong's best beer bar—not your average Brit pub, but a real gastropub, where you can sample a beer from Hong Kong's only local craft brewery, Typhoon. **Hidden Agenda**, way out in Kwun Tong, is perhaps the best place to find a local, authentic experience. Opened by local musicians who wanted a place to play, the former factory now hosts a cool, diverse lineup of local hard-core rockers and overseas indie bands.

But if you're looking for some grimy, funky hipster fun . . . nowhere beats **XXX**. Located in Sheung Wan's dried seafood market and literally underground, XXX is simply a bare room rented out to different DJs on rotating nights, ranging from dubstep to indie to dancehall. There's no bar so it's BYOB (or substances—there's no security to speak of). Nor should you expect air-conditioning.

NOTES FROM A LOCAL

Drinking on the street is legal? This wonderful piece of public policy has given birth to what we residents fondly refer to as Club 7-Eleven—great when you're broke or lazy.

VERDICT

Takes patience.

Madeline Gressel

71. Mumbai, India

SEASON: Between November and April (pleasantly tropical).
IDEAL CONDITIONS: Watch the sun set over the Marine Drive while sipping a mojito.
DAYTIME ACTIVITY: Hit Juhu or Girguam Chapuati beach.
LODGING RECOMMENDATIONS: Budget is virtually nonexistent. Try the YMCA or Airbnb. For luxury, The Taj, The Oberoi, or the JW Marriott in Juhu.
INGESTIBLES: Fancy cocktails, champagne, beer, hashish joints, and Bade Miya for spicy late-night kebabs.

I've lived in New York City for eighteen years, Montreal for four, and Hong Kong for one, and they don't hold a candle to Mumbai. Unlike aristocratic Delhi, Mumbai is the playground of new money, the bedroom of the stars. It's upscale without being snobby, thrilling without being dangerous. There is always a party, and you're invited.

Mumbai is divided into Town (South) and Suburbs (North). The suburbs are actually urban space; they are more distinctly divided into neighborhoods, the most upscale of which are Bandra and Juhu. The suburbs used to feel provincial and residential compared to Town—no longer.

Town is filled with posh clubs, rooftop bars, and tourist hangouts. Among the best rooftop bars are **Dome** along with **Aer**, atop the Four Seasons, which is filled with the rich and beautiful sipping champagne. Also notable: the **Hotel Harbour View**, which overlooks the Gateway of India, and has cheap beer.

If you want a taste of home, head to **Leopold** on Colaba Causeway, where Mumbai's tourist population congregates. Across the road is **Woodside Inn**, where expats sip beer and wine after work and listen to '90s rock. Time to dance? **Prive** is the closest Mumbai comes to snotty and exclusive—head to **blue FROG** instead. It's architecturally interesting as well as the best place in the city to hear live music and DJ sets.

The 'Burbs have a younger, looser feel. Unlike Town, the North is filled with auto-rickshaws easily available for your convenience. Hit up **Hawaiian Shack** and **Toto's Garage** to enjoy pitchers of beer and top forty among Bandra's underage.

For a grown-up time, **Olive's** on Thursday night is the place to see and be seen. It's crowded as all hell and expensive, but you're guaranteed to see an interesting cross-section of the upscale local and expat populations. **Aurus** in Juhu is similarly swank, and it's a great place to watch prostitutes work the beach below.

But if you're really ready to party, it's time to head even farther north. Most of Mumbai's best full-on clubs—most notably stalwarts **China House** and **Trilogy**—are situated near the airport, where there's more space and looser noise regulations. If you want Mumbai at it's most local and genuine, seek out the tucked-away **Kino's Cottage** in Andheri West, where no one is ashamed to blast Bollywood and break out the dance moves.

Mumbai tips:

- Bribery is always acceptable.
- Mumbaikars take great pride in their appearance, so leave the harem pants and flip-flops at home.
- Town and the Suburbs are not as far apart as Mumbaikars would lead you to believe. You can do both in one night. After midnight, traffic is nonexistent.
- Leopold is fun for a night ("Wow! Bullet holes!"), and a great place to meet people, but don't waste your whole trip there.
- If you're home before dawn, you're doing something wrong.

If you think a man is hitting on you, he is. Standards of behavior are adjusted for "easy" foreign women.

VERDICT
Everything is negotiable.

Madeline Gressel

72. Macau, China

SEASON: Spring, especially March or April (warm, not too humid).
IDEAL CONDITIONS: Winning.
DAYTIME ACTIVITY: Gambling cash at the Venetian Macao.
LODGING RECOMMENDATIONS: Ole London Hotel for budget, Pousada de Mong-Ha for hotel.
INGESTIBLES: Pastéis de nata (little egg tarts), vinho verde (Portuguese wine), dim sum.

Some call Macau the "Vegas of Asia" but this thinking is a recipe for disappointment. There is gambling for sure, but unlike the free-wheeling Western attitude, games of chance are treated more like business transactions than recreation in Macau. The idea of "free drinks for players" doesn't exist in many casinos (the **Hard Rock** seems to be the exception) and in some cases alcohol is prohibited while gaming altogether.

You don't have to gamble in the casinos to have fun. Head to the old **Casino Lisboa** for some people watching. Dig the elderly Chinese crowd playing table games you've never seen before. Working girls prowl the lobby. The Crazy Paris Show is at the **Grand Lisboa**. Stand outside the **Wynn** and watch Performance Lake. See the Tree of Prosperity in the atrium. **Lion's Bar** is the after-hours spot in the **MGM Grand**.

Largo do Senado is the town square of this former Portuguese colony. Go to Avenida Sun Yat Sen, aka Bar Street. Moonwalker is your local hot spot with a live Filipino band. Live Music Association (LMA) is where touring rock bands play. CheChe is a laid-back Portuguese-style lounge.

Cross the bridge to Cotai. You can see The Venetian from a mile away. Take pictures of strangers being serenaded by their gondola oarsman. Playboy Club is just off the gaming floor. Cool off in the wave pool at Galaxy. Wednesday is ladies' night at Cubic in the City of Dreams.

In the Taipa area, Irish Bar has Guinness on tap. You can eat suckling pig at the open-air bar at Fernando's Portuguese restaurant. Try the egg tarts at Lord Stow's.

Because you can bet on it, racing is popular in Macau. Watch the greyhounds circle the track at Canidrome. The horse races are held at Macau Jockey Club. If you're here in November, the Macau Grand Prix is rumored to have massive after-parties.

Grab a cold one in the Macau Tower. You'll want a drink before doing the 233-meter bungee jump.

General rules about Macau:

- Alcohol can be expensive, especially in casino bars. Buy airplane bottles at duty-free for mobile drinking, and a bottle for the room.
- The local currency is the Macanese pataca, but most casinos *only* accept Hong Kong dollars.
- Eating out can also be expensive. Local mom-and-pop restaurants away from tourist areas will keep you on budget.

FUCKED UP FIRSTHAND

We were drinking Super Bock outside Fernando's when our table became available. We ordered suckling pig, grilled sardines, and a bottle of *vinho verde* recommended by the waitress. After the meal, my buddies and I headed to the Wynn. They didn't want to serve us alcohol. We bribed a waitress, and, after much negotiating, she agreed to bring us cocktails under the stipulation that we stay at one blackjack table.

I was up $800 USD and then I was real up, so up in fact that after five vodka Red Bulls I nearly had an aneurysm when they changed dealers. He dealt himself blackjack three hands in a row. "They brought in a cooler!" I said, and picked up my chips.

The next day we went to the Macau Tower. It was my birthday, so I decided to do the bungee jump, which is 233 meters (764 feet). I sprung for the video, which means a guy comes up and points a camera at you one minute before jumping and asks how you're doing.

"Well," I said, "I'm hungover, I'm thirsty, and I'm getting ready to jump off a tower. All in all I'm feeling pretty good."

VERDICT
Macau is Macau and it doesn't want to be Vegas.

Noah Pelletier

73. Disney World

LOCATION: Orlando, Florida
SEASON: Anytime except summer or you're sweating balls.
IDEAL CONDITIONS: Dosed on psilocybin mushrooms, or maybe just no line at the Small World ride.
LODGING RECOMMENDATIONS: Disney's Art of Animation Resort.
INGESTIBLES: Beer, cotton candy, ham-on-a-stick.

Disney World: you might equate this place with fairy-tale bullshit, but fucking memorable times can be had here. Take your cues from the droves of stoked Brazilians and Argentines: this is a place to have fun!

Start at **Magic Kingdom** where you can glimpse the castle and steal a kiss from Cinderella.

Take the Small World ride. There's ginger representation in the form of dancing leprechauns from Ireland, and just about every other stereotype on the face of the planet. Then go watch the Dreams Come True parade.

But if you've had enough of happy families and wailing babies and cheesy grinning, for the love of god, head to **Epcot**. It's where Disney lovers come to sin. Do your own version of Round-the-World tour . . . meaning go to each country, buy a national beer, and improvise your own little pub crawl. Canada, France, Germany, Japan, and so on. Everything is adorably tacky, and by the time the fireworks ceremony starts, you'll be completely shittered.

Alternatively, you can go to **Downtown Disney**, which is basically reserved for hooligans and their shenanigans. The bonus? Complimentary parking. Order a pint at **Raglan Road Irish Pub and Restaurant** on **Pleasure Island**, or head to the **House of Blues** in the West Side. Remember that everything in Disney World is outrageously overpriced, so you must be willing to drop at least $100 in one day.

Tips for getting drunk in Orlando:

- Magic Kingdom is technically a dry park; Epcot is not. Very important to know.
- If you *must* have a drink at Magic Kingdom, you can do so at the **Be Our Guest** restaurant in **Fantasyland**. However, this is all very much against Walt's wishes, so only proceed if you wish to disrupt the dead.
- You'll find the biggest party-goers at **Universal**. Don't ride the Jurassic Park flume if you're afraid of T. rex.

NOTES FROM A LOCAL

This place used to be all pine flatwoods and swamp and they turned it into . . . money.

VERDICT

Bring friends and wreak havoc.

Candice Walsh

74. Oslo, Norway

SEASON: June through August.
IDEAL CONDITIONS: Late summer nights with the sun dropping just before you turn into a pumpkin.
DAYTIME ACTIVITY: Cross-country skiing at Nordmarka.
LODGING RECOMMENDATIONS: Allemannsloven is a law that allows you to camp anywhere in nature as long as you are a few meters away from private property. Or check the Oslo Vandrerhjem Haraldsheim.
INGESTIBLES: Rakfisk (rotten trout), Linie Aquavit, brown cheese, fresh salmon, Aass beer.

Oslo is the younger brother who's pissed off at always getting hand-me-downs from his older siblings, Copenhagen and Stockholm. Even *Osla* is suggested by Google search ahead of the Scandinavian city, as if some kind of cruel joke. It's time to put a fucked-up seal of approval on the gateway to the fjords.

Norway is famed for its terrain, and rightly so. If you travel from Sweden or Denmark by bus or train you start to see intense rock faces more frequently as you approach the Norwegian border. When you pull into Oslo and establish your base, take a walk down to the harbor. Smuggle a brew from the shop down to one of the quays and have a drink with your feet dangling off the edge. Before nightfall head over to the **Opera House**, which slants toward the water's edge. Then yodel your way toward the hipster hangout **Grünerløkka**, which is centered on a green square.

Check **Sound of Mu** for intimate live music and your first Linie Aquavit (which apparently has to cross the equator twice in oak sherry barrels). Move your way up the road to **Bar Boca**, a tiny retro spot with a '50s-style interior. If you must eat, go to **Villa Paradiso**, being prepared to queue for your pizza and Oslo's finest tiramisu. Round the corner to **Delicatessen** for a glass of wine and part with more precious kroners.

Ready for a new part of town, walk over to **Grønland**, the migrant quarter. **Oslo Mekaniske Verksted** is an industrial looking place with a courtyard in the back. There's good live music at **Datteratil Hagen** as well as the **Café Theatre**, a converted church with a stage where the altar once was.

Set your wayward sights next on the **Oslo Mikrobryggeri** (Oslo Microbrewery). Sample an organic beer in one last flailing attempt at sophistication. Then go for your few well-rehearsed, badly executed dance moves at **Blå** (Blue) resting on the bank of the Aker River. An underground alternative club with live jam sessions and sweaty crowds, this is a solid place to end the night inconspicuously.

NOTES FROM A LOCAL

Combine the beautiful nature that surrounds Oslo with a social hangout with friends. The cheapest and most spectacular way to use the few summer months in the capital.

VERDICT

Leave broke, hungover, and stoked.

Dikson

75. São Paulo, Brazil

SEASON: High season from late December to Carnaval (February or early March); cheaper tickets and good weather September through October.

IDEAL CONDITIONS: On the roof of D-Edge at sunrise after dancing all night.

DAYTIME ACTIVITY: Visit the Museu de Arte de São Paulo.

LODGING RECOMMENDATIONS: Hotel Unique or the Fasano for luxury, Ibis for budget, Vila Madalena Hostel for a chic hostel.

INGESTIBLES: Feijoada, chopp (draft beer), caipirinhas, sushi, fresh fruit.

People traveling to Brazil might be tempted to skip São Paulo. It doesn't have the best reputation among travelers: it's noisy, it's smoggy, the traffic is horrible, and there's no beach. But São Paulo's big secret is that it's one of the best places to eat and drink in the world. Unlike Rio, São Paulo isn't littered with cheesy tourist bars or mediocre restaurants; if you come to this city, you get the real deal.

Clubbing is a must in São Paulo, and Brazilians don't do it half-assed. You're either in or out. And if you're in, pack sunglasses; you'll need them in the morning. Just remember: the word for "club" is *balada*. The word for "bar" is *bar*.

For electronic music, start at **D-Edge** or the gay dance palace **Bar do Netão** in Baixo Augusta. For Brazilian music and dancing, **Santo Forte** is the place to be. To drink among the beautiful people, head to the rooftop bar of the über-chic **Hotel Unique**. If, however, you like your jeans skinny and your mustaches ironic, follow São Paulo's burgeoning hipster community to **The Alley** and **Neu Club**.

São Paulo is also home to the largest Japanese community outside of Japan, and there are tons of sushi and karaoke venues, such as the **Chopperia Liberdade**, where people of all stripes eat, drink, and belt out their favorite songs in Portuguese, English, and Japanese until 5:00 A.M.

São Paulo's drinking culture is definitely not confined to the night. Some of the best places to get liquored up during the day are in **Vila Madalena**, a bohemian-chic neighborhood packed with open-air drinking establishments, restaurants, shops, and samba bars. Check out **Genésio, Filial, Astor,** and **Mercearía São Pedro.**

You haven't truly done São Paulo until you've tried a caipirinha at **Veloso**, a hole-in-the-wall student bar in Vila Mariana that whips up the famous Brazilian cocktail, made with cachaça, a cane-sugar liquor, sugar, and limes. For a unique drink, order a *caipirinha de jabuticaba,* which mixes in a native grape-like fruit.

FUCKED UP FIRSTHAND

After whiskeys and caipirinhas and inadvisable vodka shots, we headed to Happy News, one of the most ridiculous *baladas* in the city. The clientele of Happy News is a mix of muscular dudes with *Jersey Shore* Pauly D-esque helmet hairstyles, underage teens hoping not to get kicked out, and people like me and my friends, who just want to dance and wave around a couple of glow sticks.

It's not cool. At all. But it's fun. At 5:00 A.M., we stumbled out into the near-dawn. A couple of us kept going, off to breakfast *baladas*. I went home, happy to know that São Paulo always does it for me.

VERDICT

Twenty million people and nearly as many bars.

Stephanie Early Green

76. Seoul, South Korea

SEASON: Skip the winter.
IDEAL CONDITIONS: Five days to play like a champion.
DAYTIME ACTIVITY: Hike Bugaksan Mountain.
LODGING RECOMMENDATIONS: Plenty of Western hotels, but stay in a "love motel" for a kinkier experience.
INGESTIBLES: Barbecue, soju, more soju.

Not only does Seoul have one of the most varied and interesting nightlife scenes of all the major cities in Asia, it consistently gets better.

The people here are incredible to party with—kind, well-mannered but not boring, damn nice to look at—and jesus, do they like to drink.

South Korea's been cursed with a poor domestic beer scene (something they are trying to remedy, if slowly), but they compensate for it with the ever-present, ever-potent rice wine, soju. The buses smell of it at night; the gutters are littered with the green bottles in the morning. It's cheap. It's effective. And if you drink enough of it you will most likely be missing clothing the next day.

In a culture so taken with alcohol (drugs are illegal and scarce here and not worth the hassle), a bar-goer has endless options. Visiting Hongdae you can find the college-age kids lined up for clubs **Cocoon** and **Papa Gorilla**, where the girls, and boys, just want to have fun and forget about misspent, overeducated childhoods. Rock clubs **FF** and **DGBD** have been the go-to live music spots for expats and Koreans alike for years. They're scuzzy and loud and the drinks are cheap. Don't wear white shoes; the floors have never been cleaned. **Bar Da** is Hongdae's best locals-in-the-know bar. Good cocktails and hip clientele.

If you're flush, head south of the river to Gangnam, where no one wants to talk about Psy. They're all too busy looking as though they just stepped out of a fashion magazine, except they all look as if they stepped out of the same picture—an advertisement for plastic surgery. Clubs **Ellui** and **Octagon** are massive and two of the best in Asia. Try your best to look good. The crowd will still be better dressed than you. Both clubs have world-class DJs and the Koreans are there to dance.

The center of the city is also the heart of the party scene: **Itaewon**. Once a haven for scum, both domestic and foreign, the international district is now where you find the most interesting new restaurants, bars, and clubs. At the lounge **Glam**, you'll find fancy women with perfect English looking for a boy toy, Korean men with white-girl fetishes, and a bar that puts Seoul on the same level as Tokyo, Hong Kong, and Shanghai. The club next door, **Mute**, goes all night and the music is solid.

For an unadulterated Korean clubbing experience go to **B1**—consistent crowd, good music. Visit **Homo Hill** for gay and transvestite clubs and **Hooker Hill** for, well, hookers. Even if you don't want to sample the women it's still fun to walk up the hill and watch the ladies of the night pop out from their little doors and try to lure you inside. It's the world's grossest funhouse. There are also a few G.I.-heavy bars at the end of that street. The oldest and seediest is **Polly's Kettle**, where they drink jungle juice out of two-liter plastic bottles with the tops cut off. This is a good place to get fucked up in a lot of ways.

Like the Japanese to the east, Koreans also like their karaoke, only here they call the singing rooms *norae bangs*. An average norae bang can be found nearly anywhere. Hongdae's **Luxury Norae Bang** is one of the most well-known and easiest to find. Bring a lot of cash.

For slightly less seedy versions of entertainment, Seoul has casinos, a horse track, and amusement and water parks. A common weekend pastime involves hiking to the top of a mountain to drink *makgeolli,* traditional rice wine. Just remember you have to come back down.

FUCKED UP FIRSTHAND

We started out with drinks in Gangnam, at the jazz bar Crazy Horse on Garosugil, where all the plastic surgery girls have the same faces. The band was hot, but we wanted to talk to people so we took a cab to Hongdae and got drinks at GoGos. My friend got a call from two Korean girls who had just gotten back from Italy and they wanted to meet us in Itaewon.

At Luv, the girls were wearing nice dresses, white and black, their hair and makeup perfect. We got a table and a bottle and they told us all about their travels. After the liquor ran out they wanted to dance so we took another cab back to Gangnam, to Club Answer, where most of the girls were tens. I was talking to one who gave me her name. She was tall, with short black hair and a face that looked carved out of soap. Her eyes had been widened and she spoke perfect English. I went to the bar for drinks and when I came back she had changed her dress, her hair was longer, and she had a different name. I didn't let that bother me.

VERDICT
If you can't get drunk in Seoul you can't get drunk anywhere.

Bart Schaneman

77. Singapore

SEASON: Anytime. Relatively stable (I didn't say "nice") tropical weather year-round.
IDEAL CONDITIONS: St James Power Station at 3:00 A.M. with an open bottle to drink at your own pace.
DAYTIME ACTIVITY: Botanical Garden strolling.
LODGING RECOMMENDATIONS: Swissotel and Marina Bay Sands. For budget, Hotel 81, a chain of budget hotels with an undeserved seedy reputation. Hostels: The Little Red Dot (town) and Fern Loft (East Coast).
INGESTIBLES: Chicken rice, laksa (a mild curried noodle), murtabak (meat-filled, fried "pancake"), and sup kambing (mutton soup) or bak kut teh (herbal pork rib soup). Beer, wine, and spirits available at most convenience stores. No weed brah.

For a people that are legendary for their straight-laced pragmatism, Singaporeans are surprising party animals. When you touch down, you'll head to "town," spanning a few MRT (metro) stops in all directions from City Hall Station. You'll want to go to the backpacker areas of Little India and Bugis and secure your accommodation first.

Don't be too quick to ditch the area. Many of the restored prewar shop houses have been converted to eateries (and drinkeries) with decent afternoon happy hours. **Zsofi Tapas Bar** at Dunlop

Street has fifteen different sangrias to start you down the slow road to inebriation, plus they serve free tapas with every drink. On the same street, **The Countryside Cafe** offers Western, Indian, and local food. Try the chicken hariyali kebab and the spicy fish.

The **Clarke Quay** and **Boat Quay** areas are on either side of the Singapore River. They alternate taking center stage in the local night-life scene. This decade is Clarke Quay's heyday. Go to **The Cannery** where more than twenty pubs and clubs cluster around a central fountained courtyard, and someone is getting shitfaced every day of the week. Check out **Attica** if you're into the SPG (Sarong Party Girl) scene, **The Pump Room** for live music and **Rebel** for DJs. Be warned, cover charges apply and drinks are pricey all over the area. Younger crowds usually stop at 7-Eleven for pre-party beverages, which are brought riverside.

You haven't done the club scene here until you've done at least one of the mega clubs. The household name, **Zouk**, is actually three different club experiences: **Zouk, Phuture,** and **Velvet Underground.** All are pulse pounding. Even more massive is **St James Power Station,** with five stories of sound system.

If you're looking for downtempo, head to **Arab Street** for the flipside of nightlife in Singapore. Here, al fresco dining takes place on streets that are closed (or mostly closed) to traffic. **Nabins** Ara-bic appetizer platter spans dishes from across the Middle East and their harira soup is perfect for when the temperature comes down in the evenings. **El Sheikh** and **Going Om** are chill-out café-bars, and **Blu Jaz** has a full event calendar that includes live bands, belly-dancing, and comedy nights.

Festivals take place year-round. **Timbre Rock** and **Roots** (mid-March) and **WOMAD** (August) at Fort Canning Green, and **Zouk-Out** (December) on Sentosa Island are some of the best outdoor dance events in the region. Throughout the year events such as the **Fringe Festival, Grand Prix** season (parties, pre-parties, and after-parties), and **Oktoberfest** are also great excuses to get sauced.

NOTES FROM A LOCAL

As a tourist, you can go anywhere; you won't get robbed, mugged, or molested. But if you want to see the underbelly of this place, you need a local. If you know the right people, pubs close their doors but keep their taps open. You can get "stuff" easy.

VERDICT

Safe but not fully sanitized.

Tabbi Maitland

78. Tokyo, Japan

SEASON: Spring for the cherry blossoms, or fall (after typhoon season).
IDEAL CONDITIONS: At an izakaya drinking shochu and chatting up locals.
DAYTIME ACTIVITY: Tsukiji Fish Market haggling.

Next-level karaoke in Tokyo. Bring your A-game. Photo by Ryan Libre.

Tokyo is special. Spend the day on the train or on foot, check out the different neighborhoods, such as **Akihabara, Asakusa, Shinjuku,** or **Ueno Park,** and you'll either feel like you're in a cute, small city, or the world's biggest metropolis. And it's 2050. And aliens have landed.

People say this about all big cities, but you can do almost anything in Tokyo. A ten-course Italian feast and a $1,000 USD bottle of wine? Drink beer and eat a burger while watching the Yankees game? Smoke Cuban cigars and drink Japanese whiskey? Smoky bars with salarymen drinking nihonshu until 4:00 A.M.? It's all wide open. If you don't know where to start, try this: take a deep breath, find a beer vending machine, and crack open a Kirin while you think about it.

If you happen to be there for them, make sure you catch any of the three annual **Grand Sumo Tournaments.** Buy your ticket at any 7-Eleven. Most spectators don't show up until the serious fighters appear at the end of the day, but they start selling beer at 10:00 A.M., so I say the earlier the better.

Karaoke in Tokyo can be expensive, but it's awesome. Yes, you can sing "Don't Stop Believing" onstage to a crowded Western-style bar, but you can also squeeze twenty friends into a private karaoke room, which may come with drinks and food, tambourines, and a view of the city, à la the Roppongi **Karaoke-Kan** (seen in *Lost in Translation*), or a bathtub (at **Lovenet**).

An *izakaya* is a drinking establishment, the primary purpose of which, from what I understand, is to hide from your wife and family after work. In Tokyo, like the rest of Japan, basically anywhere with a red lantern outside is going to serve either some combination of biru (beer), shochu (a Japanese liquor), or nihonshu (sake in the United States).

You probably won't see a geisha in Tokyo, unless you know a guy who knows a guy with a lot of money. Disappointed? A very different type of female entertainment, the maid café, might interest you. Mostly located in **Akihabara**, cafés specialize in different costumes and services, but they all basically have a cute young girl who looks like an anime character and pays unusual attention to you. Some wear school girl outfits, some call the male patrons "big brother," some cut your food for you, and some slap you in the face if you upset them . . . or request it.

Themes are big in Tokyo. **Ninja Akasaka, Alcatrez, Lock Out,** and **Alice in Wonderland** are probably the most popular and over-the-top examples of themed restaurants. Also, there is nothing wrong with a good old-fashioned cat café. And then there are the strip clubs of Kabukicho, the huge dance clubs of Roppongi and Shibuya, such as **Womb** and **Unit.** Tokyo also has craft beer and cocktails at **Goodbeer Faucets** in Shibuya and **Bar High Five** and **Star Bar** in the Ginza.

Remember these phrases:

- "*Nihonshu o hitotsu / futatsu kudasai*" (One / two sake(s) please.) And remember, all alcohol in Japan is called sake. Nihonshu is what Americans know as sake.
- "*Kore wa nan desu ka?*" (What is this?) If you think you're about to eat something crazy, it's always a good idea to ask.
- "*Eigo no kyoku ga arimasu ka?*" (Are there any English songs?) (Ask before you agree to sing karaoke).

NOTES FROM A LOCAL
Try not to miss your last train! Taxi rates can be expensive at night. If you missed, Internet cafés or love hotels are a good solution for staying up late. They are relatively clean and safe.

VERDICT

If the neon lights, maid outfits, ninja-themed bars, or horse sashimi seem like a dream, you're wrong. Just go with it.

Morgan deBoer

79. Washington, D.C.

SEASON: July through August is like a bad case of "swamp ass." In the winter, it's cold as balls. But events like the Inauguration, Cherry Blossom Festival, and July 4 make it worth a visit.

IDEAL CONDITIONS: Think of the nation's flag: red (a wine box on the steps of the Lincoln Memorial), white (cocaine snorted off of an unpaid intern's ass), and blue (or "blew"—D.C. is known for its history of historic blow jobs).

DAYTIME ACTIVITY: Budget several hours minimum for the Smithsonian Institution.

LODGING RECOMMENDATIONS: Duo Housing DC has a sick rooftop patio where you can mack at their weekly barbecues. High-rollers should stay at the Tabard Inn, a couple of historic houses made into a boutique hotel.

INGESTIBLES: The Rickey (gin or whiskey, lime juice, and club soda, dates back to the 1840s), Jumbo Slice pizza, DC Brau Beer, pot (legalize it!) and other overpriced drugs, Mambo sauce, Ethiopian food, half-smokes from Ben's Chili Bowl.

Amurica, fuck yeah! Every four years Washington, D.C., capital of the United States, throws the biggest party in the nation, the Presidential Inauguration. The whole city shuts down in preparation for a local holiday of drunken, patriotic madness. You can either freeze your ass off outside watching the swearing-in ceremony and the parade, or stay warm indoors and play drinking games while watching it all unfold on television.

At night, the Inaugural Ball is the hardest fete to get into, but there are tons of unofficial soirees you can attend. If you don't feel like dropping $400 to see D-list celebrities entertain you with pathetic renditions of "The Star Spangled Banner," check out $100-or-less events, such as the **Inaugural Millennial Ball** (up-and-coming musicians of the twenty- and thirtysomething generations) or **Vaudeball** (burlesque, fire-eaters, and other D.C. sideshow delights).

The political polls may have closed after the presidential election in November, but you can become President of Pole Dancing using any of the several stripper poles at **Midtown Loft.** Become the Diplomat of Douchebaggery at Logan Circle's **ChurchKey,** where you can try more than five hundred different kinds of beer from around the world.

Practice your political game-play at the **H Street Country Club,** with gut-busting Mexican food and a mini-golf course. And **Comet Ping Pong** is as amazing as it sounds—play a *real* game of beer pong (you know, with paddles and stuff) on one of their many recreational tables at this Chevy Chase bar.

Party like a president:

- **John Adams:** Drank beer for breakfast. You can, too, at Capitol Hill's **Tune Inn,** which will lovingly serve you a beer at 8:00 A.M.
- **John F. Kennedy:** Apparently dropped LSD a couple of times back in the 1960s. Feed your acid trip during the **Psychedelic Nightmare Halloween Rave Party,** going on its fourth year.
- **James Buchanan:** The only bachelor president with a penchant for gallon jugs of whiskey. Drink your weight in booze at Dupont Circle's **Irish Whiskey Public House.**

FUCKED UP FIRSTHAND

Max works at an NGO that's like the knock-off brand of the World Health Organization. He wants to be a lawyer and studies at GWU. Of all the people my gay best friend knows, he's the only straight guy. Whenever I visit D.C., he's the one I look to for some nooky in the nation's capital.

At a pub-like bar called the Black Rooster we sit outside and discuss the failing job market. Max is clean-cut, dresses in a button-down shirt and khaki pants even though it's Saturday. He's not bad looking, but if Bobby had more straight friends, I probably wouldn't give him a second glance.

"Doctors can't even get jobs anymore," Max tells me. "Only the undesirable fields are open, like proctology, or podiatry."

"I bet people make a lot of money as gynecologists, too," I reply. "I don't think you could pay me enough to stick my fingers in total strangers."

"I'd totally be a gyno," Max says to me. "That'd be so awesome."

"Really?" I say. "Even if it means staring at nasty, crusty vaginas, like, all of the time?"

He takes a swig of beer. "Absolutely. I love pussy. I seriously love it. I wouldn't care."

Max, the future-lawyer-wanna-be gynecologist, and I drunkenly make out at the bar later on. He doesn't get to see my vagina though. I wonder what he would have thought about it.

VERDICT

Seems like it would be lame, but it's actually badass.

Katka Lapelosová

7: Beach Break

No terrain creates cliché like the beach. It's hard for me to refrain from putting the phrase in scare quotes as that seems the way most people see it: "The Beach." Not an actual place (think habitat, eco-system, local economy), but an idea, a warm and effervescent fantasy constructed around sunbathing bodies, umbrellas, coolers of Natural Light, volleyball, suntan lotion, reggae. It's what makes girls wax their pubic hair and guys start thinking about the gym.

No other terrain causes this. Nobody thinks: *Damn I better get my abs in shape for the prairie.*

Meanwhile, the ocean itself is almost an afterthought.

Unless of course you're a surfer (or you kiteboard, fish, whatever), and then the whole context shifts to an almost military-style mission based around swell, wind direction, tides, currents, and everything else is of little concern.

This is also unless you happen to live in a certain kind of coastal town where your culture and livelihood depends on the ocean. The kind of place that exudes originality, independence, self-reliance, a sense that as long as there are fish left in the ocean, the rest of "The World" could self-implode and you'd still be out there hauling in nets, building boats, keeping track of moon phases and tides, and staying stoked.

In the meantime, the rest of us have to content ourselves as travelers, outsiders, let's say "students" of the beach. It's not all bad. Pertinent lessons for more advanced attitudes toward body image, priorities, and happiness are freely available if you know where to look, like small towns in southern Brazil (where beach-goers are not averse to spontaneous, three-hundred-people-in-thongs aero-

Secret spot, Pacific Ocean. Photo by Chris Burkard.

bics/dance sessions) or villages in El Salvador where there's only one local mill for grinding your corn into flour for tortillas.

Somewhere on the spectrum from Cabo San Lucas to more chill places like Raglan, New Zealand, or Atlantic Island, North Carolina, you'll find what you're looking for. And above all, respect Mother Ocean.

She plays for keeps.

80. San Diego, California

SEASON: Are you kidding? Warm, mild, dry year-round.
IDEAL CONDITIONS: Getting barreled at Ocean Beach jetty an hour after you've arrived.
DAYTIME ACTIVITY: Go deep-sea fishing.

It's easy to get jaded about San Diego as the city in California where generations of conservatives huddled together, too afraid of Mexicans to leave their homes, and have now spawned a population of suburban rebels-sans-causes paying for drinks out of trust funds. But on the flipside of that, San Diego has the best weather in the United States in terms of straight-up comfort, and it's an epic area for surfing, kayaking, fishing, etc., and their local communities that operate on stoke. Get in with them, and they'll show you spots—whether surf breaks or restaurants—you only dreamed could exist in your hometown.

Like many cities, San Diego's best but most generic time is found downtown. The **Gaslamp Quarter** has block after block of restaurants, bars, and nightclubs, such as **The Tipsy Crow** and **Star Bar**. San Diegans also love speakeasies, but they love telling people how cool they are for knowing about those speakeasies even more. On that note, try downtown's worst-kept secrets, **Noble Experiment** and **Prohibition**.

San Diego's other main hub for nightlife is in Pacific Beach. If downtown is where the yuppies go to do coke in the bathroom, then Pacific Beach is the go-to spot for slutty sorority girls attending their safety school. Garnet Avenue runs through the area and is lined with dive bars, such as **710 Beach Club** or **The Tiki House**. There's a certain charm to barhopping when the people in line ahead of you get kicked out for having fake IDs.

If going to bars feels like a dog-and-pony show, check out one of the dozens of microbreweries. **Stone Brewing** might be the best, but you'd better keep drinking just to be sure. Hit up **Monkey Paw Pub and Brewery, Karl Strauss Brewing,** and **Green Flash Brewing** for tours and samples.

Though the brand of beer you drink is a big deal in San Diego, the food you eat isn't. Waterfront restaurants with fancy names and expensive menus are everywhere. Skip that shit. The real San Diegan gastronomical experience is found in the Mexican food joints set up on corners everywhere. **Nico's** and **Roberto's** are good places to start, but really it doesn't matter. Only two rules apply: the tastiness of the food is proportional to the number of visible cockroaches, and if it's named after the *jefe* cooking in back, it's going to be amazing.

San Diego is a big city with a lot to see. It's so big that outside of downtown, most residents won't even know if they technically live there or not. Just remember if in your travels you find a bag of money, leave it be—it's probably a dead drop from the Tijuana Cartel lurking just down south of the border.

FUCKED UP FIRSTHAND

Garnet Avenue, in Pacific Beach, is actually right near Windansea, where much of California surf culture was born. When I was in college, I visited a friend who had a house on the beach, and a group of us went off to barhop. We went down the line, hitting every bar from point A to point B.

That was when we wound up on the road next to Windansea.

Windansea is a pretty nice beach, but the crown jewel is an old surf shack built back in the forties, a California historical monument. And as it happened, it was on the way. We sat down underneath it to relax. It was a warm night, and the water wasn't frigid yet at this time of the year. A few people got naked and went swimming. By just after 2:00 A.M., there were probably twenty of us gathered on the beach, having the kind of night we imagined those original surf bums had during the day in the forties.

It was obviously the perfect time for cops to show up. I like to think the surf bums who built that monument would smile on what we did.

VERDICT

Whatever it may lack in pure, unhinged ridiculousness, it makes up in waves.

Colin Heinrich

81. Raglan, New Zealand*

SEASON: December through March (summer).

IDEAL CONDITIONS: Warm and dry.

DAYTIME ACTIVITY: Surf or start learning how.

LODGING RECOMMENDATIONS: The Karioi Lodge for budget; Solscape for tepees, recycled train caboose dorms; Te Whare Farm Stay for upscale.

INGESTIBLES: Espresso, rhubarb smoothies, char sui–braised pork belly, pinot noir, New Zealand Lager, marijuana, hallucinogenic mushrooms, LSD.

Where there are waves, there are surfers. Where there are surfers, there are parties. As a beachside town with stellar point waves, Raglan attracts an international crowd of surfers and artists who never seem to get around to leaving. For a town of 2,600 amid pastoral farmland, there's a wealth of great musicians, photographers, environmentalists, and free-thinking itinerants to get wasted with.

If you stay at the **Karioi Lodge** don't miss **The Barn,** an aged cement basketball court with a thirty-foot cylindrical corrugated tin roof, with the ambience of an aircraft hangar out in the bush. The found Victorian-era armchairs, surf art lining the walls, and foosball and Ping-Pong tables add a cozy texture. Bring an eighteen-pack of New Zealand Lager, the backpackers' drink of choice. Be prepared for drinking card games like shithead, and loud Sublime on the stereo. Stray bus tours come through often, bringing in an ever-shifting mix of young, transient girls and guys to mix with. **Indicators,** a world-class point break, is just a short walk away.

In town, all the action takes places on **Bow Street.** Start at **Vinnie's,** a long-standing restaurant and bar that caters to surfers, with shapely single-fins hanging from the walls, regular First Friday shows by the surfy band The Kryptonites, and the popular "Endless Summer" pizza.

The Harbour View Hotel is another pizza spot with tap beers. Try the Monteith ale on the veranda while people watching Bow Street in the afternoons. The sports bar is in the back, where you'll find pool tables and an international crowd swapping two-on-two games and sharing jugs of beer (one liter is $11 USD). Pool is free on Tuesdays and Thursdays.

In the end, all roads lead to **The YOT Club** for its impeccable sound system, New Zealand's best bands, and freewheeling consumption of tequila. Head there for the **Sunday Sessions** for outside seating and a live DJ until nine, when the party goes inside. Worn vinyl couches around the perimeter make for intimate seating. You probably won't go home alone, or without your ears ringing. Wherever you end up, just make sure to get naked and jump off the Harbour Bridge at some point in your night.

In the morning, try **The Shack**'s hangover-curing Bloody Mary, and chat with the regulars. The Shack also has wicked burgers and smoothies, and is probably the best food in town.

The Wharf is another option at the end of Wallis Street in the harbor. Order tartar sauce with your seriously fresh fish ($10 USD) at **Boat's N',** or call the **Wahine Moe** (07825-7873) in advance to set up a sunset cruise ($39 USD) and have your fish and chips on board. It's a double-decked catamaran, complete with licensed bar, spa, and dance floor.

There is one festival in Raglan, **Boardies and Bikinis,** put on by the local radio station Tractor FM. The weeklong festival is held at the Ruapuke campground in early February for Waitangi Day. The lineup is a mix of dub reggae, tech house, and surf rock. Get some.

The real art in getting wasted in Raglan is getting away from the bars. I've had some really awesome nights in random barbecues up the back of the mountain and walking down a path along a stream, seeing glow worms. Set up a generator, a sound system, and a tent, and have a party.

VERDICT

For a small town in New Zealand, Raglan's got way more partying and music than anywhere else.

Evan Timpy

82. Bali, Indonesia

SEASON: May through October (dry season).
IDEAL CONDITIONS: Free drink hours to dawn.
DAYTIME ACTIVITY: Trek to Mount Agung at sunrise.
LODGING RECOMMENDATIONS: Komala Indah (Poppies 1) or Suka Beach Inn Hotel (Poppies 2).
INGESTIBLES: Gado-gado (boiled vegetables), nasi goreng (fried rice), Jäger bombs, mushrooms, bintang (lager).

This is where most of the three million annual travelers start and end their trips through Indonesia. Bali parties 24/7, and the two-hundred-meter stretch on **Jalan Legian** is where it all goes down. Expect everything at once: street noise, hawkers, pumping discos, ladyboy pickpockets, thousands of drunken revelers, and prostitutes. Tread carefully and enjoy the circus.

The Sky Garden Lounge is the biggest venue in town, a series of bars throughout Kuta's tallest building, and from the rooftop you see the entire city. Internationals get free drinks and table foods from 9:00 to 11:30 P.M. in the VIP Lounge, so bring your passport.

Any given night has either professional dancers, DJs, MCs, or singers performing. There are dance floors everywhere, and also lingering women for hire.

Eikon is a popular beach bar and restaurant that also has free drink hours. The young-traveler crowd, like most places in Kuta, gets rowdy. They frequently hold events here, and you'll likely find a bikini contest or some other reason for bar-top dancing. **Bounty Discotheque** is another mainstay. The dance floor is on a masted ship with a surreal blend of darkness, black lights, cages, lasers, strobes, and regular foam douses. After midnight it's standing room only. A more chill option is the **Apache Reggae Bar,** perhaps the world's only Native American–Rastafarian themed music venue. Reggae and rock cover bands perform nightly to an older mix of Australians and locals.

Beyond the raw vibes of Kuta's strip, there are classier options to the north in Seminyak, like the lounge club in **Potato Heads,** or the simple Spanish restaurant **La Plancha,** which is great for watching the sunset. Another Seminyak option is **Maria Magdalena** (Jl Dyana Pura 6), a smaller club that mostly plays minimalist house.

And you can always search out a psilocybin-laced milkshake if you're looking to trip. For breakfast the best option hands down is the English breakfast at **Alleycats Restaurant** (Poppies 2). Nights there can get pretty rowdy, too.

A few things to avoid:

- **Drug use:** Indonesia has a zero tolerance drug policy (with the strange exception of mushroom milkshakes). Possession usually leads to jail time. At the very least, don't exit a bar or walk around with anything in your pockets.
- **Local spirits, such as arak:** A number of travelers have gotten methanol poisoning and some even died from drinking bad batches.
- **Unsafe sex:** There are an estimated seven thousand cases of HIV/AIDS on Bali, according to The Bali Commission for

the Control of AIDS (KPA-Bali). Seventy-six percent resulted from heterosexual contact, with 40 percent affecting young people between the ages of twenty and twenty-nine.

VERDICT
A million places to get fucked up and a million travelers to get fucked up with.

Evan Timpy

83. Cabo San Lucas, Mexico

SEASON: Spring Break.
IDEAL CONDITIONS: Hot and oiled.
DAYTIME ACTIVITY: Diving, surfing, fishing.
LODGING RECOMMENDATIONS: If it's Spring Break, worry more about where that lucky fella or lady you're going home with is staying. Hopefully it's in the Los Cabos Corridor.
INGESTIBLES: Cerveza for the guys, fruity cocktails for everyone.

If Mexico's main export is hard-core cartel violence and terror, then its main import is crowds of horny college coeds just waiting to disappoint their parents on this year's *Girls Gone Wild*. Far removed from the strife that haunts Mexico's current reputation, Cabo is an "ultimate destination" for Spring Break. Outside this season, it's actually a pretty chill resort and fishing town with some excellent surf breaks.

Cabo is also a major stopover point for cruise lines such as Carnival, and ships will be parked offshore most days, shuttling to-and-fro the 1 percenters who belong on board. For those less fearful of really digging into the local culture (and nothing says "digging into the local culture" like getting shitfaced in a resort town), Cabo

Cabo is one of the easiest places in the world to launch epic road trips. Head north up the Baja peninsula and find/build a *palapa*. Photo by Chris Burkard.

is packed with places to stay. The best ones are located on a strip called the **Los Cabos Corridor,** a stretch of beach wide enough for any number of couples to have midnight sex without having to hear each other. Consider **The Bungalows Hotel** or **The Villa del Palmar.**

When you're ready to enter beach-club-party mode, hit up the **Mango Deck** on the beach at the extreme end of the Corridor. Its employees wander the beach spraying tequila out of squirt guns into the mouths of sorority girls who would be rolling up their windows if they drove past the same people on the street back home. It's the most crowded and most fun section of beach in Cabo, with plenty of sketchy guys just waiting to sell banana boat rides to the people too drunk to hang on in the first place.

Further inland are the **Cabo Wabo Cantina** and **Giggling Marlin.** They're less crowded than the Mango Deck, which only means the employees can spend more time forcing shots down your throat.

The Giggling Marlin has a contraption that hangs you upside down from a marlin hook while you take shots. You'll feel similar to the marlin when you're finished.

At night, those Spring Break coeds and the creepy drunkards chasing that tail will be heading to **El Squid Roe**, a multi-leveled bar near the marina that seems to be under the impression that the only sterilization they need will be handled by the alcohol spilled on the floor.

The Mexican morning heat isn't kind to hangovers, but Mexican food sure as shit is. **The Office** is a great place to grease up the stomach lining between blackouts. There are also plenty of food joints inland, like **Sharky's Tacos, Beer and Fun**, or **Tacos Gardenias**. Nicer restaurants exist for the families in resorts, but those operate on a "no shirt, no shoes, no service" policy—Spring Breakers lost those articles of clothing ten minutes after leaving the airport.

FUCKED UP FIRSTHAND

I went to Cabo for Spring Break, as did most people from my school. We all mobbed to the Mango Deck during the day, turning it into the perfect place to see that cute, shy girl from lecture letting forty-year-old Mexican men take body shots off her stomach.

A group of us found a guy on the beach in front of the Deck renting out a banana boat, so I convinced the girl to join us for a nice pleasant ride out to El Arco de Cabo San Lucas, a rock formation just offshore. The ride got bumpy—at one point I popped into the air, stretching my legs out to balance, but I recovered. Can't look too drunk for Lecture Girl.

Back on shore, I was suddenly the most popular person on the beach. Everybody wanted to take pictures with me, and even Lecture Girl seemed into me. I was plastered drunk and happy as can be. That is, until somebody finally pointed out that when I had stretched my legs to balance on the boat, I had torn my board shorts straight down the middle, leaving absolutely nothing to the imagination. I had been too drunk to notice.

I went back to the hotel to change, but people recognized me for the rest of the day as the *hombre* with no shame. In Cabo, that's not a bad thing to be. Lecture Girl certainly didn't mind.

VERDICT
Power cliché.

Colin Heinrich

84. Ibiza, Spain

SEASON: May through September (summer).
IDEAL CONDITIONS: Unlimited monetary supply for evening cocktails at Café Mambo watching the sky turn colors while the DJs spin.
DAYTIME ACTIVITY: Swimming, Castle of Ibiza.
LODGING RECOMMENDATIONS: Brisa Hotel, San Antonio.
INGESTIBLES: Wine and beer, cocktails from everywhere, chicken curry from Kanya, greasy breakfast at one of the Irish pubs around San Antonio.

In the 1950s, hippies were drawn to Ibiza's postcard beaches. The rich and famous followed suit. Now every other flip-flop-clad backpacker can be spotted shuffling to house music in **Space** or sipping a cocktail in **San Antonio Bay**. The most popular choices to stay are either in San Antonio or Ibiza Town. Choose **San Antonio**. It has beaches and more clubs than Bangkok has tuk tuks.

"But when will I sleep?" When you're retired. Or at least at home. Don't do Ibiza half-assed.

On your first day, wander the streets of **West End**. Ticketing offices and even clothing stores advertise and sell party tickets at every corner. Club promoters are everywhere. Yes, they may be annoyingly persistent, especially during high season, but they have good deals.

Choose your party purchase wisely. Particularly in late May (opening parties) or early September (closing parties), high-end clubs such as **Pacha** and Space charge €40 to €80 ($52 to $104 USD) per ticket. Topping this, the average price for a standard drink (e.g., vodka lemon) costs $15 USD. And since clubs are scattered all over, you'll have to budget for a taxi, too ($13 to $40 USD depending on location).

But not all is crazy expensive in Ibiza. For dinner and a pre-party beer, go to **Kanya**, a funky restaurant and bar at the furthest tip of Sunset Strip. Get there early and snag yourself a spot by the pool.

At night, club promoters will come up to you offering amazing drink deals to one up their many competitors. Particularly, new and not-yet-known clubs are a steal. **Es Paradis** is located in central San An and offers discounted or even free entry on some nights. Look out for flyers.

If you need a change of scenery, hit **Playa D'en Bossa Beach** and check out **Bora Bora** club, which has daily beach parties free of charge. Think all day chill tunes, with the party getting started at 5:00 P.M. and finishing around 5:00 A.M.

Ibiza Town (also known as Eivissa) is overrated, but if you have an urge to check it out, go to **Zoo Bar**, located opposite the port for some relaxed cocktails in their massive outside seating area.

Things to remember:

- Supermarkets are your friends. Buy booze before you go out. Don't rely on getting fucked up in a bar unless you've got bank. Same goes for food.
- It's impossible to overdress. Look sloppy and you may not get into high-end clubs.
- It may be pricey, but splash out on at least one big party in a major club. You are in Ibiza after all. Watch the film *It's All Gone Pete Tong* to get a feel.

FUCKED UP FIRSTHAND

No longer squashed between strangers' sweaty pits, boobs, and balls, I finally have space to dance. The *doof doof* sound of David Guetta's record scratching makes my arms fling awkwardly back and forth.

"You're the most beautiful girl in here!" he says to me. I roll my eyes and laugh at this. Pacha is full of gorgeous girls. I smile at my best friend, who has a guy's arms wrapped around her waist.

At 10:00 A.M. we leave the club. Pacha is stunning, it's high ceilings and chandeliers making it seem like a castle. Once we hit the concrete outside, I shield my eyes from the sun with one hand while unfastening the sweaty straps on my heels with the other.

VERDICT

Forget you have a boyfriend or girlfriend.

Larissa Peuckert-Coleman

85. Melbourne, Australia

SEASON: December through March, especially January and February (summer).
IDEAL CONDITIONS: Peak of summer festival season.
DAYTIME ACTIVITY: Hiking the Dandenongs, just outside the city, accessible by bus.
LODGING RECOMMENDATIONS: The Nunnery hostel (budget), Middle Park Hotel (boutique bed and breakfast), passing out on St. Kilda Beach.
INGESTIBLES: Victorian Bitter, Melbourne Bitter, goon, whiskey and marijuana, Chinese dumplings, falafel souvlaki, and breakfast at Collective Espresso in Camberwell.

To experience Melbourne in all its liver-ruining glory, take advantage of the highly efficient tram network, which combined with the city's relatively small size and endless number of bacchanalian hangouts, ensures that a single delirious odyssey covers a lot of ground without the risk of sobering up in between pints. And unlike most public parklands in which even a rum–and-raisin gelato is likely to be seized by the police, **Edinburgh Gardens** in North Fitzroy is generally left to its own devices. To keep Monday-morning blues at arms' length, spend the Sunday-after idling under a haze of pot smoke enjoying an acoustic session from local musicians among the trees by the bandstand.

Fitzroy is Melbourne's hipster central and there are lots of pubs serving craft beer. **The Grace Darling** on Smith Street, named after a nineteenth-century heroine, has a thoughtful selection of draft brews, a basement bar dedicated to whiskey stupors, and a seasonal menu whose Sunday roast is served in cast-iron pots. It's rad.

For something entirely local, try finding the elusive **Standard Hotel** on Fitzroy Street. It's Melbourne's best beer garden, with a take-out beer menu and a strong emphasis on real bands and musicians, so there's no risk of being molested by pretentious synth-heavy art-house trendies.

Behind the tiny bar at the **Black Cat** on Brunswick Street they'll rustle up fresh pizza. Outside in the beer garden, a Hunter S. Thompson mural encourages subversive thoughts.

There are boundless BYOB eateries but the manic dumpling houses in the Central Business District (CBD) Chinatown are the best, with endless menu options and no-nonsense service. Goon (cask wine) is the cheapest option for group BYOB but beware of gnarly hangovers.

The CBD is also the place for panoramic views of the city. Being served Pimms by staff in 1950s lawn tennis attire at **Madame Brussels** on Bourke Street is a novel experience, or try the **Campari House** rooftop on Hardware Lane for beering, hot dogs, and the occasional open-air movie.

When climbing stairs to rooftops becomes a struggle, try **Section 8** in Tattersalls Lane, a stone's throw from Chinatown. The graffitied brickwork, wooden pallet benches, and a shipping container serving as an outdoor bar strikes the perfect balance between brown bagging it in a back alley and stumbling across a once secret hip-hop syndicate.

As you descend toward corporeal ruination, venture further south to St. Kilda for some skid row wantonness. A beachside mix of backpackers, prostitutes, tattoo shops, late-night bars, and the Jewish quarter of Balaclava, St. Kilda seems to be the natural conclusion on any serious drunk. **Yellow Bird** on Chapel Street is a must on Tijuana Tuesdays for margaritas and homemade Mexican food. The cavernous **Esplanade Hotel** is a key music venue, while **The Vineyard** is possibly the drinking equivalent of Dante's Inferno. If you need a breather, pull up a milk crate and join the local hobos for whom the grass outside is both home and pub. You might find yourself wishing you'd brought a dictaphone because you sure as hell won't remember any of their outrageous tales come morning.

NOTES FROM A LOCAL
If you've failed to fully ingest enough alcohol, weave your way to Chinatown's dankest, most uninviting laneway that is Croft Alley and the **Croft Institute** therein, apparently the materialization of a mad scientist's chimera. Leave a trail of bread crumbs in order to find your way back.

VERDICT
A bridge between Europe's left-of-center haunts and the young boisterous Australia's drinking culture.

Tom Ansell

86. Puerto Vallarta, Mexico

SEASON: November through May (dry season).
IDEAL CONDITIONS: Nonstop fiestas during Christmas and New Year's.
DAYTIME ACTIVITY: Explore the Rio Cuale.

Don't just stay in Puerto Vallarta; head south along the coast for wide open beach spots to set up camps with your crew. Photo by Chris Burkard.

LODGING RECOMMENDATIONS: Hotel Posada de Roger (budget), Blue Chairs for an ocean-side room in one the most storied gay hotels in town.
INGESTIBLES: Tacos de pastor (marinated pork), chicharron, ceviche, camarones (shrimp) on a stick, paletas (popsicles), Pacifico beer, tequila, and Suero (fermented cream) for the hangover.

With 322 sunny days per year, a gay-friendly vibe, and a loose interpretation of liquor laws, Puerto Vallarta (PV) is up there on the list of party cities. If you're a gay man, proceed directly to the area of Los Muertos Beach that's called **Blue Chairs** (named after the famed gay hotel it abuts) and get cruising. You can lay out a towel or take a chair under an umbrella, but roped-in areas are hotel run and you'll be required to order from a waiter. Either way, you can enjoy the beats and eye candy.

Lesbians might want to book for February and hit the annual

Vallarta Girl party. No matter when you visit, make sure you get to **Frida's,** if only for their second-floor balcony seating and to say hello to mucho-friendly barkeep Blanca.

The **Zona Romantica** (aka Old Town) is Vallarta's tourist hub. Packed with hotels, restaurants, bars, and taco stands, this historic cobblestoned neighborhood backs into the mountains and is shaped like an amphitheater, making the Zona-after-dark a contained and social place to party. In the daytime, come here to find souvenirs: blankets, silver, and tequila, the latter of which you can find in every flavor and strength as you walk the *malecón* (boardwalk). While there, fuel up on nacho-wrapped hot dogs, *elote* (corn, mayo, cheese), and *churros,* all of which are conveniently absorbent.

Stop at any OXXO and grab a six-pack of Pacifico, or step into one of the many locals for *"un litro."* Drop your butt into the sand and watch the sunset (drinking in public is technically illegal but almost uniformly unenforced). Local mariachis will walk the beach and serenade the sun under the horizon. Around 20 pesos ($1.25 USD) will buy you a song.

The hours between sundown and dinner can be deceptively long, so do as the locals do and siesta. Vallarta will wake you promptly at nine o'clock every night, when the pirate ship anchored in Banderas Bay sets off fireworks. Your nap is over. Got to your balcony and open a beer.

Expect to eat late and take your time. In the Zona, have dinner or pre-drinks on the rooftop patio at **Joe Jack's Fish Shack;** order the ginger mojito, seriously. Once you're fed and lubricated, head over to **Bolero's.** This is a decent place to start the tequila tour, but if you insist on the bar rail, ask for sangrita to cut the aftertaste.

La Noche is a martini bar with table dancers going off to loud music, and televised gay porn. Expect to pay premium prices for drinks. The Zona club crawl will take you to **Paco's Ranch** (locals and drag performances) and **CC Slaughters** (all-night rave). Those looking for camp should visit **The Palm** or **Reinas,** and male strippers can be found at **Antropology.**

Sometime in the morning hours, you're going to get hungry. Time for the taco tour. Here's a taco-stand primer: Each *taquero(a)* serves a different specialty; get the *cebollitas* (fried green onions) if they have them; try the salsas, carefully; *cabeza* means head; and gringo(a) palates will probably like *barbacoa* (barbecue), *birria* (stew), and tacos *de pastor*. By many accounts, the very best *pastor* in town is at **Takos Panchos**, which is not a stand at all, but a small restaurant. Ask anyone, or look for the line on Olas Altas.

Puerto Vallarta tips:

- If you visit over the holidays, don't get sloppy with your accent. *Feliz ano nuevo* means "Happy new anus." Unless it's a very specific kind of New Year's party, you mean *Feliz año nuevo*.
- Street drugs like cocaine, ecstasy, and weed aren't hard to find in Vallarta, but they are illegal and the local policia don't look the other way. You've been warned.
- Get out of Vallarta and party in any of these nearby places: Yelapa (you have to take a water taxi), Sayulita, or Punta de Mita.

FUCKED UP FIRSTHAND

I was invited out to Punta de Mita, a small town about forty minutes north of Vallarta. Mita shows up in the news occasionally because Bill Gates, Ben Affleck, and Kim Kardashian vacation there (separately), and though there's a Four Seasons and a handful of swish restaurants, the village itself is really only a few gravel roads.

After an evening drinking red wine and tequila shots, a bunch of us wobbled into the night. As we passed a house party, revelers called out to us, "*Vamos a bailar!*" so we let ourselves into their yard and I inexpertly led a woman through a frantic salsa in the shadow of the DJ's crackly speakers.

Light and music and people spilled out of **Brenda's Place**, the only joint open at that time of night. Inside the restaurant—Brenda serves breakfast from 9:00 A.M. to noon—a drag queen with a Benatar vibe MC'd a relentless karaoke show.

"Red wine with grapefruit juice, *por favor*." My friend placed her order and turned to me. "It'll help with the hangover."

It didn't, but even my inexorable headache couldn't erase the memory of a Mexican drag queen crooning "Total Eclipse of the Heart" in my ear.

VERDICT

You don't have to be gay to party in Vallarta, but it helps.

Keph Senett

87. Atlantic Beach, North Carolina

SEASON: Summer, especially June and July through early fall.
IDEAL CONDITIONS: Sun, offshore winds, six-foot swell.
DAYTIME ACTIVITY: Surfing, fishing, boating to nearby islands.
LODGING RECOMMENDATIONS: Palm Suites or Sand Dollar Motel for budget.
INGESTIBLES: Cans of Natural Light for boat drinking (don't forget a coozie), hush puppies, coleslaw, Bojangles fried chicken, sweet tea, bourbon.

Located on the Crystal Coast of North Carolina, Atlantic Beach has a certain laid-back vibe that is uniquely Southern. The beach crowd starts the night at **Amos Mosquito's**, where the waitresses have names like "Buttercup" and "Cutie Pie." The **Tackle Box** is your quintessential beach bum bar for cheap drinks and cornhole matches out back. Go to **Monkey Bar and Grill** for $3.50 margaritas on Wednesday. Drop some money in the jukebox at **Beach Tavern**. Sit at the bar or get hustled by a local at one of the pool tables.

The largest crowds will be across the bridge at the Morehead City waterfront. Drop by **Jack's Waterfront Bar** for a drink on the deck. The **Arendell Room** is a traditional cocktail bar with more than thirty varieties of bourbon, and there's live music on the back porch on Tuesdays. Grab some fish tacos at **Ruddy Duck Tavern**.

Cross the other bridge toward the Beaufort waterfront. **Backstreet Pub** is filled with sons of sailors catching a microbrew. If you're looking for that special hole in the wall, cut over to the **Royal James Cafe**. If the sun is setting (or even if it's not) hit up the "rhum bar" at **Front Street Grill** and stand on the back patio overlooking the inlet. **The Dockhouse** is your best chance for chatting up the captain of that yacht that just docked.

After an all-nighter, head over to **Georgia B's** for French toast.

If you're here in the summer, rent a boat or, better yet, hitch a ride to **Shackleford Banks** (locals call it "Shack"), a small barrier island inhabited by wild horses. You will see people gathered on one boat, and then abandon ship for another vessel when the beer runs out. On the shore, people play horseshoes and bocce while grilling out. On the waterway, people ride jet skis way too fast after drinking too many Natural Lights. Bring sunscreen.

Rules for Atlantic Beach:

- Booze is permitted on the beach. No glass.
- Hard liquor is only sold at ABC stores.
- Be sure to secure a ride back from Shack. Many a sloppy drunk has gotten marooned there overnight.

NOTES FROM A LOCAL
Your tourist experience isn't complete until you've gotten a sunburn, had a few boilermakers at BT's (Beach Tavern), and staggered to the ocean for a night swim.

VERDICT
Hard-pressed to find nicer people anywhere.

Noah Pelletier

88. Utila, Honduras

SEASON: December through April, August for Sunjam.
IDEAL CONDITIONS: Any breeze keeping the sandflies away.
DAYTIME ACTIVITY: Diving.
LODGING RECOMMENDATIONS: Mango Inn (hostel/budget), Caribbean Dream (cheap furnished apartments), and hammocks on the UDC (Utila Dive Center) dock for siesta.
INGESTIBLES: Local brews Salva Vida and Port Royal, eighteen-year Flor de Caña rum, baleadas from street vendors. Hangover-abolishing "diver's breakfast" (Munchies). Caught-an-hour-ago lobster (Babalu). Cocaine, rendering food irrelevant.

Known as "The Rock" by backpackers, dive bums, and functioning alcoholics alike, the smallest of the Bay Islands is harder to leave than Alcatraz. There are only a few bars scattered down two streets,

Synchronized floating at Cayos Cochinos, Honduras. Photo by Scott Sporleder.

but with a constantly changing crowd of travelers, the party never ends. Salva Vida, Port Royal, and Flor de Caña are pretty much the same price across town (34 lempira; 20 lemps equals $1 USD). Every dive shop has dorm beds and a bar.

Kick things off with a few sunset Salvas on UDC's dock following your afternoon dive—the bar is conveniently located between the boats and the gear room.

When it gets dark, check out **Babalu** (Utila's oldest dock bar), made of pieces of sheet metal, old pipes, and various other flotsam. Pick a fresh lobster from the heap on the bar ($10 USD). Try the home brew *ron ponche* if you're feeling bold. Ask Dado for the whole two-liter plastic bottle if you're feeling suicidal.

Main Street Lounge serves wicked enchiladas. **El Picante** has nachos and homemade guac. Try **RJ's** for barracuda, snapper, and whatever else someone caught that day. Vegetarians can order a plate of sides—potatoes, rice, and salad—from most places. Carnivores? Get a steak from **Driftwood**.

After dinner, go to another dock bar—**Tranquila** or **Coco Loco**—and start drinking Flor de Caña if you haven't already. Switch to Cuervo during happy hour. Head up Cola de Mico to **Treetanic** where Neil, owner and artistic genius, has spent over a decade creating a ship among the mango trees from beer bottles, shells, and other shiny fragments. Stumble to **Bar in the Bush** on Wednesdays and Fridays. No one remembers what happens here.

Go home. Stop at the corner for a *baleada*—cheese, eggs, and some kind of meat in a fresh tortilla. Hydrate and pop an Utila-style 1,000mg ibuprofen. If/when you wake up, head to **Munchies** or **Bundu** for breakfast. Get a plastic bag full of freshly squeezed *jugo de naranja* from the guy at the corner of Main and Cola de Mico.

Skid Row is home to the infamous Guifiti Challenge: four shots of traditional Garifuna herb-infused moonshine and a T-shirt for $10 USD. Tuesday is ladies' night at **La Pirata** and Bay Islands College of Diving hosts a weekly karaoke. Look for the **Cake Lady** pushing her bicycle down Main Street most afternoons; she sells homemade chocolate cupcakes, as well as ganja cupcakes with rainbow sprinkles.

Upon getting Dive Master certified, most shops make you endure a snorkel test: strap a mask over your face, put the snorkel in your mouth, and swallow whatever gets poured into the cut-off two-liter plastic bottle taped to the top—rum, beer, hot sauce, the occasional raw egg.

During **Semana Santa** (Easter week), **Carnival** (July), and **Sunjam** (August), prices skyrocket and accommodation books up. Plan ahead.

FUCKED UP FIRSTHAND

I'm so high I can't even eat the olives off my pizza. Maya and Fernando and I finish our rum and climb onto his motorbike. I wrap my arms around Fer's bare stomach; my chest sticks to his back in the heat. Maya, her hands on my waist and her chin over my shoulder, starts singing Queen's "Don't Stop Me Now."

Treetanic's mosaic-tiled stairs are cool beneath my bare feet; the floorboards are sticky with rum and beer. Maya hijacks the stereo and Freddie Mercury reclaims the song she started. She drags me behind the bar, pouring Cuervo down my throat and over my chin.

I don't remember getting to Bar in the Bush. I'm trying to leave until Ollie places me on his yellow dirt bike: "I can take you home, or I can give you some MDMA and bring you back to the party." I wake up to Maya speaking in heated Spanish to Fer, and then in English: "Don't fucking touch me." She leaves and slams the door. I try to sit up; black static blooms before my eyes and I almost throw up. My flight leaves in an hour.

The sun's hammering the airstrip's old black tarmac and throbbing up through the soles of my feet, my stomach and brain, and the backs of my eyes. My heart rate is still out of control. I haven't owned shoes in six months; when I board the six-seater plane, I'm wearing my neoprene booties.

VERDICT

Kind of place where you can do shots with a dude in an Aloha shirt who later turns out to be the attending physician.

Alana Seldon

89. Zanzibar, Tanzania

SEASON: February, July through September.
IDEAL CONDITIONS: 90 degrees Fahrenheit (32 degrees Celsius) and sunny, with a salty sea breeze.
DAYTIME ACTIVITY: Zanzibar was central to the nineteenth-century slave trade and spice trade fusing Moorish, Arab, Persian, Indian, and European elements; do some sightseeing.
LODGING RECOMMENDATIONS: Princess Salme Inn, Annex II Guest House, Warere (cheap, Stone Town), Africa House Hotel, Zanzibar Coffee House, Serena Hotel for more luxe. East Coast Beaches: Teddy's Place. North Coast: Kendwa Rocks.
INGESTIBLES: Octopus, calamari, fish, lobster, coconut bread, Konyagi (gin-like substance served in sachets), pilau, spices, herbs (legal and illegal), sugar cane juice.

There are three things you need to know about Zanzibar. First, it has insanely pristine beaches. Second, it's where pirates and sultans came to party. Third, Freddie Mercury was born here.

Stone Town, the small district of Zanzibar's capital and a seventeenth-century UNESCO World Heritage Site, bustles with burqa-covered women, speeding scooters, annoying touts yelling "Jambo music? Snorkeling? Dolphins? Spice Market?" along with old men on their way to pray in one of the city's many mosques.

Arriving by ferry from mainland Tanzania, **Mercury's Bar** (no relation to Freddie) awaits just outside the gate. Beers are reasonably priced ($2 USD), sundowners on the patio are a must, and an evening's entertainment is watching foreign tourists attempt to dance "African" to live music on the weekends.

Diving a little deeper into the winding archway, **Tatu Lounge** is a good place to start a night. A rickety wooden three-story bar/restaurant/lounge with ocean views, it's where foreign chicks go to get seriously hit on by muscular Zanzibari dreads. The hardest part is making it back down the practically vertical wooden staircase. A buddy system is recommended, even for the sober.

There's no skipping the **Forodhani** food market to pad the stomach for inevitable shots of Konyagi soon to follow. **Livingstone Beach Restaurant** is just a few meters down the beach from Forodhani, and has a killer renovated beachfront patio, live music, and a dance floor that picks up around midnight. Stock up on drinks early; securing a cold Kilimanjaro beer isn't easy when the place is packed.

If you can get to Stone Town in February, there's no excuse for missing **Sauti Za Busara** ("Voice of Wisdom," in Swahili), a massive five-day music, culture, seafood, and booze-fueled party held in the supreme setting of a seventeenth-century Omani fortress.

There's a sandbar a few kilometers off Zanzibar that disappears during high tide, but is known to have occasional DJ parties. Ask around for DJ Nani, he'll know what's up.

Don't go to **Bawani Club** sober. It's Zanizibar's only real "club," and often described as a place to avoid until your judgment is impaired enough to actually love it. Pool tables and drinks are upstairs, Bongo flava (Tanzanian rap and hip-hop) music and strobe lights heavily pound the dance floor downstairs.

Kendwa Rocks, an hour and a half drive to the north tip of Zanzibar, hosts a sloppy and picturesque full-moon party every month, usually on the closest Saturday. It's the best place to find blond girls with British flag bikinis on their gap year, get wasted on the beach, and dance until sunrise. Don't even bother booking a hotel. You won't sleep, and can catch a dala-dala bus back to town in the morning.

A few things to note about partying in Zanzibar:

- It's still a conservative Muslim island. Off the beaches, keep your clothes on. Be respectful.
- Condoms are difficult to find. Plan ahead.
- The bribe for getting caught having sex on the beach by police is around $20 USD, after serious negotiations.

NOTES FROM A LOCAL
You can't party in Kendwa without "dipping skin."

FUCKED UP FIRSTHAND
I woke up soaked in boozy sweat and bloody sheets. With fifteen people crammed into a rented four-bedroom apartment, the competition for mosquito nets was fierce, and I had evidently failed. As I stumbled my way through an orgy of bodies scattered across the floor in search of water, my friend Paige was making her way out as well. "I just woke on the floor covered in octopus tentacles and money and have no idea what happened, or where I've been. I assume it was a good night," she said.

I attempted to piece together my memories from the night before: tequila shots, several empty Konyagi bottles. Skinny-dipping with a group of Iranians as, unbeknownst to us, hotel guards leered on. Going clubbing soaking wet—or, wait, did they kick us out for that?

Assuming I didn't contract malaria, it was a good night.

VERDICT
Ganja-smoking rastas with horny middle-aged European divorcées, volunteer medical students from Berlin with greasy Italians, all amid conservative Muslim culture and seventeenth-century sultan architecture as you stagger your way home to the call of prayer.

Jonathan Kalan

8: Baller

We've almost made it home. Which, as one author in this chapter put it, is "where you were headed all along." By now you know that there are all different places and styles for getting fucked up. Many of these have been global cities—places whose cultures, geographies, expatriate communities, and histories have progressed in a certain way as to become, as the saying goes, "infamous" for nightlife.

We've saved this last selection though for places that have some other indefinable ingredient. What is it about Tel Aviv or San Francisco or Buenos Aires that enables—all out normalizes—behavior that would land you in jail most anywhere else? Is it just the way populations have evolved? What is it they've come for, or migrated from, that has created this environment?

You'll have to go find out.

90. Buenos Aires, Argentina*

SEASON: March through May (fall), September through November (spring), beautiful days, less heat.

IDEAL CONDITIONS: A Sunday afternoon stroll up Calle Defensa to Parque Lezama holding hands with your new lover.

DAYTIME ACTIVITY: Check out the Reserva Ecológica along the Costanera Sur for a quick escape from the pavement.

LODGING RECOMMENDATIONS: Airbnb (or similar) for an apartment (San Telmo or Palermo) to live more like a local, Circus Hostel, Pop Hotel, ChillHouse, Millhouse Youth Hostel.

INGESTIBLES: Locally raised steak, cheap marijuana, cheap delicious Malbec and other vino tinto, empanadas, chorizo stands, caipirinhas, Quilmes Lager.

Sexy *tangueros* are in all of Buenos Aires's touristy plazas, like Plaza Dorrego in San Telmo or Plaza Serrano in Palermo. Photo by Kate Siobhan.

The rumors are true. No matter how fucked up you've ever been, the place to test out your all-nighter skills is Buenos Aires, where the weekend has very undefined boundaries and 6:00 A.M. is the perfect time to head to the next party, not to bed.

Local *porteños* are professionals at going all night on a Tuesday and still looking fucking good at work come Wednesday. To keep up, you're going to need a whole lot of energy drinks (or even better, habituate to drinking mate), some swag clothes, and the ability to let go of any notion of an itinerary—spontaneity is key.

Drinking can start in the daytime. Happy hours are a great place to kick back, generally from 3:00 to 7:00 P.M. The rookie mistake is eating dinner at a "reasonable" hour. Locals don't eat until 9:00 or 10:00 P.M. Take in a few happy hour drinks from 3:00 to 6:00 P.M. (often accompanied by a *merienda,* usually mate and pastries or a platter of meats, cheeses, olives, nuts, etc.). Then nap and gear up for an epic night. *Boliches* (nightclubs) start grooving about midnight or 1:00 A.M., but you'll likely hit a few lines. Dress for the weather if you'll be waiting, but always dress well. The last thing you want is an epic invite but get turned down for wearing sneakers.

As far as which *boliche?* **Niceto Club** has stood the test of time. **The Basement Club,** which lives below the **Shamrock** (an Irish pub), has cheap drinks (can be hard to come by), and decent tunes. It caters to both *porteños* and ex-pats, and can be a better "entry" into BsAs nightlife. Another easy entry is **Crobar,** a guaranteed good time with talented DJs and an always packed house. **State** at Alsina is another solid place to see visiting international DJs.

Some alternative-style *boliches:* **The Roxy Disco,** for the more rock 'n roll vibe, and **Bahrein** is multi-leveled with different music from commercial to dirty/sexy/sweaty, as well as a chill-out room on each floor. **Amerika** is epic, a huge gay disco that's hetero-friendly, with two dance floors. **Jet Lounge** has more of a lounge vibe, and **Congo,** a grittier, basement-like bar and unpretentious crowd.

There are other options if dancing isn't your thing. **Ocho7Ocho** is a "secret" bar with no sign, just an address and a doorman. It's lower key, but great for groups looking to drink and chat. Or, there's **Squat House.** They take over a space and throw a party, but the location isn't announced until the day of. You have to Google it. Another option is **La Ferona Social Club,** which is literally an apartment. Funky and trendy, there's lots of mingling and it gets jampacked.

Is it 6:00 A.M. yet? Congratulations. You've made it to afterparty hours. That's right. It's not over. If you've been working hard, you're hopefully off to someone's private after-party but if not, no problem, head over to **Miloca.** You can keep on dancing and watch the sun come up. If 7:00 or 8:00 A.M. isn't quite enough for you, try **Cocoliche,** where the dance party keeps going until 1:00 P.M. Is 1:00 P.M. not enough? There's also **Caix,** a concrete dance haven where on Sundays, hard-core party people pay $50 USD to keep on going until (seriously?) 3:00 P.M.

Buenos Aires is huge. The idea here is not to hit up every place on this list, but rather hit up one or two, and let the night take you wherever it may.

BsAs tips:

- There's a secret bar within the secret bar of Ocho7Ocho. Just walk all the way to the back of the first bar. Sometimes there's a private party back there, but, hey, that makes for an even better story.
- Don't take what you can't lose. As with any nightclub anywhere, snagging a wallet or purse is a piece of cake.
- BsAs is not cheap, nor are many of these party places. If you want to go all night long, be willing to fork out the cash.

FUCKED UP FIRSTHAND

Freshly arrived in Buenos Aires, friends of ours called us up. "To-night," they said, "it's on." After a midday nap, we binged on carne at Don Julio. I literally shed a few tears.

After dinner we lined up at Congo, near our apartment in Palermo. Thirty minutes in line was enough to make friends with those in front and behind us, so once we got in, around 1:00 A.M., it was go time. Congo is a bit gritty, but the dancing was hot and sweaty and the drinks were reasonable.

Somewhere around 4:00 A.M., as I started to get delirious (my average bedtime being ten o'clock), we snagged a taxi with a group of about twenty others. We went to another bar whose name no one is certain of anymore. There was no line at 4:00 A.M., but the place was jammed with sweaty bodies and the scent of youthful people being alive. Rotating between the dance floor and some couches (don't sit too long or it's all over), before I knew it, it was 7:00 A.M.

By BsAs standards, this was a regular weeknight. I, however, felt like a champion.

VERDICT
Practice makes perfect.

Kate Siobhan

91. Barcelona, Spain

SEASON: March through August (spring and summer).
IDEAL CONDITIONS: On the streets after an FC Barcelona win.
DAYTIME ACTIVITY: Architecture touring, check out Sagrada Familia, Casa Batlló, and Casa Amatller.
LODGING RECOMMENDATIONS: Rent an apartment through ViveBarcelona .com.
INGESTIBLES: Fishy tapas, jamon iberico (cured ham), Manchego cheese, sangria, mojitos, coconuts on the beach, paella, cortados, chupitos (shots), cava.

Throughout the year, wanderlusting, multi-generational party-seekers travel to Barcelona, or BCN as cool people abbreviate it, many remaining to embrace the Mediterranean and the opportunity to nap on a daily basis without tan lines or scorn.

On a clear day, nurse your hangover at **La Barceloneta**, a seminude beach where you can take in the sights of sexy students and saggy Spanish man-boobs or doze off while soaking in the healing effect of the Spanish sun (just keep your belongings within reach). When the coastal drizzle falls, explore the indoor forest at **Sagrada Familia**, Gaudí's famous, ethereal, and offensive cathedral, or check out **Museu Picasso**.

BCN is well known for its nightlife, but day drinking is a well-practiced, acceptable, and even encouraged way to lead into your siesta. Stacked buildings line narrow streets, and each block usually harbors a few, if not several, family owned cafés; scope all of them, or better yet, settle on one near the beach and get to know the staff. Failing to do this can mean your order of sangria is a pitcher laced with a Dole fruit-cup. For a sure bet, try **Café de Los Angelitos** in La Barceloneta and order a mojito.

Swim or drink your way to an ample appetite and try a mass consumption of whatever is being sold or served at the **Mercat de Sant Josep de la Boqueria,** BCN's most famous and over-the-top market. You can find fresh juice, local produce, live crab, candies, cured meats, cheeses, and an assortment of animal parts on ice. If you're interested in something a little more traditional, most restaurants will serve a "*menu del dia,*" a three-course meal often including a glass of wine for €10 to €15 ($13 to $20 USD).

Dinnertime arrives late; between nine and ten o'clock is typical. Tapas restaurants serve a handful of house plates and every menu includes a salty and spicy combination of *patatas bravas,* Spain's version of a French fry. As the majority of tapas restaurants do not have a printed menu, mealtime is the occasion when you need to speak Spanish or have a companion who can. Otherwise you're stuck with a crude "pick and point method" at the bar-top cabinet display. Finish with any form of espresso; I strongly suggest a cortado, you'll appreciate the caffeine when you are still drinking and dancing early into tomorrow.

Well-fed and a little buzzed, request *la cuenta* and leave an additional 10 percent for gratuity. If it's early in the week take the train to **Sala Apolo** on La Rambla. The long-ass line and pricey cover are worth the rave-like experience with badass DJs and a light show, complete with stiff-as-fuck cocktails and possible key bumps in the bathroom. If it's the weekend, head to **Razzmatazz** or the *discotecas* on the beach. These clubs give you astounding sunrises on the *playa* as you stumble out at 5:00 or 6:00 A.M. Younger travelers insist on **Espit Chupitos** in L'Eixample. The shots are weak but cheap and served on fire or in flare fashion. Order "The Boyscout" and leave within twenty minutes to avoid boredom and a newbie-style hangover.

Barcelona will silently share its passion during the daylight through nap-taking and sit-ins, and then throw you on your face with amazing festivals and nightlife. It's always cool to eavesdrop or join in.

FUCKED UP FIRSTHAND

The crowd stood thick and smelled of booze and sweat. We found the most comfortable and ambiguous seat in the bar; in truth it was a windowsill on the stairway supporting an old air conditioner with just enough room for four of us. We had an expansive view of both stories, along with the big-screen TV.

We swallowed pints of Guinness and tumbled into a love for soccer. We had thought an Irish pub would be less crowded than others; in fact, we were among the last few allowed to enter the building.

The crowd busted out a surprising "We Are the Champions," as Barca seized the World Cup. We flowed to the streets to celebrate. Red light spewed from all directions and blanketed the crowd as people lit flares. Flags rose, horns shrieked, kids shimmied up light poles and shouted. A mere six hours earlier we had escaped the same block in haste as police fired rubber bullets at young protesters, all to prepare the park for an astounding achievement or soul-crushing defeat.

VERDICT
¡Olé!

Sarah Briggs

92. Brighton, United Kingdom

SEASON: April through September (fair weather, late spring, summer, and the first color of autumn).
IDEAL CONDITIONS: A sunny weekend day, drifting aimlessly through The North Laines.
DAYTIME ACTIVITY: Tour the funky interior of the Royal Pavillion.
LODGING RECOMMENDATIONS: Kipps Hotel in Old Stein (really a hostel) or a bed and breakfast in Kemp Town.
INGESTIBLES: Ale and lagers, fresh vegetarian food, Sunday roasts.

Even the Prince Regent knew where to get fucked up in England. Two hundred years ago he built a tacky home modeled on the Indian Taj Mahal known as **The Brighton Pavillion** where he'd go down for the weekend with mistresses to drink, gamble, and test the mattresses. Hence the term a "dirty weekend" in Brighton. You will see it there today, a monument to mischief.

The hub of the city is called **The North Laines.** It's a network of small streets lined with bars, restaurants, shops, and stalls selling bric-a-brac goodies. Go to **Bill's Restaurant** for some seriously tasty fresh food. The walls are decorated with hampers of chutneys, jams, and oils (you will feel like you're eating in a giant chef's cupboard).

Duck into **The Basketmakers Arms** for a pint of quality ale, checking the notes customers have scribbled on and stuffed into old tins on the walls. Stop off at **The Dorset** for a cold pint and some prime people watching. Across the road is **Komedia** (a place to keep an eye on for any live music or comedy). Wind around the corner on an evening and try to catch some free live jazz or blues by the crusty old guys at **Fitzherberts**. You'll want to check out **The Great Eastern,** too, whose arsenal of whiskey will contribute to your enjoyment and slurred-word levels. **Las Iguanas** often has two-for-one deals that hover just above £5 ($6.50 USD) on potent cocktails.

Head two minutes south by foot and you'll come to **The South Laines.** The pathways are narrower and they lead to a few great pubs. **The Hop Poles** is one of Brighton's oldest and is rightfully known for its food. After a swift pint there you'll be about ready to see the seashore. About fifty paces south and you're clambering your way along the pebbled beach. Go to **The Fortune of War** and order a plastic pint of something cold before you nestle into the beach and watch the sunset behind the burned skeleton of **The West Pier.**

Don't go to West Street. It's like the characters from the *Jersey Shore* multiplied and took over a small chunk of the city. Go for a grimy night of shuddering basslines, sweat, and laughter at **The Volks. Concorde 2** is always worth a visit, too; it's a massive venue that dots its calendar with live music and funky dress-up and themed events.

Hand in hand with getting fucked up in Brighton is the Sunday roast. Go to the **Setting Sun** if the time of day coincides with the name and you'll enjoy a top-class roast with a good array of wine, beer, and numerous stronger options. If there's live football on and you want to get fucked up with fanatics while tucking into a roast, go to **The Geese,** which is in the same area (Hanover). Overall, Brightonians put a lot of effort into keeping the entertainment calendar eclectic, and the close proximity of everything allows you to stumble your way blissfully through town.

NOTES FROM A LOCAL

Duck in and out of as many pubs and bars as possible.

VERDICT

Dirty weekend.

Dikson

93. Montreal, Quebec

SEASON: May through September, especially June and July.

IDEAL CONDITIONS: Warm enough for terasse drinking.

DAYTIME ACTIVITY: Kayaking, surfing the Lachine Rapids (or just hanging out by the river).

LODGING RECOMMENDATIONS: Hotel Quartier Latin for budget, Hostel Alexandrie-Montreal for hostel.

INGESTIBLES: Wine, microwbrews, marijuana, sangria, poutine with squeaky cheese curds (La Banquise), a smoked meat sandwich (Schwartz's), a Montreal bagel (St. Viateur).

Montreal is the greatest party city in Canada. Maybe in all of North America. Maybe the universe. If you're a tourist, you'll go to **Crescent Street** where women in nine-inch hot pink heels spill out onto the streets and plainclothes firemen drive by on their trucks seemingly at random. If it's *terasse* season, watch the scene unfold from **Sir Winston Churchill.** Go to **Brutopia** for cheap $5 USD pints on a weekday, or **Hurley's** for Irish music.

Montrealers know that the best parties are on **Saint-Denis Street** and **Saint-Laurent Street.** Saint-Laurent has more posh clubs, like **Café Méliès,** where the sangria comes garnished with a slice of orange. **Tokyo** has the best outdoor *terasse,* but you wouldn't know it until you made it past the disco. **Big in Japan** is a Japanese-themed whiskey bar where you're led through a weird hallway covered in fabric to the back where food and drink are served cafeteria

Montreal is a juxtaposition of poutine, cold winters, and some of the world's biggest river waves, which people surf right in the city. Photo by Alex Rykov.

style. Just outside is **Patati Patata** with $5 USD burgers and $3 USD beers.

Saint-Denis is the pub hub. **La Distillerie** is for when you want mason jars filled with alcohol that will make you blind. **Le Saint Bock** is for microbrews and the best nachos you've never had. **Mâche** also has moderately priced beers and kickass $6 USD *poutine*.

In the Old Port, go to a rooftop bar. **Suite 701** is filled with sexy businessmen catching a drink after work. If those views don't excite you, you'll have a panoramic look at the city's oldest buildings, including the Notre-Dame Basilica.

If you're here in the summer, go to the TamTams drum circle at **Parc du Mont-Royal.** When you first see it you might think there's nothing but weirdo hippies and losers banging on drums and getting high as fuck. But then you'll notice the thousands of Montrealers sprawled out across the field on blankets or tossing Frisbees in the grass. A DJ booth is set up at the **Mordecai Richler Gazebo** for impromptu dance parties, and there's a larping area further into the woods if you want to sign over your virginity.

Check for festivals. **Grand Prix, Osheaga, Jazz Fest,** etc. Montreal is a festival city. Come to **Piknic Electronik** at **Parc Jean-Drapeaux.** Live DJs spin for hipsters and party people from 3:00 to 9:00 P.M. If you pack a picnic, you're allowed to bring wine and beer. The admission is $14 USD. Bring condoms.

Finally, remember these general rules about Montreal:

- Booze is ridic cheap compared to the rest of Canada—you can buy a twenty-four-pack of beer for $15 USD.
- You can purchase alcohol at the *dépanneur* (convenience store).
- As soon as spring hits, it becomes *terasse* season . . . meaning almost every restaurant, pub, and club has a patio, deck, or rooftop area.
- Thursday is a big party night out, with lots of happy hour specials. Plan accordingly.
- *Apportez votre vin* means "Bring your own wine." You can do this at many restaurants.

FUCKED UP FIRSTHAND

Sunday evening. I'm disheveled and unshowered and working away at my laptop in the devastating summer heat. My apartment is a shithole. I sleep on a dirty mattress with a pillow that smells like breakfast.

My roommates—two dudes I found in a classifieds ad—are fantastic. James, the American, shows up and announces that some people are coming over for a barbecue. I pull on some decent clothes as a hoard of people show up. Tons of handsome men—Moroccans, Belgians, French—they all speak French, and barely English, but they're friendly and offer me beer.

We barbecue on the back deck, then gather a collection of paper plates and cutlery and head up to the illegal rooftop. A French guy living in the upper apartment pops his head out the window and introduces himself. Soon, he joins us. What I didn't know about this rooftop is that there is an abandoned bar space. We eat our barbecue and I sit cross-legged on the floor with a girl from Quebec City. She tells me she's terribly self-conscious of her English, and is embarrassed to be speaking to me. And here I am, in her French province, barely able to muster a "*Comment ça va?*"

Somebody has boxed wine and the French guy from the other apartment has tequila. The only light we have is from Saint-Laurent, and surprisingly, the stars.

VERDICT

Poussez means "push."

Candice Walsh

94. Las Vegas, Nevada

SEASON: April through September.
IDEAL CONDITIONS: Winning.
DAYTIME ACTIVITY: Get up to the Spring Mountains National Recreation Area, only thirty minutes from downtown.
LODGING RECOMMENDATIONS: All the world-famous resorts you already know by name.
INGESTIBLES: Any cocktail you can drink too many of, whatever food room service claims will cure a hangover fastest.

Ah, Vegas, where the everyman can escape monotonous life into a world of flashing lights and old people shitting themselves because the next pull is gonna hit a jackpot . . . it has to. This town's come a long way since the days of mob bosses breaking your legs after a lucky streak; these days, naïve families photograph the Bellagio

Fremont Street, with its barrel vault canopy for those intoxicated enough, plus pedestrian mall and casino. Photo by Holly Clark.

fountains for their scrapbook while trying desperately to avoid staring at armless Fred Flintstone peeing on the tree behind them. At night, flocks of drunken singles with more hair product above the neck than brains wander through the streets like a well-dressed zombie apocalypse.

Those looking for wholesome family fun will be staying in fringe resorts like Circus Circus and New York, New York, or worse . . . off the Strip entirely. But nobody goes to Vegas to see the suburbs. Jump straight into the action by staying at the **Aria Resort and Casino**. As the hub of Vegas's new CityCenter initiative, the Aria is the nicest hotel in Vegas. It's the first choice for married businessmen when it comes to bringing prostitutes back to the penthouse suite they took out a second mortgage to afford.

Next door is **The Cosmopolitan**. It's not as lavish, but it leases several floors and a patio to **Marquee Nightclub and Dayclub,** which books world-renowned DJs like Avicii and Calvin Harris. On the other side of Las Vegas Boulevard is the world-famous **MGM Grand,** the oldest resort on the Strip. Here, unattended toddlers pound on the glass to the lion exhibit while their parents sip cocktails they think Muhammad Ali or Frank Sinatra would have liked. The pool area hosts the MGM's seasonal dayclub, **Wet Republic,** where bad tattoos might as well be mandatory. Splash around in the pool and try not to think about what that water's been through, or rent a cabana and watch as beautiful women flock to your alcohol supply, only to disappear entirely when it's gone.

Get out of the resorts and hit the sidewalks. **The Fremont Street Experience** is the biggest congregation of people looking to dull their senses on the Strip. A zipline runs down the length of Fremont Street itself, so it's safe to say the risk of an aerial vomit bomb is omnipresent, but that just adds to the thrill, doesn't it?

The next day, nurse your hangover at the popular breakfast stand **Hash House A Go Go.** It's where the celebrities go to look their worst, so be prepared to wait for a table. For a more substantial meal, head to **Jimmy Buffett's Margaritaville,** where you'll enjoy food, giant margs, and the simple pleasure of watching Tommy Bahama–clad retirees eating homefries.

Each resort features some kind of seasonal show. If your taste gravitates toward watching giant muscled men gently lift each other with body parts not meant for lifting things, try any of the Cirque du Soleil's shows. Or, their aquatic performance at the Bellagio adds a surreal water theme for those looking to be confused about their fetishes.

Of course, there's plenty to see away from the illumination of the Strip's neon signs. **Red Rock Canyon** and **Valley of Fire State Park** are just outside the city. Finally, **The Neon Graveyard,** where old Vegas landmarks are stored after obsolescence, is great for a little context.

FUCKED UP FIRSTHAND

I went to Vegas for the first time in 2011 for a friend's twenty-first birthday. His grandmother is a fairly large gambler and so casinos try and keep her—and those she vouches for—as comfortable as possible. In this case, we were comped a penthouse suite in the Aria. Nothing beats walking into a hotel room the size of an apartment and having the curtains automatically open to reveal the entire Vegas Strip glittering like a jewel outside.

Later, we went to Wet Republic to party during the day. We had a cabana and $500 worth of alcohol to drink. We made friends with the neighboring cabanas and ended up with a giant party within the already insane party that was Wet Republic. At one point, every person there was either making out with somebody else or puking. Of course, we were spending money so the club staff simply cleaned up the puke and brought out more shots.

One of the people enjoying the party just happened to be Tiësto, one of the biggest DJs in the world. Clearly he could do a better job than the DJ spinning at the time, so he simply walked up to the booth and asked if he could man the turntables for a bit. Who would say no to that? We were treated to a free show by Tiësto simply because the man wanted to spice up his own vacation. Now that's Vegas.

VERDICT

All about the winning streak.

Colin Heinrich

95. Edinburgh, Scotland

SEASON: Characteristically rainy all year-round, but as long as you're drinking, who cares?

IDEAL CONDITIONS: Drunk enough to hold your liquor while stumbling around the Royal Mile, with a ruddy-faced Scot who really wants to bang but will probably pass out before getting the chance.

DAYTIME ACTIVITY: Check out the Edinburgh Castle.

LODGING RECOMMENDATIONS: Castle Rock Hostel, University of Edinburgh.

INGESTIBLES: Scotch whiskey, haggis, black pudding, shortbread, skirlie-mirlie, rumblethumps, bridies, clootie dumplings.

Edinburgh is like the burly dude who comes to your party, drinks whiskey straight from the bottle, punches a hole in your wall "to prove he can," and then hooks up with the girl you've been trying to make it with. Scots are rowdy. They know how to make excellent booze. And they drink it all of the time, all day long, because they fucking can.

The biggest shitshow in Edinburgh is **Hogmanay,** celebrated on the last day of the old year and continues well into the first day of the new one. The event hosts killer bands from around the world, street theater performances, a torchlight procession, a crazy carnival in the middle of the city, and fireworks at midnight. You are free to purchase libations at one of the many outdoor bars serving up tasty food and beverages in the freezing cold, but it's totally okay to BYOB as long as it's in a plastic container.

If you've got the balls, participate in the Hogmanay **Loony Dook** tradition. Dress in your favorite costume, strip down to your skivvies, or just get wasted and cheer on the **Dookers Paraders** who willingly plunge themselves into the icy River Forth. You are guaranteed to see some erect nipples and shriveled dicks.

Edinburgh is also one of the most haunted cities in the world. Tons of venues, like hoity-toity **Itchycoo Bar,** claim to be haunted, but the dopest place to see a ghost is on a tour of the **Vaults,** where the scum of Edinburgh used to live back in the olden days. If you haven't pissed your pants from getting spooked, lots of tours end with drinks at the pub.

All scotch is whiskey, but not all whiskey is scotch. Sample at stores like **Cadenhead's Whisky Shop** or **Whiski Rooms,** near Edinburgh Castle; **28 Queen Street** is a fancy-pants venue where you can become a member of the **Scotch Malt Whiskey Society,** and prove your dedicated alcoholism by participating in some of their blindfolded whiskey tastings.

Finally, other than being a badass piece of menswear, here's what you need to know about Scottish kilts:

- Although people will tell you that Scots traditionally free-ball it, it's okay to wear undies beneath your kilt (but do you really want to?).
- If you're Scottish, do your ancestors justice and find the tartan pattern that matches your clan.
- The jockstrap for your kilt is called a *sporran*. It's like a man purse that covers your junk so you don't get sack-tapped while playing the bagpipes.

NOTES FROM A LOCAL
Make the trek over to the Black Rose Tavern on Rose Street, Edinburgh's best punk bar. No Dave Matthews Band allowed!

VERDICT
In the United Kingdom, you get more alcoholic the farther north you go.

Katka Lapelosová

96. New York City, New York

SEASON: Autumn: foliage in Central Park, drunk. Winter: ice skating at Wollman Rink. Spring: rowing on the lake near the Loeb Boathouse. Summer: Shakespeare in the Park.
IDEAL CONDITIONS: Lost on the subway toting a water bottle of vodka, a Groupon for Babeland tucked into your bra, standing next to your inebriated bestie who keeps screaming, "I fucking love New York!"

DAYTIME ACTIVITY: Walk the Meatpacking District all the way up to 34th Street via the Highline.

LODGING RECOMMENDATIONS: Couchsurfing.org or dorms at Hostelling International.

INGESTIBLES: Brooklyn Lager, $2 "dirty water" hot dogs, bagels (duh!), pizza, a sample of Checker Cab Blonde Ale after your free tour of the Chelsea Brewing Company.

London's pubs close at 11:00 P.M. Tokyo's Metro is donezo after midnight. All-night diners do not exist in Dubai. But in Manhattan, you can have it all—a lapdance, overpriced drinks, greasy plates of chicken and rice from a street cart, ecstasy at a warehouse party—twenty-four hours a day, seven days a week. New York—the city that never sleeps (with you unless you buy it a drink).

Being one of the most expensive places in the world to live, you'll meet a lot of poor-ass artists in New York City. Live vicariously through them while sipping cocktails and enjoying art at the Metropolitan Museum of Art's **Rooftop Garden Café,** open in summer. Or pretend to be a trust-fund baby while nursing a $15 drink at **Top of the Strand,** ogling at toothpick-thin socialites or their fantastic view of the Empire State Building. Perhaps struggling improv actors are more your type? Get trashed at **UCB East** bar/comedy theater, where drawing giant wieners on their chalkboard-covered walls is expected.

Kinkier types should head to **Chelsea** and the **Meatpacking District,** where you can drink, dance, make out with total strangers, purchase the perfect dildo, etc. Pick up some BDSM gear at **Purple Passion/DV8** and screw your brains out with a random stranger you'll meet at **XES Lounge**'s karaoke night.

Happy hour was practically invented in Manhattan; just follow whoever's in a suit after five oo'clock and you're set. Head to the **Upper East Side** to get smashed and horny on $1 oysters and $6 G&T's at **Fulton,** from 5:00 to 7:00 P.M. But if you want to pay happy hour prices all day long, head to **123 Burger Shot Beer** in **Hell's Kitchen** (stands for $1 burger sliders, $2 shots, and $3 draught beers).

Start out with a boozy brunch complete with dance party and sparklers at the **West Village's Bagatelle**, then head to **Greenwich Village** and grab free hot dogs, happy hour–priced drinks, and see a drag show at the historic **Stonewall Inn**. End your evening at 3:00 A.M. with omelettes and mimosas at **Maison**, a fancy little bistro near the former trash capital of Manhattan, Times Square.

And what would be a trip to Manhattan without visiting a strip club? Drop yo' dolla bills at **Sapphire New York,** where you can see titties and watch UFC, or catch some retro-sexy stripteases at the **Penthouse Executive Club.** Channel your inner stripper at **Harlem's Le Femme Suite** (ladies only, sorry perverts), an intimate pole dance studio near mouth-watering **Manna's,** where you can soak up your binge drinking with Southern-style soul food.

Bonus: What are the "Five Boroughs"? Manhattan is only one. Be adventurous (or miss your subway stop) and get sloppy at a few of these off-the-island venues:

- **Brooklyn: Post Office** (Williamsburg), the **Wreck Room** (Bushwick), **Minor Arcana** (Prospect Heights)
- **Queens: Bohemian Beer Garden** (Astoria), **Tap House** (Forest Hills), **Press195** (Bayside)
- **The Bronx: Bronx Ale House** (Kingsbridge), **Bruckner Bar and Grill** (South Bronx), **Stan's Sports Bar** (outside Yankee Stadium)
- **Staten Island: Duffy's Tavern** (West Brighton), **Drunken Monkey Bar and Grill** (Westerleigh), **Lee's Tavern** (Dongan Hills)

FUCKED UP FIRSTHAND

The Chrysler Building swirls around in front of me. But fuck, it's hard to remember how drunk you can get when you're doing sake bombs and sloppy karaoke for two hours at a seedy karaoke bar in Koreatown. My friends want to go to a club downtown, but I stumble around, trying to get my bearings.

"Are you all right?" Theresa asks me. "No, no way," I admit.

I decline her offer to walk me home, hubris taking over; of course I know my way home, dammit! It's uptown, uptown is north that way. I know because I know that lamp post, wait why is the Empire State Building getting smaller, when did the Upper West Side start hanging Peking Ducks all over the place? . . . Oh, shit, I'm in Chinatown.

The stench of raw fish is overwhelming, and I begin to gag. Normal people would just throw up into a trash can, but I'm so wasted that I scatter my wallet, ChapStick, and cell phone across the ground and puke straight into my handbag.

Two young men wearing flashy shirts walking down the street stop. They want to hit on me. "Hey there, pussycat," says one. "What's your name?" I wipe my mouth on my arm.

"Kat," I reply. "My name really is Kat." I hold out my purse to them. "And there's vomit in my purse."

VERDICT
Meatpacking.

Katka Lapelosová

97. Prague, Czech Republic

SEASON: Getting schwasted is awesome here year-round, but cold winters provide a good excuse to check out clubs and pubs and get toked.

IDEAL CONDITIONS: The basement of a potraviny, a nightclub that only plays music from the 1990s. Your babička's house.

DAYTIME ACTIVITY: Walking Charles Bridge, possibly looking for weed.

LODGING RECOMMENDATIONS: MadHouse Hostel, Hotel Cerny Slon for a hotel that makes you feel as if you're on the set of *Game of Thrones*.

INGESTIBLES: PIVO (duh), Becherovka (herbal bitters), Slivovice (plum brandy), Absinthe, smažený sýr (hunk of fried cheese), vepřové (pork), knedlíky (pork cutlets and bread dumplings), Pribináček (addictive kids' yogurt/mousse thing).

"Prague is the party capital of Central Europe," says basically every traveler you'll ever meet. Where else can pretentious study-abroaders black out on beer that's cheaper than water or sleazy Austrians dance half-naked to drum and bass in cave-like clubs, and wanker Brits indulge in quality sex workers during traditional "stag night" adventures?

Most of the super crazy party spots are located near **Old Town** and **Wenceslas Square.** Sure, you'll have a great time making out with Slovenian tourists at places like **Lucerna Music Bar** or **Karlovy Lázně,** but for an authentic Czech experience get out of your fucking comfort zone and head to **Futurum.** Participate in the insane Czech tradition of shotgunning your $1.50 USD pint of beer and shattering it on the dance floor. The patrons don't seem to care—they are too busy publically groping each other under the strobe lights and fog machines.

Lushes and study-abroad frat douches congregate at **The Pub,** where each table is equipped with a device that ranks how much Pilsner Urquell you've slurped down against your table mates. It's all fun and games until someone gets roofied, but that's tallied up on a different machine. If you are the type of drunk that gets so shit-faced you start climbing on things, the half-pub, half–rock climbing facility **Boulder Bar** will fuel your desire.

Get toked and head to **Chapeau Rouge** where, even on a humdrum Tuesday night, shit gets real. The myriad of secret passageways and spiral staircases lead you to intimate DJ caves and crazy rave rooms. Score drugs near the restroom and be shocked at how cheap a bag of weed will cost you (have you ever paid $12 USD for dope? You will now!).

If you're desperate for some drunk grub, the sausage stands at the foot of Wenceslas Square are your best bet. The inebriated swear by their delicious crispness and fulfilling currywurst taste. Fancy yourself a scoop of cannabis- or absinthe-flavored ice cream? Treat yo'self to some at the **Absinth Shop**. The tunnel under the Legerova overpass also offers late-night, weird-ass eats such as **Pizza Grosso**'s New York-style pies, sugar doughnuts, and shaved meats, but you'll have to dodge some junkies to get to them.

Couple things about Czech drug culture:

- It's weed. Any other drug will land you in jail and will also make you look like a total douchebag, since an estimated four hundred thousand Czechs are regular pot smokers.
- People smoke joints freely on the streets and in the parks of Prague, no big deal. Some establishments will even let you light up inside. **Střelecký Island** is a secluded spot where no one will bother you, except for some swans looking to get in on the action.

FUCKED UP FIRSTHAND

Tom and I ruminate over our last bag of Czech weed. Tomorrow we'd cross over another country's border by plane; taking it with us, was out of the question.

"Petr would probably take it," I suggest. He worked at the café below our school, and was integral in accompanying us to the best of Prague's party scenes. He force-fed me "Magic Eye" (shot of crème de menthe hidden in a stein of Gambrinus beer) my first week in the city. Afterward, we danced to Aqua's "Barbie Girl" in PoPo Café Petl's underground music club.

"Oh, yes, I'll take it," Petr tells us via SMS. "But right now I'm out of town. Can you maybe put it somewhere and I'll pick it up?" Just put a bag of weed somewhere in Prague and hope Petr finds it?

"I got it," Tom tells me. He starts walking toward Charles Bridge. The most famous bridge in Prague is at its most beautiful at two o'clock in the morning. The daytime tourist crowds have all dispersed, and all that's left are some wrought-iron lanterns posted in between thirteenth-century bronze sculptures of saints.

We hid the weed inside an empty lantern on Charles Bridge.

"Found the bag!" Petr texts us the next day. "Man, this is good stuff! *Děkuji vám!*"

VERDICT
Fucking genius.

Katka Lapelosová

98. Rome, Italy

SEASON: Rome is mild year-round except July through August, when temps reach upper 80s.
IDEAL CONDITIONS: International Worker's day, on the first of May. On May Day a concert takes place every year: Thousands of people, mostly unemployed, gather in San Giovanni to celebrate work.
DAYTIME ACTIVITY: Viewing Colosseum, dated AD 72, Forum, Domus Aurea, and Pantheon.
LODGING RECOMMENDATIONS: The Yellow and M&J hostels have lively bars.
INGESTIBLES: Pizzas, Birra Peroni, caffé corretto with Sambuca, Romanella, grappa, greasy porchetta sandwiches.

Way back in the day, while most of the world was chasing rabbits dressed in fur, Romans were already getting fucked up on their tricliniums, inventing debauchery and A-plus substances abuse. After a couple of millennia, echoes of that very same decadence can be found on the cobbled alleys of Rome.

A typical night revolves around sitting in a square drinking beers, and then bar hopping while intermittently harassing passersby. There are four main areas where this drunken vagrancy takes place and, since public transport did not evolve much since the triclinium days,

When in Rome, keep an eye on your crew when people suggest entering fountains. Photo by Paolo Margargari.

you will not have an easy time changing between them on a night out. One option is a mini-marathon, one night for each district.

The most popular district among students is **San Lorenzo,** close to La Sapienza University and decimated with bars. Here people gather to drink, play music, and meet strangers on the steps of **Piazza dell'Immacolata.**

Close by is **Celestino,** the main watering hole, always crowded and very, very cheap. For the same back-slapping vibes, but less of a crowd, you can go to **Bar dei Brutti.** If money is not the issue, then go to **SAID,** an ancient chocolate-factory-turned-bar where food is also served.

I Porchettari, a typical Roman *fraschetta* where you can mishandle red sparkling wine (*romanella*) while eating unpretentious food, is also a worthy option. **Pourquoi** has a vast beer selection and serves an infamous *birramisu,* tiramisu made with beer instead of coffee, a delicacy to some, but a depravity to others.

To finish off the night you can go to **Jolly Roger** where you will find die-hard alcoholics, or **Locanda Atlantide**, which hosts live music and DJs.

If you want the student ratio to drop in favor of a more diverse crowd go to **Trastevere,** where the nightlife revolves around **Ponte Sisto, Piazza Trilussa,** and **Piazza Santa Maria.**

Bar Mariani, close to Ponte Sisto, and **Bar San Calisto,** opposite Santa Maria, are where you can get your Sambucas, or caffè corretto for as little as $1.50 USD. Along the alleys joining the two squares there are bars to fit all tastes. Safe bets are **Mr. Brown** and **Cinema America.**

Close to Trastevere is **Campo de Fiori,** where you can find bars popular among foreigners, such as **The Drunken Ship,** home to most American students abroad, and **The Scholar's Lounge.** The bar of the squatted **Teatro Valle** is where you can buy your wine with a free offer and **Piccolo Teatro Campo d'Arte** is another squatted theater where, on selected nights, you can buy rotten vegetables to throw at the performers.

In this district you will also find palatable clubbing options, such as **Anima** or **Mood** where you can try to get the shift.

The **Pigneto** area is also popular and good options are the **Cargo** and **Tam Tam,** the latter with a pulp-trash, jungle-themed décor.

Try the **Cube,** or the more exclusive **Goa** and **Art Café** if you want to put on your dancing shoes and go clubbing. For live music check out the programs of squats such as **Villaggio Globale, Forte Prenestino,** and **Brancaleone.** It's all about forming a solid little crew to start the night in your local square, and then checking where the vibe takes you.

NOTES FROM A LOCAL

A Roman proverb states: inside the small barrel is the good wine, but in the big one there is more.

VERDICT

"Timeless."

Pietro Buzzanca

99. West Hollywood, California

SEASON: Mating.
IDEAL CONDITIONS: Summer nights, Gay Pride, Halloween.
DAYTIME ACTIVITY: Celeb watching on Sunset Plaza or just go to the beach.
LODGING RECOMMENDATIONS: The Ramada West Hollywood for the sound of action through your walls, Sunset Marquis for star fucking.
INGESTIBLES: Strong drinks in plastic cups, same-sex tongues, mimosas in the afternoon.

WeHo is where the gays go. The main strip sits just west of La Cienega on Santa Monica. It's a good twenty bars worth of crazy action that gets kicking after ten and goes late, especially on the weekends.

The Abbey remains the beam of the scene, an indoor/outdoor concoction at which Liz Taylor used to drink wine in the afternoon with her queer friends. Loose pours in the house drinks make everyone equally loose, the bathroom is the scene of almost every crime imaginable. The Abbey is also girl friendly, a place where lipstick lesbians walk confidently past gym teacher lesbians, who nearly faint at the sight.

The strip on Santa Monica runs the gamut. **Micky's** is where old people go to lust after strippers. **Here Lounge** is where young people go to lust after strippers. It should be noted that most of the strippers are straight and have enhanced one important feature with hard-on drugs. They're also working on acting careers.

The strongest drinks in West Hollywood are poured at **Mother Lode,** a bar that hasn't been updated since the seventies and wears it like a badge. It's a bar kind of bar, with no dancing and a pool table.

You'll piss in a trough here, not a urinal with penis-blinders shielding you. And you'll get some looks.

Hamburger Mary's is the home of Drag Queen Bingo, which is exactly as it sounds. It's a good place to fuel up with bar food and watch men in skirts who are "undergoing the process" with quick trips to Mexico. Most straight people seem fascinated with the place, so point your arrow here if you have a hetero in tow.

Dive-bar drinkers worship **Fubar**, which is seedy and cocksure. It has the aroma of ammonia covering up the smell of sweat and sex. Thursday to Sunday, this place is packed full of a combination of queens, hipsters, daddies, average joes, and hot motherfuckers. The photo booth up front has documented many wasted nights, but the bathroom has certainly seen some action, too.

You're guaranteed to get a strong drink at the **Gold Coast Bar**, which opens at 11:00 A.M. on weekdays and is heaving by noon. It's hardly a tourist attraction. The windows are blacked out, and not for effect. Nicknamed "The Old Coast" by locals, this is the place to go if you've got a penchant for daddies, who are more than happy to buy you a drink. They have a much different plan for their retirement money than most older gents.

When hitting WeHo remember not to tempt fate. Take a cab. Don't worry, they're lined up on every corner just dying to take you (and the trick you've picked up) back to your hotel. Book early for Pride and Halloween, and know that the days start early and go late. Many of the roads that go in and out of WeHo close and parking is ridiculous, so find a hotel nearby and walk/stumble.

FUCKED UP FIRSTHAND

I lived one block from Fubar for two years. Not being too into the super-gay scene, I preferred this bar and their stiff drinks over the trendier ones west of La Cienega. Friends and I would usually pre-game at my apartment and show up at 11:00 P.M., then close the place at two.

We'd most often go for "Big Fat Dick," the Thursday night soiree that is everything your mother has ever warned you about. Upon entering I'd usually be eye level with one or two strippers' banana hammocks, and within seconds I'd have a strong-ass Stoli soda in hand. But it's what goes on in the back that is interesting.

Early in the evening, patrons are allowed to have photographs taken of their weenie. I was always too shy to whip out my junk but many of my friends did it, especially because your contribution lands you a free drink. What happens with the photos? They're developed, then hung across the room on a clothesline for everyone to see.

The saying on Fubar's Web site is "Not your father's gay bar" and they're right.

VERDICT

The biggest sausage party on the planet.

Tom Gates

100. Tel Aviv, Israel

SEASON: June through September, when young Israelis hit the beach with friends, blankets, booze, and guitars for long afternoons of sweating, surfing, and matkot (ping pong without the table).

IDEAL CONDITIONS: Friday nights on Shabbat, a rooftop terrace, cold beer, solo travel. Locals willing to teach you how secular Israelis celebrate the holy Sabbath with music, dancing, sex, and arak.

DAYTIME ACTIVITY: Get learned at the Museum of the History of Tel Aviv, or walk around the neighborhoods Noga, Gan HaHashmal, and Florentin.

LODGING RECOMMENDATIONS: Florentine Hostel at 10 Elifelet. Guests vie for cheap bunks or couches and hammocks on the terrace.

INGESTIBLES: A mystery blend of "incense" that will drop you, pale lagers like Maccabee and Goldstar (certified kosher), shots of anise-flavored arak and fig-flavored fidg.

Tel Aviv is where business licensing is lax and young entrepreneurs open a bar and a dance floor overnight that fills with tanned legs and sweaty shoulders and swaying heads. News spreads in passing on the beach, in a group of friends sharing a beer on the rooftop terrace of **Florentine Hostel**, between travelers and the young, tattooed kiosk guy on the corner, and people line up and it's big. For now.

Most of them fold within a year or two, only to be scooped up by the next entrepreneurial spirit. You have to talk to Israelis to know where to go for your party, because the hot shit your guide book raves about may already be pulsing to another beat.

If you're a broke backpacker, they'll tell you to head south, far from the swank cocktails on the trendy stretches of **Rothschild** and **Dizengoff**. They'll tell you to go south to **Florentin** and **Jaffa** where the eves are dripping and the uneven streets are filled with kids who came straight from the beach, with artists smoking cigarettes, watching the action from their garage studios, with baby-faced IDF soldiers on leave, with rich kids from the northern suburbs who want to feel the irreverence of the city for themselves, after a long, reverent Shabbat dinner with their grandmothers. They go to **Hoodna** where secondhand chairs and sagging sofas spill out onto the sidewalk and beer bottles and cigarettes hang lazy from their fingers.

The South is where bars like **Anna Loulou** with a handful of stools and no room to breathe somehow manage to squeeze in a stage for live Balkan music and spoken word performances and boast arak quietly sourced from Ramallah. It's where kids drink their beer on the curb with their eyes trained upward toward the reggae band jamming out on the roof of the latest hole-in-the-wall. It's where every other Israeli walks a dog that looks like a horse down Florentin Street to grab a slice at **Basilikum**.

It's where you'll catch a guy's eye as you scoop your hummus standing up outside a tiny joint on **Abarbanel**, and he'll come up to you and smile and tell you that he likes your glasses. It's where you'll only look lost for a second before someone scoops you up to take you with them to their friend's rooftop party, or to see the latest European DJ at **The Block**, where the sound system is famous and the party isn't over until the sun comes up.

The call to morning prayer from the Jaffa mosques will echo through the narrow streets, telling you when it's time to sleep.

FUCKED UP FIRSTHAND

I woke up bleary eyed and realized that we had traded the dirty streets and industrial garages outside of Comfort 13 south of Tel Aviv for the silence of a Shabbat morning in the leafy northern suburbs, and a bed in his house in Ramat Aviv. His mother was moving around the living room. We tiptoed out the front door when she was busy in the back bedroom.

"Looks like you had a better night than the other American" the hostel owner mumbled when I wandered back to my bunk the next morning. The other American, a redheaded thirtysomething guy, had come home to the hostel and crawled into his bed. Around the time that the Jaffa mosques alit with calls to morning prayer, he stood up, sleepwalking, and confused the nearby double bed for a toilet.

"*He's peeing on meeeeee,*" the Norwegian guy snickered at the breakfast table, imitating the German girl's horrified screams as she woke up to the feeling of warm piss on her leg.

The German girl lay in a nearby hammock looking haunted. I secretly thanked the American guy for making my bad decisions look like great ones.

VERDICT

Sweetly A.D.D.

Matador Network

101. San Francisco, California

SEASON: August through November looks like fall, feels like summer.
IDEAL CONDITIONS: Visiting wealthy locals.
DAYTIME ACTIVITY: Head to Ocean Beach in the Outer Sunset.
LODGING RECOMMENDATIONS: Lavish hotels or a van parked in Golden Gate Park. None of it's cheap.
INGESTIBLES: Craft beers, custom cocktails, medical marijuana, hippy-grade acid, lawyer-grade cocaine, pure MDMA, and cutting-edge sex toys.

San Francisco is divided into districts. Distinctly. Cross the street from the towering cement skyscrapers of the Financial District into the ancient Asian architecture of Chinatown and you'll definitely know it. Up the hill to the swanky North Beach cafés and across the park to the hippy hills of Haight-Ashbury Dylan-strumming buskers: each zone presents a theme party of local culture. And any good night should include at least three districts.

Over an extended stay, SF is best discovered via an attrition of surgical strikes: key shows at legendary music venues like **The Warfield, Great American Music Hall,** and **The Fillmore;** celebratory feasts at world-renowned eateries like **The Stinking Rose** (garlic!), **Tommy's Mexican** (tequila!), and the seafood at **Farallon;** and random wonders like ball games at **Pac Bell** on the bay, doobies in **Golden Gate Park,** and the underground raves only the cool kids know how to find.

You can spend a lifetime discovering secret basement jazz and one-night warehouse blowouts. But you've only got a few days, and you barely know where to start. Here's how you do it:

- **Pick a district.** North Beach. Haight-Ashbury. Mission. Whatever's outside your door, really. They're all on fire. Walk no more than two blocks before entering a bar. Sit on a stool and order something strong. Talk to the bartender. Tell him you're thirsty, then buy him a drink.

- **Change districts.** Quickly. As if you're trying to throw off a tail. Jump a cable car, skateboard down the hill, or head underground to the MUNI. Public transportation is great here. Use it. You'll stumble out in the gay **Castro District,** or the bum-crazy **Market Street,** the delightfully seedy **Tenderloin.** Enter the first bar you see. Order something that scares you. Put music on the box. Compose a limerick on the bathroom wall. Confess your love to a stranger.

Talk to locals. What are they doing next? Maybe they're heading to one of the *Matrix*-like club scenes at **Ruby Skye, Temple,** or **1015 Folsom.** Maybe tracking down some dive bar shots at crazy **Uptown** (Mission), the fishy **Hi Dive** (Marina), or the greasy **Tee Off,** where you can stand on the Ping-Pong table wailing on a borrowed electric guitar. Maybe they're heading to bonfire on **Sunset Beach** or a stony stroll through **Golden Gate Park** . . . doesn't matter really, just say, "Can I come with you?"

Your last stop should be someone's house. There you'll find a clean glass bong, fresh cocaine, and a bottle of scotch; jazz on vinyl and a view of the city lights. This is where you were headed all along. Home. New Yorkers stay out all night because their apartments are too small to sleep in, but San Franciscans love going home because that's where they hide their stash.

Remember the rules:

- Most San Franciscans think weed is legal. It's not, but there's power in belief.
- The beach here is not romantic in any way.
- Public transportation rules. Use it. And assume that odd dude is an undercover cop.

The hangover: it might take a Bloody Mary or two to recall your new friend's name. Break the ice with some Frisbee golf and a joint in the park, then go lazy vintage shopping in the Haight or Mission districts. Somewhere between the lazy sun and bitter wind, the temperature is just right and too much to bear. Lie down. Wherever you are, just lie down. You won't be going out again tonight. It's not that type of city.

FUCKED UP FIRSTHAND

The long walk through SF's twisted streets gets further tangled by the onset of psilocybin mushrooms. Glowing fog. Shadowy strangers. Troll-bridge hobos. I arrive at the converted opera house of the Great American Music Hall with my jaw dragging behind me.

Who goes out like this alone? I do. And, okay, nobody wanted to see the weird Australian instrumental band I was into. No one, except the other drugged-up freaks in the building, all just gaping into the lights as violinist Warren Ellis babbles mad intros then shatters our brains with his telepathic laments and unbearable torrents of sound. Glorious. I lean against a pillar and imagine the entire building will crumble without my support.

When I step outside the fog is gone. The stars have assembled to listen to the show. A slurry-eyed troubadour is playing sad Tom Waits covers in the piano bar up the street, and I drink scotch until the drugs go home. Someone locks the doors and I sleep behind a jukebox. Crushed by a lullaby.

VERDICT

A treasure chest at the bottom of the sea.

Nathan Myers

Last Call

A big *gracias* to all the authors who sacrificed their time and organs for this. Also a big thanks to Holly Schmidt for thinking of Matador.

If you're incredulous that we've left out Montañita or Daytona or La Libertad, wherever it is, or if they've added new beers at Gallagher's Pub and you just can't wait to let everyone know, you have a chance to add your knowledge, photos, video, and stories by visiting **101places.com**. We look forward to seeing you there.

And that's it. We've checked all the dive bars and danced to all the bass drops and scarfed all the late-night food we can for now. Our ears are ringing. We've made it home. It's time for bed. How about one last *salud* and let's catch each other downstream.

About the Authors and Photographers

Hal Amen sucks at writing witty bios.

Tom Ansell resides on Queensland's Sunshine Coast as part of his Pommie-turns-salty-surf-bum reincarnation.

Luke Maguire Armstrong (TravelWriteSing.com) is a travel writer who plays the guitar like a tiger.

Keith Bain is a writer with nomadic tendencies who lost his heart to Cape Town, South Africa.

Blissom Booblé is an ordinary schoolteacher turned burlesque performer.

Corey Breier is an avid explorer of both the wilderness and the Web; find him on Twitter @itsCoreyB.

Sarah Briggs is currently slinging drinks in Portland, Oregon.

Chris Burkard, a photographer, feels at home submerged in arctic surf.

After climbing the ranks of Rome's underground boozing scene, **Pietro Buzzanca** was last sighted in Dublin, losing a beer chugging competition to an Irish truck driver.

Dalton Campbell is an Austin-based portrait photographer (www .daltoncampbell.com).

Holy Clark is a photographer, writer, and traveler from Philadelphia.

When **Liam Cusay** isn't poking around castles in Europe, he lives, writes, and avoids rigorous exercise in Sydney, Australia.

Morgan deBoer is based in Hayama, Japan, where she writes about food, travel, and her experiences as one half of an American military family.

Dikson is a nomadic Zimbabwean performance poet, travel writer, and all-around sound cat.

Cody Forest Doucette has spent the past six years circling the globe in pursuit of images from the ice of Svalbard to the jungles of Sumba.

Zak Erving's first foray into human flight was when he was six. He fell like a rock, but his head stayed in the clouds (sparkpunk.com).

James Fidelibus's passion for photography is only surpassed by whitewater, mountain biking, and bacon.

Tom Gates is a Los Angeles–based writer who loves to go far away whenever he can. His book, *Wayward,* has been number one on both the iTunes and Kindle travel charts.

Steph Glaser is a freelance writer, traveler, and teacher who lives with her family in Salida, Colorado.

Natalie Grant is a writer from San Francisco who has been to over twenty countries with her trusty backpack, Morris.

Stephanie Early Green is a writer based in Washington, D.C., who has lived and worked in Brazil, Argentina, and South Africa.

Madeline Gressel is a writer and journalist born in New York City.

Colin Heinrich lives in southeast Asia and enjoys guacamole, music festivals, and that place in Joshua Tree that looks like a Salvador Dalí painting.

Joshua Heller is very funny.

Abigail Higgins is a journalist based in Nairobi, Kenya, and her hometown of Seattle, Washington (abbyhiggins.com).

Becky Hutner is a writer/editor based in Venice Beach, California.

Tereza Jarnikova sometimes lives in the Czech Republic and always rides her bike.

Josh Johnson is a travel storyteller with a penchant for strong ales and aimless wandering.

Jonathan Kalan is an award-winning independent photographer and journalist covering east Africa and the Middle East.

Priyanka Kher loves to travel, write, and eat—in that order (www.roadiswheretheheartis.com).

Katka Lapelosová is a contributing editor at Matador Network living in New York, and is the coolest person you will ever meet.

Ryan Libre can be found traveling around Asia looking for new kinds of homemade alcoholic beverages. His current favorite is *tsabi* from Kachin State in Burma.

Tabbi Maitland is a border-crossing, party-crashing introvert.

Nina Mashurova is a writer because notebooks are the most portable form of gear.

Christopher J. Miller is an editor at the Kyiv Post in the former Soviet state of Ukraine and a returned Peace Corps volunteer originally from Portland, Oregon.

Suze Morris has lived/worked/studied on three continents, where she has developed her skills of navigating places where maps don't exist.

Nathan Myers is the leading authority on guacamole combat.

Larissa Olenicoff is a travel adict and iPhone photographer.

Chicago-based writer **Sarahlynn Pablo** likes 'em neat, dirty, and with egg whites.

Noah Pelletier has a certificate in creative nonfiction from UCLA. He lives in Germany.

Jessica Peter is a Canadian who loves writing, travel, craft beer, and fish jokes (www.jessicapeter.net).

Larissa Peuckert-Coleman is a kindergarten teacher and writer (www.larissacoleman.wordpress.com).

Nick Rowlands lived in Egypt from 2006–2012, working as a tour leader, travel writer, and journalist. He is currently based in San Francisco.

Suzanne Russo is a New York–based writer and wanderer with an affinity for ghost and palimpsest chasing, historical reenactment crashing, and joining parades.

Kate Santoro studied journalism at Boston University, and her degree goes to good use each time she writes an email from her corporate cubicle.

Bart Schaneman lives and writes in Seoul, South Korea.

Alana Seldon is a Canadian writer living elsewhere.

Keph Senett is a Canadian writer whose passions for travel and soccer have led her to play the beautiful game on four continents.

Sarah Shaw is a travel writer, artist, and English teacher from southern Maine, currently residing in Colombia and blogging about life as an expat at www.mappingwords.com.

Kate Siobhan is a freelance writer and photographer based out of Vancouver, Canada.

Scott Sporleder is a photo snapper.

In 2011 **Evan Timpy** took his American dollars and left the country, devoting his time and energy to global independent travel, surfing every day, reading, and writing.

Candice Walsh is a Professional Experience Collector and full-time inventor of job titles that don't make much sense.

Mark Walsh is an educator and wallet-maker who has been freezing his ass off in Antarctica since 2009.

Miranda Ward is the author of *F**k The Radio, We've Got Apple Juice: Essays on a Rock 'n' Roll Band*. She lives in Oxford and can be found online at www.mirandaward.co.uk.

Ben West abandoned the sterile world of pharmacy ownership to pursue his love of climbing mountains, exploring, blogging, and dancing terribly in far-flung countries.

About the Editor

David Miller is the Senior Editor of Matador Network, two-time winner of the Lowell Thomas Award for excellence in travel journalism. Follow him @dahveed_miller.

About Matador Network

Matador Network (**www.matadornetwork.com**) launched in 2006 with the vision for a travel site and community based not on airline reservations and hotel rooms, but the real cultures, people, and places we encounter. We've since evolved into the largest independent travel publication on the Web, and developed a new media school for the next generation of travel journalists.

Index